COMING OF AGE IN JEWISH AMERICA

COMING OF AGE IN JEWISH AMERICA

Bar and Bat Mitzvah Reinterpreted

PATRICIA KEER MUNRO

RUTGERS UNIVERSITY PRESS
New Brunswick, New Jersey, and London

Library of Congress Cataloging-in-Publication Data
Munro, Patricia Keer, 1957–author.
Coming of age in Jewish America : bar and bat mitzvah reinterpreted / Patricia Keer Munro.
pages cm
Includes bibliographical references and index.
ISBN 978–0–8135–7594–0 (hardcover : alk. paper)—ISBN 978–0–8135–7593–3 (pbk. : alk. paper)—ISBN 978–0–8135–7595–7 (e-book (epub))—ISBN 978–0–8135–7596–4 (e-book (web pdf))
1. Bar mitzvah—United States. 2. Bat mitzvah—United States. 3. Jewish teenagers—Religious life—United States. 4. Jews—United States—Social life and customs. I. Title.
BM707.M86 2016
296.4'5424—dc23   2015032495

A British Cataloging-in-Publication record for this book is available from the British Library.

Visit our website: http://rutgerspress.rutgers.edu

Manufactured in the United States of America

From generation to generation: to those who came before, especially my grandparents, Sophia and William Keer and Ruth and Herman Davis, of blessed memory; and to those who follow, especially my grandchildren, Lilianne and Theodore Casner (and those who, God willing, will come later). And, as always, to David Munro, who has walked beside me on the journey.

CONTENTS

ACKNOWLEDGMENTS

This book would not exist without the people who shared their time, thoughts, and rituals with me. The rabbis who welcomed me into their congregations and brokered introductions to staff members and congregants deserve a special mention: their time and consideration made it possible for this book to exist. Rabbis, education directors, and administrators all answered my questions thoughtfully. In the busy life of a synagogue, this is no little thing. Families welcomed me into their homes and gave of their time. Each offered a different view of the ritual and what it meant to family members. Their words convinced me of the value of bar and bat mitzvah. Other congregants helped me understand the rich pattern of Jewish life that surrounds the ritual's place in the congregation. Their generosity provided me with a vast quantity of data, from which this book has emerged.

My research apprentices and assistants provided invaluable assistance in developing the research and analyzing the data. The University of California, Berkeley, encourages undergraduates to participate in ongoing research through the Undergraduate Research Apprentice Program. Under the guidance of Claude Fischer, I supervised David Reder, Alina Goldenberg, and Kate Morar as they gathered and analyzed website data and helped me develop the final set of interview questions.

In 2011–12, I received a Berman Foundation Dissertation Fellowship in Support of Research in the Social Scientific Study of the Contemporary American Jewish Community. I particularly want to express my thanks and gratitude to the Berman Foundation. The award enabled me to hire three research assistants, Kendra Nervik, Cora Tobin, and Crissy Chung, who diligently transcribed the resulting interviews and assisted in coding them. Kendra then worked on the project as a volunteer, ultimately collecting her own data and collaborating on a joint paper. She has since entered graduate school in sociology at the University of Michigan, and I look forward to her growth as a scholar with pleasure and pride.

Teachers, colleagues, and friends provided support, advice, and helpful critiques. From the beginning, Ann Swidler saw the potential of this research, and her questions helped me understand the broad patterns that underlie the research. Claude Fischer shepherded me through the nitty-gritty of the project, encouraging me to take a more expansive approach to the research through the congregational surveys. David Hollinger gave a historical perspective from outside the Jewish community that allowed me to be confident that I was communicating my findings to a broad audience. I am also especially grateful to Fred Astren, who first encouraged me in my academic career; Rabbi Stu Kelman, who pointed me toward Stuart Schoenfeld's work, which inspired me to think about bar and bat mitzvah; and to Stuart Schoenfeld himself. I have learned from and worked with many others, especially Hanan Alexander, Jerome Baggett, Irene Bloemraad, Chava Boyarin, Daniel Boyarin, Arnold Dashefsky, John Efron, Arnie Eisen, Marion Fourcade, Eric Gruen, Josh Holo, Arlie Hochschild, Mike Hout, Shaul Kelner, David Nasatir, Nurit Novis, Bruce Phillips, Naomi Seidman, Sandra Susan Smith, Dina Stein, Barrie Thorne, and Robb Willer. The Van Leer Institute's 2013 Summer Workshop for Young Researchers on Jewish Culture and Identity, "Rituals and Symbols in Contemporary Jewish Cultures: Between Preservation and Change," gave me valuable feedback as the book developed, and I am especially grateful to Yehoyada Amir, Naftali Rosenberg, and Chaim Waxman for their comments at the workshop. The Berkeley Institute for Jewish Law and Israel Studies has given me a home and colleagues as I have completed this book. Thanks especially to Ken Bamberger, Rebecca Golbert, and Miri Lavi-Neeman for welcoming me to the program. My colleagues in sociology have made the journey pleasurable and interesting. My thanks to Corey Abramson, Zawadi Ahidiana, Hana Brown, Sarah Garrett, Daniel Laurison, Greggor Mattson, Damon Mayrl, Jennifer Randles, and especially my writing and mutual support buddy, Heidy Sarabia.

A book does not happen on its own, and there are many people at Rutgers University Press who deserve my thanks. Marlie Wasserman saw the potential for my research to become a book and encouraged me to finish the dissertation and write the book. It took longer than anticipated, and I greatly appreciate her patience and gentle persistence. I could not ask for a better editor or press. Marilyn Campbell ably directed the process from manuscript to book, and Jeanne Ferris ensured that my words actually said what I meant.

I have saved my family, friends, and community for the end. My path to academia was not typical: I came to graduate study with half-grown children and a full life in my community and congregation. For more than ten years, I have tried to balance that full life with my academic work. While this has never been easy, the support and encouragement from friends and family have made it possible. Thanks to all the folks who make up Congregation Beth Emek; Karen Holtz, Miriam Miller, and Valerie Jonas; Aziza and Leo Mara; Phyllis Lasche, Steve Hatchett, Jim Green, and Molly Bang; Elynn and Marty Finston; Melissa Reading and John Castor.

My entire *mishpocha* (family)—from my great-grandparents and grandparents who emigrated to the United States in the early twentieth century, to my far-flung family, including my parents, Barbara and Leon Keer, and my siblings and their families: Jackie and Steve; Harold, Amy, Adam, Sam, and Jacob; and

Michael, Cindy, Corinne, and Erika—has made me who I am. My grandmother, Ruth Davis, of blessed memory, held all our dreams and wishes. She always wanted to read this book—I wish I could have given her a copy.

My children finished high school and college while I was in graduate school. Miranda married Daniel, and together they had Lily and Rory. Deborah traveled around the world, entered graduate school, and married Aaron. They have supported me, mocked me, cheered me on, and cheered me up. They are the very best children any mother could want.

After thirty-five years of marriage, I am still blessed to share my life with Dave. His confidence in my ability enabled me to find it myself, and his humor, kindness, respect, and love sustain me every day.

NOTES ON KEY TERMS

In a book intended for use by multiple audiences, there are inevitably a few terms that benefit from clarification. In particular, the terms bar or bat mitzvah and Torah take on a range of meanings, so I clarify them here. Other terms are defined in the text.

Literally, bar mitzvah combines Aramaic and Hebrew to mean "son of the commandment(s)", with the plural being b'nai mitzvah for a group that includes at least one male. Bat mitzvah is the corresponding term for a girl ("daughter of the commandment[s])," with the plural for an all-female group being b'not mitzvah. These translations show that the phrases refer to a person or people, rather than to a ritual. Indeed, that is one usage: a boy becomes a bar mitzvah on turning thirteen; a girl becomes a bat mitzvah at thirteen in liberal American Judaism or at twelve in Orthodox Judaism. Yet these definitions expanded over time.

Bar or bat mitzvah also refers to the ritual in which the boy or girl participates, which symbolically represents a new status. In common parlance, it often refers to the party celebrating that symbolic moment. It also serves as all-inclusive term that covers the entire event, from the beginning of the service to the end of the celebration.

In this book, I use bar or bat mitzvah as an adjective: bar or bat mitzvah student or child describes the individual; bar or bat mitzvah service, ritual, or performance describes the ceremony itself; bar or bat mitzvah celebration describes the party; and bar or bat mitzvah event describes the entire day. B'nai or b'not mitzvah also appear where plurals are appropriate.

Torah, too, has several meanings. "The Torah" refers to the Five Books of Moses or the Pentateuch, handwritten on a scroll. The content encapsulates the fundamental narratives, values, and practices of Judaism, while the scroll itself is a concrete and sacred symbol that represents the heart of Judaism. "Torah" (without the definite article) often has a more general meaning, encompassing Jewish learning through the millennia to the present. Though Jews of all denominations use this broader definition of Torah, the phrase "Torah Judaism" refers to Orthodox practice that follows rules (Halakhah) derived from this definition of Torah.

In this book, I use "the Torah" when referring to the Five Books of Moses, "the Torah scroll" when discussing the scroll itself, and "Torah" when discussing general Jewish learning.

COMING OF AGE IN JEWISH AMERICA

1 · IT'S NOT DUDDY KRAVITZ'S BAR MITZVAH ANYMORE

Bar and Bat Mitzvah in the Twenty-First Century

The most memorable moment in the 1974 movie *The Apprenticeship of Duddy Kravitz* is the video montage shown at a bar mitzvah party. It is "a riotously abrasive home-movie that cross-cuts between shots of Bernie's nice, middle-class bar-mitzvah and shots of Zulu rites, Hitler, a circumcision ceremony, storm troops marching, the bar-mitzvah feast and a man eating razor blades" (Canby 1974). The movie epitomizes one stereotype of the American bar mitzvah that was common in the twentieth century: a strange ethnic rite of passage far outside the mainstream, enacted within a minority community composed largely of immigrants or their children and grandchildren. In the twenty-first century, bar or bat mitzvah continues to be a central ritual in American Jewish life, and it still evokes images of a glitzy, excessive party, at which both teens and adults dress and celebrate inappropriately.[1] Yet celebration and ritual are not the same: a reception is not a substitute for a wedding, nor is a wake a substitute for a funeral. Similarly, underlying the flash and fanfare of the bar or bat mitzvah party is a ritual that has profoundly shaped the American Jewish community and American Jews alike.

When thirteen-year-old bar or bat mitzvah students stand before family, friends, and sometimes community in a public ritual, they exemplify the core values of Judaism, uphold the family honor, and symbolically represent the Jewish future.[2] Some students manage a flawless performance, while others struggle through with whispered help, yet the family almost always deems the ritual a success. Parents and grandparents are amazed and awed; students stand a little taller and prouder. But the stakes are high: a failed ritual would embarrass both child and family and diminish Judaism itself.[3] So congregations and families alike invest substantial effort to ensure the ritual's success.

Bar and bat mitzvah have affected who joins synagogues and how they participate, the way Jewish professionals allocate their time, what Jewish supplementary schools teach and why, and what comprises the regular religious service into which the bar or bat mitzvah ritual is embedded. In short, the ritual has changed how American Jews understand and engage with Judaism.

At the same time, the content and meaning of the ritual has changed in response to the cultural shifts of the late twentieth and early twenty-first centuries and the needs of the participants. The nineteenth-century writer Ahad Ha-Am famously wrote: "More than the Jews have kept the Sabbath, the Sabbath has kept the Jews." That is, through observing Shabbat, Jews reinforced common values and stories, while keeping shared connections alive. In a similar way, bar mitzvah has played a crucial role in creating and sustaining American Judaism, so much so that it can be said that as much as American Jews have created bar mitzvah, so has bar mitzvah created American Jews. This book tells the story of that persistent relationship.

BAR MITZVAH IN AMERICA: MAKING THE BAR MITZVAH BARGAIN

From its earliest incarnation the bar mitzvah ritual developed from the needs of the people. Only later was it accepted by the Jewish elite: the leaders and teachers. Tracing the ritual's history is not easy; the historical record is sparse, particularly with regard to bar mitzvah's beginnings.[4] We do know that the ritual began to take shape during the twelfth century, when the adult responsibility of taking a vow was connected to puberty, as defined both by physical changes and turning twelve or thirteen, depending on gender (Hilton 2014, 1–34). It developed as a ritual more for parents than for children, with the central moment taking place when the father recited a blessing that relieved him of responsibility for his son's religious obligations. The parallel actions of the child's reciting a blessing before and after reading from a Torah scroll, as well as reading from the scroll itself, were also early additions. By the sixteenth century, a speech and a celebratory party had been added to the ritual, and with those additions came attempts by the leadership to define and control the ritual: "For four hundred years there have been battles between families who want the minimum educational import and synagogues who demand the most they can get" (Hilton 2014, xvi).[5]

These battles have characterized the history of bar mitzvah in America as well. The American bar mitzvah was a ritual that percolated up from the laity and forced itself on the Jewish leadership, which attempted to control its perceived excesses and use it to educate the laity. In one common pattern from the early twentieth century, a modest ritual took place on a weekday. The bar mitzvah boy donned tefillin (phylacteries) and tallit (prayer shawl), read three verses from the Torah scroll and a section from the Haftarah (associated reading from the Prophets), and delivered a memorized commentary to the congregation, after which his father recited a blessing that released him from ritual responsibility for his son. A more or less elaborate reception followed this short ceremony (Fishbane 1995a, 157–58). Even then Jewish leadership resisted and scoffed at this relatively modest event, labeling it a cliché-driven exercise of conspicuous consumption (Levitats 1949, 153). Despite resistance from leaders, the Jewish laity have continued to claim bar mitzvah as an important part of the Jewish life cycle. Others have wondered why this ritual retains such a powerful presence, concluding that it provides a way to mediate between Jewish and dominant cultures (see, for example, Hilton 2014; Schoenfeld 1986 and 1993). I would elaborate on that conclusion, adding that the ritual provides a particularly strong symbolic means of bridging the contradictions between Jewish and American culture.

Like other immigrants to America in the early twentieth century, as Jews adapted to life in America they had to demonstrate economic success through material means, assimilate into the American cultural melting pot, and adopt an American value system that placed both voluntary affiliation and self-creation at its heart. Although surrounded by Jewish ethnic culture, these immigrants faced an existential crisis with regard to their American children: "Will my child be a Jew? How can I ensure that my child doesn't break the chain of tradition?" The bar mitzvah helped answer that question: the ritual itself, including the speech, demonstrated formal loyalty to the Jewish people, explained and interpreted Judaism in the American context, and capped the process of raising a child who was both Jewish and American. The celebration following the ceremony demonstrated another, more obvious, form of success: that of the immigrant who makes good.

The Jewish religious elite, particularly rabbis and educators, had a different perspective. By inclination, training, or role, this group has always been more immersed in the Jewish world than the laity, and thereby more able to resist American norms. In their leadership roles, which often included teaching and interpreting Judaism to the laity, members of this elite attempted to ensure the reproduction of Jewish beliefs and practices. The existential questions the elite struggled with were not only those of the individual family, but also those of preserving both religion and people: "What is the best way to maintain an authentic

Judaism in America? Will Judaism continue to exist in America?" For these leaders, a bar mitzvah ritual was, at best, a distraction from real Judaism. At worst, because preparation for the ritual was minimal and focused on specific training for a single event, it was destructive to authentic Jewish continuity. Leaders saw the same actions—reading from the texts (Torah and Haftarah) and reciting a speech—that symbolized continuity to families as a hollow display of an ersatz Judaism. When attempts to discredit the bar mitzvah failed to stem its popularity, religious leaders used that popularity to strike a bargain: rabbis would formally sanction the ceremony with their presence in return for time to educate the children religiously. This bar mitzvah bargain was stated explicitly by Judah Pilch, a Jewish educator in the mid-twentieth century: "Bar Mitzvah represents a powerful motivation, a goal which children and their parents readily understand, and will work to attain. Recognizing the value of this motivation, increasing numbers of Jewish educators and rabbis have sought to direct Bar Mitzvah preparation from mere coaching for a performance, to education for living as American Jews" (quoted in Schoenfeld 1987, 73).

Thus, bar mitzvah became the primary means of inculcating Jewish belief and practice, with the hope that the students' engagement in Judaism would continue beyond the event. The rabbis in the twentieth century largely accomplished part of their goal: they successfully used the bar mitzvah as a lever to increase the number of children engaged in formal Jewish education. In the first half of the twentieth century, the portion of children receiving formal Jewish education doubled, from about 25 percent to more than 50 percent, and almost 90 percent of these children enrolled in the synagogues' schools, rather than enrolling in unaffiliated community schools or preparing with private tutors (Schoenfeld 1986). Mid-twentieth-century requirements for a synagogue bar mitzvah ritual typically included three years of religious training; the ability to understand some Hebrew, read prayers, and follow the service; some knowledge of Jewish customs and practice; and an introduction to Jewish history (Levitats 1949).

The existential concerns of the twentieth century have shifted as Jews integrated into American society and have increasingly understood Jewish identification as a matter of choice, one more area of self-creation that characterizes modernity and the American worldview (Bellah et al. 1996). Responsible parents, as part of modern child rearing, teach their children to make good choices, and through making those choices, their children learn to create their adult selves. Yet with that freedom comes the possibility that the child's choices may contradict the parent's values and choices (as when the child of a banker becomes a performance artist). Therefore, it is not enough for parents to teach their children to make choices; truly successful parents teach their children to make choices that also reflect parental values and choices (see, for example, Fischer 2010; Giddens 1991; Tobin et al. 1989).

According to this logic, a successful American Jewish parent is one who raises a child who can demonstrate both a freely chosen sense of self-identity and an affiliation with Judaism and the Jewish people. This tension, typical of American Judaism more generally, was expressed by one student in my study: "I don't think my parents and me [sic] talked about what it [bar mitzvah] means, but I know that they really wanted me to do this and they did give me a choice—that I could or I couldn't—and I made the choice that I wanted to. I made that choice." What this young man understood from his parents was that bar mitzvah mattered to them and so did the act of choosing. It is hardly surprising that he "chose" to do what mattered to them.

Two major cultural shifts of the late twentieth century also contributed to heightening the symbolic importance of the ritual: rising rates of intermarriage between Jews and gentiles and the egalitarian effects of feminism.[6] Jews who married gentiles had long been seen as rejecting the Jewish people by marrying out of their faith, so it is not surprising that increasing intermarriage rates alarmed the Jewish community and Jewish elites in particular.[7] Though the effect of intermarriage on the Jewish future remains a matter of intense debate in the Jewish community, the Reform movement's 1983 resolution accepting patrilineal descent changed the place of these families in congregational life. As part of that change, bar or bat mitzvah became an important symbol by which intermarried families could demonstrate that they had raised Jewish children.[8] The effect of second-wave feminism on parents of daughters also had a profound effect on the ritual's meaning. These parents, particularly mothers, wanted their daughters to claim all of Judaism, recognizing that being able to participate fully and equally was not something they could take for granted. Though the nature of the existential concerns have shifted, bar or bat mitzvah still represents a symbolic claim for Jewish identity and affiliation and the bar mitzvah bargain remains central in American Jewish community life.

That bargain underlies the relationship between the community, the ritual, and the participants (both leaders and laity). It affects the content of Jewish education (particularly, but not exclusively, in congregational supplementary schools), in which the desire to teach a broad spectrum of Jewish studies competes with the requirement to learn specific skills necessary to enact a bar or bat mitzvah ritual. It affects how rabbis and cantors allocate their limited time. The ritual becomes part of a regular congregational service, changing the nature of the service and attendees to a greater or lesser degree as the service accommodates the ritual. It can even affect synagogue design, which can include space to host bar and bat mitzvah celebrations.[9]

The ritual changes family life as well. Most synagogues require families to join and enroll their children in religious school for a number of years prior to the event. That act of affiliation implies some level of commitment. At a minimum, it costs money to join, and it takes time to schlep children to religious school. Whether a family joins a congregation just to fulfill the ritual's requirements or for other reasons, that affiliation provides the opening for education. At the same time, bar or bat mitzvah preparation is a normative part of that education, so the ritual itself shapes students' and parents' perceptions of Judaism's content and meaning. And, as more than one student in my study noted, the lengthy preparation for bar or bat mitzvah increases students' sense of its importance and meaning.

Training for the ritual also takes time and money. Planning and ensuring a successful celebration, while outside the formal purview of the congregation, is an important parental responsibility. There is, in fact, a parallel between the responsibilities of the students and those of the parents. Both children and their parents work to demonstrate new skills and/or status: the student formally commits to a new degree of Jewish responsibility (whether or not that will be enacted in the future), while the parent demonstrates successful parenting of a Jewish child.

Bar and bat mitzvah rituals are peculiarly individual, yet they take place in a community setting. As peak events in family life, each ritual brings together a group of people connected by kinship or friendship to the individual student and his or her nuclear family. This personal community witnesses the ritual. Through this process, the public ritual itself is affected: what happens in one bar or bat mitzvah can be appropriated, reinterpreted, or rejected by other families or by the congregational leaders. Thus, the personal elements of bar or bat mitzvah are infused with public meaning, and the public elements of the ritual are invested with personal meaning.

As a result, the shape of the ritual is fluid, with its elements varying over time and across places. It shapes and is shaped by the nature of the congregation; the expectations of the participants; and the congregation's size, location, culture, and denomination. As the symbolic meaning of the ritual changes, so do the elements and participants. Thus, though the ritual has retained key elements over time, participants and congregations also shape its content, the way in which it is enacted, and who participates in it, resulting in differing expectations over time.

For example, one congregation may encourage students to lead the whole service, while another may restrict their participation so that congregants can lead it as well. The San Francisco Bay Area has a culture of bar and bat mitzvah rituals taking place on Shabbat morning, whereas in some other parts of the United States, Saturday afternoon or evening services are also options.[10] There are differences across countries as well. Michael Hilton (2014, xii)—reflecting British (and perhaps European) custom—lists four "traditional" elements of the ritual: (1) reciting a blessing (*aliyah*) before or after reading from the Torah and chanting the final few verses of the weekly portion; (2) chanting the Haftarah, the associated reading from the Prophets; (3) having the father recite a blessing releasing him from responsibility for his child's (Jewish) behavior (*sheptarani*); and (4) a celebration following the service, during which the child delivers a speech. However, in liberal American Judaism the ritual follows a different pattern: the child leads one or more prayers, chants from both Torah and Haftarah texts in varying amounts, and delivers the speech during the service itself (rather than at the celebration).[11] Only in the Orthodox case is the *sheptarani* recited regularly, although parents almost always speak to their child, giving a speech or blessing him or her, which arguably fills that space.[12] While these changes may seem inconsequential, each has symbolic value. *Sheptarani*, for example, is one of the earliest elements of the ritual, but liberal American Jews find its wording, in which the father renounces his responsibility for his son's actions, difficult, as its frequent absence shows.[13]

I began my research by thinking about these differences: How do students prepare for the ritual? How are students expected to participate in the service? How does the ritual affect the rest of the congregation? Yet because bar or bat mitzvah is a moving target, such descriptions date quickly: even as I collected data, some rabbis explained that revising their programs was an ongoing process. In fact, the key question became one of understanding the relationships between these moving parts. In other words, how does the congregation shape the ritual and its participants, and how, in turn, do the ritual and its participants shape the congregation? That question led me to create a model by which to understand the relationships among the ritual, participants, and congregation.

FROM RESEARCH TO THE BAR AND BAT MITZVAH SYSTEM

In designing the research, my focus remained on the areas of preparation and ritual itself, largely excluding the celebrations.[14] My work took place in the San Francisco Bay Area.[15] Like the areas around Washington, D.C.; Philadelphia; and Boston, it has a population of around 215,000 Jews (Kotler-Berkowitz 2013).[16] The Bay Area Jewish community had its origins in the California Gold Rush of 1849, and since then it has developed a culture of acculturation and diffusion (A. Kahn and Dollinger 2003), as well as a distinct lack of the ethnic enclaves that shaped Jewish communities like those in New York, Chicago, and Los Angeles. The rate of intermarriage between Jews and gentiles in the Bay Area is somewhat higher than national norms, while the rate of synagogue affiliation is much lower. Denomination distribution is also substantially more liberal than

US averages. Only the percentage of Conservative congregations is similar to the national average, while there are far more Reform, independent, and Renewal congregations and far fewer Orthodox congregations. High intermarriage rates strongly affect the composition of these congregations. While the percentages of families in such marriages in Bay Area Conservative and Orthodox synagogues are similar to the national averages, that is not the case in Reform and similar types of congregations, where in the Bay Area 40–70 percent of the members are in such marriages (as opposed to 26 percent nationally).

In sum, compared to the national averages, the Bay Area has a smaller percentage of Jews who join synagogues; the synagogues are more liberal; and in those synagogues, particularly with regard to younger families, the intermarriage rate is higher. At the same time, the region supports an active Jewish cultural life that includes many Jewish film festivals, street fairs, day schools, centers for specific types of Jewish learning (meditation, for example), a regionwide adult education program called Lehrhaus Judaica, and synagogues of various sizes and denominations.

Jews in the Bay Area are an example of one of the many different types of American Jewish communities. Though New York—which has the largest, densest, and most Orthodox (by percentage) Jewish community in the United States—is often imagined as the paradigmatic American Jewish community, it does not represent the variety of practices, beliefs, and identities found in other American communities, such as Chicago, Minnesota, or the Bay Area. By the same token, studies based in small and isolated Jewish communities (for example, Albuquerque) capture the issues facing such communities but not those of a large ethnic enclave. History, the surrounding culture, size, and density all contribute to Jewish life, and each results in people's different engagement with Judaism.

As a research site, the Bay Area offers much more than simply one choice among many. Its size offers one obvious advantage: there are fewer than a hundred congregations in the region, making it possible to describe completely the Jewish congregational landscape of the area. Understanding bar and bat mitzvah across a complete region provides the opportunity to understand how different variables—notably, size and denomination—shape the ritual in the context of a particular regional culture.

More significantly, both the American religious landscape (see, for example, Hadaway 2011; Putnam 2010; Pew 2013 and 2014) and the American Jewish landscape (Kosmin and Keysar 2013; Pew 2013 and 2014) show increasing levels of individualization and secularization nationally. With its low rate of congregational affiliation and its continuing cultural norms of religious pluralism and individualism, the Bay Area exemplifies these current trends. Examining it provides a window into the American Jewish future.

Precisely because affiliation is low, choosing to join a synagogue requires some self-justification on the part of congregants, with regard to both time and money. Both lay and professional leaders of these synagogues are well aware of the difficulties in recruiting new members, which results in some synagogues taking substantial pains to make the case for joining. High intermarriage rates introduce another issue that affects congregational dynamics: how do congregations remain distinctively Jewish yet also include non-Jewish participants? Bay Area congregations are an example of how minority communities—whether religious or ethnic—in a pluralistic society negotiate the tension between distinctiveness and inclusiveness.

This research used two primary modes of investigation: interviews with leaders of Bay Area congregations and observations and interviews at five representative congregations.[17] At each congregation, I requested interviews with rabbis, education directors, and administrators or executive directors. People in each of these roles provided different information about and different perspectives on bar and bat mitzvah.

From this pool, I chose five representative synagogues at which to observe services, religious school classes, and preparation for bar or bat mitzvah and to interview congregants, students preparing for bar or bat mitzvah, and their parents and tutors. This enabled me to understand the families' viewpoints, to consider both preparation for and enactment of bar or bat mitzvah, and to compare the bar or bat mitzvah service to an ordinary Shabbat service. Of the five congregations, four—a Conservative, an Orthodox, a Reform, and a nonaffiliated or independent congregation—had memberships of 200–400 families. The fifth was a very large Reform congregation, with a membership of well over a thousand families and a cohort of around eighty students, which represents the effect of size.[18] At each congregation, I observed Shabbat services, tutoring sessions, and religious school classes, while also drawing on content from websites, bar and bat mitzvah booklets, and bar and bat mitzvah speeches. In total, I interviewed over two hundred people, including forty-two rabbis, thirty-three education directors, thirty-six administrators or executive directors, members of twenty-eight bar or bat mitzvah families, and twenty-nine other participants (lay leaders, tutors, teachers, and congregants).

The different perspectives offered by both my in-depth observation and the leadership resulted in a wealth of information about supplementary school curricula, preparation for and participation in bar or bat mitzvah rituals, and Shabbat services more generally. I often felt that my informants were filling the roles of the blind men and the elephant: in feeling different parts of the animal, one thought he held a snake, another a palm frond, and a third a rope. In listening to people who played different roles and in observing different aspects of preparation and performance, I saw, if not the whole elephant, at least most of it.

As I listened and observed, it became clear that rabbis and teachers, congregants, and families were part of an interdependent system that included these participants, the nature of the ritual, and the institution of the congregation—its denomination, size, location, and history. That system was structured by a set of inherent tensions that included:

- Negotiating meaning: Participants ascribe different meanings to the ritual that depend on their roles, experiences, and knowledge. Leaders and families negotiate these different meanings through the course of preparation and performance.
- Balancing process and performance: Rituals symbolically enact the narratives and values that bind communities together. Without a competent performance, any ritual fails in its purpose, so the bar and bat mitzvah students must be adequately prepared for that performance. At the same time, leaders (and, at least to some degree, families) expect the ritual to represent a corpus of Jewish knowledge. Thus, in the limited time available to them, Jewish professionals balance the process of inculcating Judaism with the need to ensure a competent ritual performance.
- Raising or lowering community boundaries: With changing demographic characteristics and cultural expectations, congregations attempt to include previously excluded groups—women in Orthodox Judaism, and intermarried families in liberal Judaism. This inclusive attitude is balanced by the need to develop boundaries that protect the symbolic nature of the Jewish ritual.
- Managing public and private ritual needs: The ritual is integrated into the regular community service. As a result, congregations balance communal needs for a regular public Shabbat service with the private elements of a family life-cycle event.

When pointed out, this structure is clear and seemingly obvious. However, the participants most often do not understand the structure this way, focusing instead on the solutions that result from negotiating these tensions. Thus, they talk about how the service attendees are guests of the family, rather than about the tension between public service and private ritual, or discuss why (or why not) a non-Jewish parent can help pass the Torah, rather than the tension between inclusion and preservation of Jewish boundaries.

Approaching bar and bat mitzvah as a system makes it possible to understand how and why change occurs, taking into account the full range of participation. These four tensions not only shape the system, but they also characterize American Jewish life more generally, providing a lens through which to understand how Jews manage the often contradictory aspects of Jewish and American life. Furthermore, they can be used to understand the nature of American religious life, providing a framework for approaching change in congregations more generally.

FROM INDIVIDUAL STORY TO SHARED EXPERIENCE

It is common for research projects to develop out of personal experience, and this one is no different. My personal experience of American Judaism, much of which I took for granted as I lived it, developed into a broader understanding of the forces that shaped that experience. This chapter concludes with my personal story as means of introducing these larger issues.

The book is organized in three sections. Chapters 2 and 3 introduce the constituent parts of the bar and bat mitzvah system: the congregation, the ritual, and the participants. Each of chapters 4–7 examines one of the four inherent tensions. After summarizing these tensions, Chapter 8 concludes by addressing the relationship between bar and bat mitzvah and the Jewish future and, with some trepidation, offers policy suggestions. A caveat: while I refer to these topics covered in these chapters throughout the narrative that follows, they are not presented in order.

When my husband and I married in 1980, we joined the increasing number of intermarriages that resulted in the Reform movement's 1983 decision regarding the children of intermarriage. We settled on the eastern edge of the San Francisco Bay Area, where our family joined the small local congregation. Too small to support a rabbi, the congregation flew student rabbis up from the Reform movement's Hebrew Union College every other week to lead services, while congregants filled in on other weeks. When we joined, much of the work was done by volunteers, and I became one of them. I learned to lead services, attended Torah study, and served on the congregation's board.

Though these choices seemed individual, they were shaped by the nature of the times, characterized by second-wave feminism, the embrace of ethnic identity, and an increased sense of individual expression. When I declared that I could both practice Judaism and marry a non-Jew, I was making a particularly American choice that arose out of that time. We joined a synagogue on the basis of location. But its size and denomination mattered in shaping our family's Jewish experience. Small congregations need congregant participation to survive (Baggett 2009, 176–78). They also offer intimacy and encourage innovation. All of these factors enabled me to learn, participate, and develop a web of relationships. At the same time, the congregation assumed we would join as a Jewish family, rather than that I, as the Jewish partner, would join alone, which meant that our family felt accepted in that community, as we might not have had we joined another denomination. Yet joining a Reform congregation had other consequences: Reform practice determined the congregation's approach to Judaism. The American milieu and the varieties of American Judaism are discussed in chapter 2, which also introduces the five congregations that I observed.

Through my years of experience on my congregation's board, I became part of the lay leadership. I learned how synagogues are financed, members are recruited and retained, different factions in the congregation interact, and children's education is planned and enacted. I also learned to focus on the common goal of creating and maintaining a Jewish community in a Jewish space, a matter of ongoing negotiation. The Education Committee struggled with the question of whether to focus on Hebrew for its own sake or to prepare students for bar or bat mitzvah. The Religious Practices Committee debated how to balance a long-standing Torah study group with an increasing number of bar or bat mitzvah services.

Like most congregants who negotiate these issues, I saw them simply as problems to solve. Yet determining what kind of Hebrew to teach is part of the larger tension—discussed in chapter 5—between ensuring a capable performance and the process of inculcating Jewish identity, belief, and practice. Determining where the bar or bat mitzvah service fits into the congregation's Shabbat morning routine is part of the larger tension—discussed in chapter 7—between the public service and the private rite of passage. At the same time, there was little debate about the role or content of bar or bat mitzvah service itself: its place in congregational life was taken for granted. It was in this environment that our daughters prepared for their bat mitzvah services.

Our family's experience was typical of those at small congregations. With only a few bar or bat mitzvah services a year, each daughter could individualize her service, making it uniquely meaningful. Around half of the students in each girl's cohort came from intermarried families. Like them, we had to consider, in conjunction with the congregation, how to include a non-Jewish spouse (and his family) in the event. We had to plan the events surrounding the service, which included deciding how to handle difficult relatives with different needs in the larger context of family and friends.

The preceding short paragraph encapsulates much of the book. In individualizing our daughters' services, our family wrestled with different meanings of the ritual—discussed in chapter 4—trying to integrate the change of status, the welcome by a Jewish community of a new Jewish adult, the completion of a difficult task, and the personal celebration into the content. Finding ways to include my husband, the father of these Jewish children, while still respecting the integrity of the Jewish rite of passage resulted in decisions that, as it turned out, were common among other congregations. The tension between including previously excluded groups and preserving the Jewish nature of the service is the subject of chapter 6.

My daughters' bat mitzvahs were overwhelmingly personal events: each was differently shaped by preparation, performance, and celebration; each took place in a different extended family environment marked by births and deaths. In this we were as ordinary and unique as every other family. All Jewish families face challenges that result from differences between children, changes in family composition, and changes in the synagogue. There is a reason that bar or bat mitzvah evokes so much emotion: every family has these responsibilities to manage.

At the same time that my daughters were preparing for bat mitzvah, I had begun work as a bar and bat mitzvah tutor. These tutors vary substantially in their training, ranging from cantors who have years of formal training to people who, like me, are largely self-taught. My role as a community leader enabled me to understand the congregation's needs, and my role as parent gave me an individual perspective. Tutoring brought a third dimension to the process: the relationship between text, teacher, and student over a period of time, a topic discussed in chapter 5. It is a relationship similar to that of a music teacher or individual athletics coach, one in which an expert teaches an individual student. Each tutor begins with the individual student, an approach to the subject, and a goal. I taught students who varied in their learning styles, Hebrew or musical abilities, and interests. I found myself balancing meeting these individual needs with mastering the material by the date of the bar or bat mitzvah service. In almost all cases, I had the pleasure of witnessing my students' transformation from trepidation to competence.

It was through living the three roles of parent, community leader, and teacher and understanding that each role provides a different view of bar and bat mitzvah that I began to understand the ritual's role in American Jewish life, an understanding that later informed my work as a scholar.

As a congregational leader, I was concerned with the effect of the ritual on the community, taking Rabbi Eric Yoffie's words to heart: "The Shabbat morning bar or bat mitzvah . . . in most cases has alienated the uninvited, young and old, and appropriated the worship service as a private affair of the bar mitzvah family. This is far from a simple matter. For many Reform Jews, the rite of bar mitzvah is the single most significant religious event in their lives, and we should be respectful of its impact. Still, Judaism is a collective enterprise, not a private pursuit, and we must be troubled by the prospect that a family celebration is displacing Shabbat morning communal prayer" (1999).

As a parent, I was concerned with my family's individual event, ensuring that the needs of the child, members of her extended family, and friends were met. And each moment was powerful. When I stood in front of the guests at our older daughter's bat mitzvah, I felt surrounded by all the communities of which we were a part and felt their love and support. It is a feeling that is with me still.

When I stood with my younger daughter as my grandmother placed my grand-father's tallit on her shoulders, my heart overflowed with both joy and sorrow—joy at the continuity of generations and heartbreak at recent losses in our family. Bar or bat mitzvah provides these powerful moments for families, moments that are unique to each family.

As a tutor, I was concerned with the student and the service, attempting to forge a connection between text and student while ensuring that the student was prepared for the day of the ritual. I took delight in those moments when a student asked a particularly insightful question, mastered a piece of text, or otherwise showed a spark of the Jewish adult he or she could become. However, tutoring also connected me to the greater Jewish future, and like other teachers, I hoped these students would go on to maintain their Judaism as adults.

Much of the work on bar or bat mitzvah comes from the standpoint of the leaders, particularly those engaged in Jewish education. This is not surprising: while the experience of preparing for and enacting bar or bat mitzvah happens no more than a few times in a family's life, it profoundly shapes the lives of Jewish professionals. As a result, families' individual experiences are often overlooked by the professionals. While this book examines the tensions that are inherent in the relationships among congregation, ritual, and participants, part of my goal is to bring out the individual voices and stories of parents and children. Ultimately the ritual developed from the people, and it is maintained because it offers something meaningful to them. Hearing their voices matters, both intrinsically and because bar and bat mitzvah is a symbolic statement about the Jewish future, a future I turn to in chapter 8.

Though bar and bat mitzvah is obviously a topic of interest to Jews, the bar and bat mitzvah system has implications for the sociology of religion. Bar and bat mitzvah rituals exemplify how American religious rituals enable individuals and groups to negotiate between individual and public meanings. Through generalizing the bar and bat mitzvah system, this book thus provides a model to use in considering the interplay between personal and public ritual.

In addition, congregations, despite losing membership in recent years, are still the places where religions are enacted and reproduced in community. The four tensions negotiated between congregation, participants, and ritual can be applied to religious organizations more generally. Rituals take the sacred beliefs of a community and—through investing words, actions, and objects with meaning—bring these beliefs to life, thus reproducing the social and moral underpinnings of that community. The ongoing process of making meaning from rituals, whether peak moments or daily actions, is a necessary part of maintaining the life of a religion, particularly in a secularized society.[19] At the same time, ensuring that those who perform these rituals do so competently and respectfully is another aspect of maintaining the symbolic core of the community.

Participants in the process matter as well, whether they are leaders or attendees. Through playing their parts, both performers and witnesses are strengthened as individuals and as part of their community, while the sense of community is reinforced. That reinforcement happens not only formally, through religious services and classes, but also informally, as congregants and religious leaders negotiate their competing interests. Thus, understanding the interactions among bar or bat mitzvah, congregation, and participants leads to understanding the process of change and continuity within religious groups more generally.

2 · DESCRIBING THE CONTEXT

Congregations and the Bar or Bat Mitzvah Service

The four tensions that make up the heart of this book are the result of interactions among the congregation, the ritual, and the participants. However, these constituents do not have equal roles. Though both congregation and ritual are affected by these tensions, they are often seen as givens—part of the social and structural fabric of community life, which the participants must navigate. Both the congregational characteristics and the symbolic nature of the ritual set the limits for what is possible, but it is the different participants—rabbis, congregants, parents, and students—who negotiate the tensions. In this chapter, I consider the first two constituents, the congregation and the ritual; in the next, I describe the participants.

American Judaism exists in the context of American culture and religion. The first half of this chapter presents that context and discusses how American Judaism has adapted to it; then it describes each of the five congregations that I observed. This serves two purposes: it introduces the differences across the congregations in terms of size, culture, denominational approach, and Shabbat service practice, and it illustrates denominational approaches to modernity and the American context.

The second half of the chapter discusses the relationship between the bar or bat mitzvah service and the regular Shabbat morning service. It begins by outlining the underlying similarities in service structure and symbolism shared by all Shabbat services (regardless of denomination), goes on to describe the two distinctly different ways that these services are enacted, and then explains how the bar or bat mitzvah ritual adapts the Shabbat morning service to accommodate the peak rite of passage.

Through describing the elements of American Jewish life that are often taken for granted, I hope to clarify the nature of the constituent parts and their relationship to each other and the broader American context. The American milieu is the sea in which American Jews swim: understanding its effect enables both laity and leaders to make informed decisions and better understand the decisions of others. Similarly, understanding the relationship between regular Shabbat and bar or bat mitzvah service clarifies the reasons for conflict between the participants.

FROM AMERICAN RELIGION TO AMERICAN JUDAISM IN THE TWENTY-FIRST CENTURY

The American congregational model is in many ways a good fit for the traditional functions of the synagogue as a place where Jews gather to pray, learn, and build a community. Synagogues share with other American congregations the characteristics of composition, membership, meetings, and activities.[1] Families and individuals choose to join a synagogue and decide if and how they will participate, depending on their level of Jewish knowledge, identity, and observance and their comfort with a given congregation's culture and customs. Lay leaders, drawn from the congregation's membership, provide governance; rabbis, cantors, and education directors provide expert knowledge and establish the overall approach to congregational life, with rabbis, like ministers, being responsible for the religious content of services and interpretation of practices and texts.

Like other American congregations, synagogues provide spaces for congregants to gather at regular and (usually) predictable times as well as places to engage in communal activities. Some activities (most notably Rosh Hashanah and Yom Kippur services) engage virtually all members, some (often civic or social service activities) engage only a persistent few, but by definition, synagogue activities are communal, rather than individual, acts. As is the case in other American congregations, in synagogues these activities fall into three categories: religious practice, education, and social gatherings. The goal of both formal and informal religious education is to ensure the religion's survival in the future. These activities range from classes for children through adult choir practices to sewing a curtain for the Ark. Religious practice may include regular services in the congregation's building and home practice that relates to and deepens congregational religious practice.[2] Other activities serve to build or maintain relationships among members. These can be purely social in nature, but they can also include elements of education or practice (for example, belonging to a choir includes aspects of education, worship, and community).

These similarities mask an important difference between church and synagogue: the synagogue also acts as a particularly Jewish space in which Jewish
identity and peoplehood can be expressed.[3] The synagogue is tribal in ways that
few Christian congregations are.[4] Synagogues demonstrate this by using Hebrew,
referring to a common past and future, invoking connections to the greater Jewish people, and encouraging individual modes of Jewish identity. Each of these
elements symbolically reminds Jews of their connection to a people and its history.[5] The synagogue is also the place where Jewish communal life is enacted and
shaped, children are educated, and life-cycle events are observed. Unlike joining a church, membership in a synagogue is predicated on the assumption that
members are Jewish by birth or conversion (or, in the case of a family, that at least
one parent is Jewish).[6] Unlike in a true tribal society, American Jews can and do
choose when or if to join a congregation. As both a Jewish space in a non-Jewish
world and a group formed by voluntary affiliation, the congregation is caught
(as congregants are) between maintaining an exclusively Jewish space, thereby
losing potential members, and competing for members by being open and inclusive. Different denominations take different paths to manage this conflict.

Though the American cultural context affects all synagogues, individual congregations are shaped by region and location in that region, by past history and
current demographic characteristics (members' age, diversity, rate of intermarriage, and socioeconomic status), internal politics, and cultural norms. These
characteristics make each congregation uniquely interesting, but ultimately they
matter less for understanding bar and bat mitzvah than do the characteristics on
which I focused: size and denominational affiliation.[7]

The size of a congregation (the number of either families or individual members) affects resources, both monetary and human; the degree of bureaucracy
necessary for the institution to function; the number and variety of programs;
and the degree of congregational engagement. I noted above my own experience
in a small congregation. This personal experience was confirmed by rabbis of
small congregations, while a different experience was reported by some (though
hardly all) of the congregants at the large Reform Beth Jeshurun,[8] who felt alienated from the community.[9]

The size of the bar or bat mitzvah cohort, a related number, also largely determines the ritual's effect on the congregation and the ability of the congregation
to individualize the ritual and preparation for it.[10]

Denominations set expectations for relationship to authority—whether
ascribed to God or tradition—or individual choice, to Jewish practice, and to the
Jewish people. Denominations set policy, publish prayer books that shape how
liturgy is enacted, train new rabbis or other Jewish professionals, and develop
educational material for both children and adults.[11] Though each congregation
is different, these policy and practice norms underlie congregational life to the

point where virtually every congregation includes its affiliation (or lack thereof) on the synagogue website.

Modern Judaism, of which American Judaism is one variation, developed through attempts to reconcile two contradictory value systems. Judaism is an ethnic religion with group boundaries defined primarily by heritage. The resulting Jewish people are viewed as chosen by God for a special relationship that includes a set of obligations or commandments. This sense of chosenness contrasts with the rationalistic worldview that characterizes modernity. The three primary branches of Judaism—Reform, Conservative, and Orthodox—originated in nineteenth-century Germany as different approaches to negotiating this contrast. The particularly American expression of modernity, emphasizing voluntary choice and the assumption that all people have the right to make their own choices and, in so doing, create themselves (Eisen 1983), has shaped all three movements in distinctively American ways.[12] During the twentieth century other approaches to Judaism have developed: Reconstructionist, Renewal, Humanist, and a postdenominational or independent approach. In the Bay Area, most congregations are affiliated with one of the three primary denominations, with the independent or nonaffiliated congregation making up the fourth largest group.[13]

These different approaches to Judaism have consequences for congregational practice. A Modern Orthodox congregation will no longer be considered Orthodox if men and women sit together in services. A Conservative congregation must keep a kosher kitchen to remain part of the Conservative movement. Reform congregations may differ in their approaches to kashrut but must allow egalitarian worship. Whether a congregation's relationship to a given movement is tight or loose, that movement's directives shape congregational practice. This includes liturgical content and presentation. All Jewish prayer has a common set of rubrics, but how those are realized and interpreted varies from movement to movement, although each denomination has a common siddur (prayer book) used by member congregations. This affiliation also shapes each congregation's approach to liturgy, texts, and their interpretation when preparing students for the bar or bat mitzvah ritual.

In choosing my observation sites, I focused on the shared characteristics of size and denomination, using information gathered from interviews with leaders and recent scholarship on congregations (Raphael 2011). Each congregation I observed demonstrates a different approach to Judaism, one largely representative of the denomination with which it is affiliated. The distinctions between denominations and the nature of each congregation are discussed in what follows.

Reform Sukkat Shalom: Making Choices

Reform Judaism incorporates individual choice into its structure, seeing Jewish law as a reservoir of fundamental practices and beliefs with which individual Jews choose to engage as individuals. In 1999, following a more general cultural trend, the Central Conference of American Rabbis, the rabbinical association associated with the Union for Reform Judaism, adopted a set of principles that encouraged more engagement with Jewish learning and practice (Central Conference of American Rabbis 2004). These practices are not a matter of obligation but of choice, with each Jew adopting those practices that are individually meaningful and each congregation determining what level of traditional adherence is appropriate in its services. This has resulted in a complex, pluralistic approach summed up in the introduction to the recent prayer book, *Mishkan T'filah* (Tent of Prayer): "The challenge of a single liturgy is to be not only multi-vocal, but poly-vocal—to invite full participation at once, without conflicting with the keva [fixed] text. Jewish prayer invites interpretation; [some of] the . . . material was selected both for metaphor and theological diversity. The choices were informed by the themes of Reform Judaism and Life: social justice, feminism, Zionism, distinctiveness, human challenges" (Frishman 2010, ix).

This quote does not apply only to prayer but also to the choice of words such as "invite" instead of "command," the offering of multiple interpretations, and the inclusion of secular as well as traditional Jewish sources. Thus, it exemplifies the Reform approach to Judaism more generally. Although this approach assumes a range of practice and belief from fully engaged to minimal, and all Reform congregations have some members who engage in intensive Jewish practice, Reform rabbis described their typical congregants as minimally observant.

There are about thirty Reform congregations in the Bay Area, the smallest of which contains under 100 families, and the largest of which contains around 2,500 families. In addition to following the approach to Judaism shared across Reform congregations, these Reform congregations are distinct from the others in my study in two ways. First, the percentage of intermarried families in these congregations is high, with rates of 40–70 percent and even higher in families with young children. Second, the pluralistic and voluntaristic approach described above extends to congregational governance. While rabbis are the congregational leaders, decisions—often including those regarding religious practice—are more likely to be shared with lay leaders than is the case in Conservative or Orthodox congregations.

With a membership of about 300 families and a typical bar or bat mitzvah cohort of twenty-five students each year, Sukkat Shalom is representative of medium-size Reform congregations in the Bay Area, with a strong rabbi, a few full-time employees and more part-time teachers, and a strong partnership with volunteers.[14] The congregation is led by Rabbi Doron, its founding rabbi. After many years of service, his voice and presence carry much weight, particularly with regard to the content and performance of religious services. A staff of six (including Rabbi Doron, the education director, and the cantor) oversees the supplementary school, adult education, different types of Shabbat religious services, and other types of programs. Additionally, part-time employees teach Hebrew and religious school for a few hours each week during the regular school year. Volunteer committees take on governance (finance, facilities, and communication) and plan social actions and religious and educational activities.

As is the norm for Reform congregations, the primary Shabbat service takes place on Friday evening.[15] In Reform congregations of this size, Saturday morning services without a bar or bat mitzvah ritual can vary from none to a lay-led service or, as at Sukkat Shalom, informal services led by the rabbi. These services take place in the small library with chairs set in a circle, and there are usually between ten and twenty attendees who participate actively and comfortably. The service changes dramatically when there is a bar or bat mitzvah, which takes place in the ample sanctuary, with most but not all of the attendees being invited guests. Despite encouragement from the cantor, only a few of these attendees participate actively in the service.

Like most supplementary Jewish religious schools, irrespective of denomination, Sukkat Shalom's school begins in kindergarten and extends through seventh grade (and bar or bat mitzvah).[16] Supplementary religious school takes place on Sundays and one weekday, for a total of four and half hours each week. It includes both Hebrew and Jewish studies, with the older grades more focused on bar or bat mitzvah skills and content.

Reform congregations vary substantially in their expectations of the amount of participation in the bar or bat mitzvah ritual, but their approach to the material is similar. At Sukkat Shalom, students lead about half of the service, read twelve to fifteen verses of the weekly Torah portion, chant four or five verses from the associated Haftarah, and discuss the Torah portion in a brief speech.[17] Students begin to learn this material about six months before the day of the ritual, first meeting weekly with Cantor Waldman to solidify their parts in the service and learn their Haftarah readings, then adding meetings with Rabbi Doron to learn their Torah portions and develop their bar or bat mitzvah talks. Students' families also meet together three times during the year to discuss parental roles with regard to the ritual. Finally, students have the option of participating in a program that encourages individual students to try out different types of Jewish practice: learning about personal Jewish history, doing charitable work, and practicing ritual behavior.

Orthodox Adat Yitzhak: Encouraging Torah Judaism

While Reform and Orthodox Judaism both assume a unique relationship between Jews and God through Torah, Orthodox Judaism has at its core the absolute authority of Torah and the associated set of rules and laws, called Halakhah, that has been developed and interpreted through the past two millennia. Orthodox Jews account for a little more than one-tenth of the Jewish population in the United States; however, their rate of synagogue affiliation is much higher than that of Jews who identify with more liberal denominations, and thus Orthodox Jews make up around 20 percent of the American Jews who belong to congregations.[18] Unlike Reform Judaism, with its seminaries, publishing house, and governing body, Orthodox Judaism encompasses a wide range of beliefs and behaviors, from the ultra-Orthodox Jews who claim to completely reject modernity to the Modern Orthodox Jews who—like Reform and Conservative Jews—attempt to reconcile modernity with Judaism. Orthodox Jews have origins in Eastern Europe, Spain, Syria, and Iran. Modern Orthodoxy accounts for somewhat more than two-thirds of this branch of Judaism.

Relative to some other parts of the United States, the Bay Area's Orthodox population is small. There are eighteen Orthodox congregations, which range in size from under 50 to around 200 families, with ten falling into the parameters of this study. Although both Sephardic and Karaite congregations exist, most Bay Area Orthodox congregations (certainly the larger ones) identify themselves as Modern Orthodox.[19]

In theory, Orthodox practice dictates the shape of everyday life, from food and clothing to religious observance, which includes observing the dietary laws of kashrut, emphasizing the observance of Shabbat and holidays, and dressing and behaving modestly. In addition, there are distinct gender roles with regard to religious practice: men and women sit separately, and men are allowed to participate in ways that women are not.[20] Because of its encompassing nature, it requires a community of close neighbors to reinforce and support practice, a difficult proposition in the Bay Area, which has no geographic concentration of Jews. As a result, Bay Area Orthodox congregations include families who do not necessarily observe strict Orthodox practice in their homes but affiliate with a particular congregation because of an attachment to the rabbi, the community, or some elements of Orthodox practice.

This is the case at Adat Yitzhak, which has two distinct segments: those who are Orthodox in practice and therefore affiliate with the congregation because of that affiliation and those who, whatever their home observance, belong because of the rabbi, the supportive culture, or the kind of practice and learning that the congregation provides. Thus, the membership is diverse, encompassing Reform, Reconstructionist, atheist, Conservative, and Orthodox Jews. Rita Cohen's attachment to the congregation is representative:

We really, really like Adat Yitzhak. . . . There are Orthodox, there are nonobservant people. The Orthodox can't have a shul without the non-observant because they need each other. Not only that, but we can't have the kind of shul we have without the Orthodox. So because we need each other, we're very respectful to each other . . . and it makes for a very healthy—moderation for each. . . . The group is better than any individual; each person rises when engaged with people at Adat Yitzhak. That's my experience of it, and I find that really remarkable and wonderful.

With a membership of about 200 families and a bar or bat mitzvah cohort of about twelve students each year, Adat Yitzhak is representative of the Bay Area's Modern Orthodox congregations. In addition to the charismatic and energetic Rabbi Teitelbaum, the congregation employs two assistant rabbis (or rabbinic interns) who help lead and teach, along with an administrator. The synagogue houses a large preschool, with a director and teachers, and there is an active adult education program. Unlike the case in other branches, almost all Orthodox families send their children to Jewish day schools, so the congregation has no supplementary school.[21] As at Sukkat Shalom, volunteer committees take on governance (finance, facilities, and communication) and plan social and social action activities. However, Rabbi Teitelbaum is solely responsible for religious practices and educational decisions.

Adat Yitzhak's primary Shabbat service takes place on Saturday morning. These services are well attended; Rabbi Teitelbaum says that he sees every congregant at services at least once a month. During my observations, attendance rarely dipped below 150 adults, with about two-thirds of those present being men.[22] Services at Adat Yitzhak are largely lay-led—only by men—with Rabbi Teitelbaum reserving the role of interpreting the text for himself. The service is highly participatory, with both men and women reciting the prayers and following the texts.

Because Rabbi Teitelbaum individualizes bar or bat mitzvah preparation, students vary considerably in how they enact the ritual. However, most chant some verses from the Torah and all of the associated Haftarah portion, which they learn from an approved tutor. Most students also give a speech on the Torah portion or a lesson on a specific topic (for example, the role of the priestly class—Cohens and Levis—in modern Judaism). Students study with Rabbi Teitelbaum or his wife (in the case of girls) for several months to prepare these speeches. When a bar mitzvah takes place, there is little change in the service content or participation. A bat mitzvah, on the other hand, does not take place during the main service. The complications that result are discussed in chapter 6.

Conservative B'nai Aaron: Claiming the Center

Reform Judaism integrates Judaism into American mainstream culture, and Orthodox Judaism emphasizes Jewish practice and belief. The Conservative movement balances these two approaches, arguing that while Jews and God are bound in a relationship shaped by Torah and Jewish law, each Jewish community lives in a particular historical moment, and in each moment, Jews can interpret Torah to allow some flexibility. As a result, Conservative Jewish practice sometimes looks like Reform Judaism and sometimes like Orthodox Judaism. For example, on one hand, both Reform and Conservative Judaism embrace egalitarian practice, with men and women filling similar religious roles; on the other hand, both Orthodox and Conservative Judaism reject equilineal heritage, in which the child of a Jewish parent (not only a Jewish mother) is considered Jewish. In other respects—for example, the use of Hebrew, observance of dietary laws, and Shabbat restrictions—Conservative congregations fall between Reform and Orthodox Judaism, encouraging stricter observance than the former, but allowing more lenient observance than the latter.

There are fifteen Conservative synagogues in the Bay Area, representing about 20 percent of the congregations (compared to 23 percent nationally), with membership at each Conservative synagogue ranging from 300 to 700 families. B'nai Aaron is a Conservative congregation consisting of around 400 families and with a bar or bat mitzvah cohort averaging twenty students each year. The congregation is led by two rabbis—Rabbi Rosen, the senior rabbi who has served the congregation for more than two decades, and Rabbi Josephson, a young rabbi who appeals to younger families. The staff also includes two administrators, the education director, and a rabbinic assistant. The professional staff members oversee the supplementary school and the part-time teachers, adult education, different types of Shabbat religious services, and other types of programs; a large volunteer board governs the congregation. The congregation is proud of its outreach to young adults and young families, but older families and couples still predominate.

As at Orthodox Adat Yitzhak, the primary Shabbat service takes place on Saturday morning, with around 120 people attending. The service at B'nai Aaron is largely lay-led—although, in an important difference from Adat Yitzhak, both men and women act as service leaders. The rabbis alternate in introducing the weekly Torah and Haftarah portions. Toward the conclusion of the service, one or the other rabbi delivers a *d'var* Torah (a commentary on the Torah portion; literally, a "matter of Torah"), with a printed handout summarizing the talk. As at Adat Yitzhak, attendees participate actively in the service, and most age groups, including small children, are represented.[23]

The rabbinic assistant acts as the congregational bar or bat mitzvah tutor and is responsible for all preparation except for the bar or bat mitzvah talk.

Students study with her for six months prior to the ritual to learn to chant the Torah, Haftarah, and expected prayers. Unlike at most congregations, the rabbis do not work with students individually, but they teach the seventh grade class, which enables them to focus on difficult topics, such as the Jewish response to death. Students develop their bar or bat mitzvah talks over several meetings with mentors, congregants who have volunteered to work with students and, ideally, develop an ongoing relationship with them.[24] For the ritual, students are expected to lead some sections of the Shabbat morning service, chant around fifteen verses of the Torah portion and all of the Haftarah, introduce both Torah and Haftarah readings, and deliver a brief bar or bat mitzvah talk. In many congregations, this speech replaces that usually given by the rabbi, but at B'nai Aaron, the rabbi prepares and gives a speech as well, so that although the student displays his or her learning, the congregation can also hear a more mature interpretation of the texts.

Independent Or Hadash: Enacting Jewish Pluralism

Independent congregations have intentionally chosen not to affiliate with a specific denomination, instead encouraging members to "take practices from the full spectrum of Jewish tradition, and look for the challenge of building their own traditions within the broadest parameters of traditional Judaism."[25] Although they incorporate elements from different denominations, the congregations emphasize the individual's responsibility to develop a personal Jewish practice, which—both theologically and practically—results in these congregations being most similar to Reform in observance and congregants' philosophy and practice.

There are twelve independent congregations in the Bay Area, representing about 16 percent of the total (compared to 5 percent nationally); their membership ranges from 100 to 400 families. These congregations tend to be more idiosyncratic than affiliated congregations, so it was difficult to choose a typical independent congregation. I chose Or Hadash, because of the rabbi's intentional approach. Or Hadash has a membership of around 300 families, with a typical annual bar or bat mitzvah cohort of twenty-five students. Led by Rabbi Melmed, a rabbi who incorporates aspects of Reform, Conservative, and Orthodox Judaism into his practice, the congregation prides itself on its high level of volunteer participation and governance in all aspects of congregational life.

Most congregants who attend services do so on Friday night, but Rabbi Melmed holds weekly Torah study, and some of the congregants who attend that also stay for Shabbat morning services. The rabbi encourages lay leadership, and congregants often chant from the Torah or lead portions of the service, a practice more common in Conservative or Orthodox congregations than in liberal congregations.

Rabbi Melmed has invested much time and effort on developing an intensive bar and bat mitzvah program, which requires substantial effort from both parents and students. Students must attend regular services and keep a service journal, individualize the bar or bat mitzvah service, write a booklet that interprets the Hebrew texts they will read, translate a prayer, and write a separate speech that introduces a discussion that the student will lead. Families are required to attend an eight-session family class that not only prepares the whole family for bar or bat mitzvah but also includes more general information about Jewish values and practice. Students lead most of the bar or bat mitzvah service, chant around twenty lines from the Torah and the entire Haftarah portion, and deliver the speech that leads into the discussion.

Large Reform Beth Jeshurun: Judaism on a Large Scale

The four congregations described above represent differences in denominational practice, but all four are medium-size. Reform Beth Jeshurun is different: it represents the effect of size. Congregational size (and institutional size more generally) affects the nature of rules, relationships, access to leaders, and institutional bureaucracy. Time constraints prevented me from observing a very small congregation, but my interviews with rabbis at a number of these congregations showed them to be more idiosyncratic in practice, engage a higher proportion of congregants (although a lower total number), and encourage more personal relationships with the leaders. In contrast, very large congregations have no choice but to develop policies, schedules, and lines of authority to keep track of different needs and activities.

Bar and bat mitzvah preparation and enactment is a particularly clear example of how these large congregations negotiate the needs of a large population. While all congregations must manage the ritual's logistics, problems related to the logistics are more pressing in large congregations. In very small congregations, ongoing personal relationships mean that students' progress can be tracked informally. However, as overall class size and the number of bar or bat mitzvah students increase, the competing needs of different populations also increase, while tracking students' progress becomes more difficult.

In large congregations, the professional leadership is responsible for organizing and tracking students' progress. On the one hand, this can result in smooth performances; on the other hand, families can feel like, as one parent said, "cogs in a machine." There are six or seven (depending on precisely where the line is drawn between one size and the next) very large Reform congregations in the Bay Area, each of which has developed extensive and varied programs for bar or bat mitzvah preparation. Of these, I chose to observe Beth Jeshurun, a congregation with a membership of well over 1,000 families and a bar or bat mitzvah cohort of about eighty students a year, equal to the combined total of the other four congregations discussed. Beth Jeshurun is served by several rabbis of different ages and with different styles, skills, and responsibilities, along with a large and expert staff. Decisions are made by the staff, with input from the board, although the large pool of congregants also can generate and enact new ideas.

As at most Reform congregations, Beth Jeshurun's primary Shabbat services take place on Friday night. With substantial resources, the congregation offers several services to accommodate different interests: in addition to the ongoing contemporary service, the congregation offers different services tailored to the needs of young families and young adults.

Saturday morning services are filled largely, but not exclusively, with bar or bat mitzvah families and their guests. Here, because there are more students than weeks in the year, the congregation must make decisions about how to allocate space. Some large congregations do this by having bar or bat mitzvah rituals in which two or more students share time and space. Beth Jeshurun has enough space to hold two services simultaneously, so on many Saturday mornings, two or even three Shabbat services take place.

Like Or Hadash, Beth Jeshurun developed an elaborate bar or bat mitzvah preparation program. This begins eighteen months prior to the day of the ritual and includes family classes that explain parts of the service, short classes to teach essential prayers, and eight sessions with one of the rabbis to work on an extensive speech, as well as an introduction to both the Torah and Haftarah portions. Students are expected to chant around twelve verses from the Torah and a few from the Haftarah, lead one or two central prayers, and deliver a speech.

These five different congregations represent most of the range of practice in the Bay Area. Each was chosen to typify either denomination or size. The Bay Area skews substantially more toward Reform than does the national norm, so in some sense, my results skew that way as well. However, the reality is more complicated: Bay Area denominations are, like those in other regions of the United States, bound by denominational norms and rulings. People who join these congregations have different expectations of the different denominations. As a result, these congregations do represent the breadth and differences seen in American Jewish practice. At the same time, they all exist in one region of the country and so there are distinct regional similarities of language and approach across the congregations and denominations. Whether more similar or more different, all must answer the same questions: How do we ensure that our students are adequately prepared? What should the content of the ritual be? How do we ensure that we both protect the ritual practice and welcome members and guests? How do the different goals of the ritual and the Shabbat morning service complement or conflict with each other? The constraints of the different denominations and sizes result in different answers to these questions.

FROM WEEKLY SERVICE TO PEAK EVENT: CONSTRUCTING THE BAR OR BAT MITZVAH RITUAL

While many religions have coming-of-age rituals, these most often emphasize the new adult status in ceremonies that are distinct from regular religious practice. The same can be said for other Jewish rites of passage: all have rituals separate from the regular service.[26] The bar or bat mitzvah ritual differs in that it explicitly incorporates (or is incorporated by) that regular practice, with students mastering and leading all or part of the regular service to emphasize the individual Jew's ability, responsibility, and right to lead the service. The result—that on this day a child leads the community in prayer—is a powerful and profoundly democratizing event. But a bar or bat mitzvah, precisely because it is a rite of passage, is not simply a community religious service but at once more (a peak event) and less (a service led by a teenager). It is necessary to clarify the relationship between the two services to understand the context for what bar or bat mitzvah students do and how that service affects other aspects of congregational life.

The Shabbat Morning Liturgy and D'var Torah

Like Muslim and Catholic prayer, Jewish prayer is highly structured. Whether recited on a weekday or Shabbat, in the morning or evening, it repeats the same sections, with minor variations that depend on time of day and day of the week.[27] On Shabbat, this daily service changes to incorporate the distinctive qualities of the sabbath: the weekly Torah reading and accompanying Haftarah are chanted and explained, and (in Conservative and Orthodox practice) the Musaf section, a modified recapitulation of the morning service, is added. Although presentation and interpretation vary, in all denominations the Shabbat morning service consists of five sections, with the Musaf section added in Conservative and Orthodox practice.[28] Afternoon services (typically held only in Orthodox congregations) include a brief selection from the next week's Torah portion.[29]

The liturgy was developed over several centuries and is preserved—or modified—within the prayer books, or siddurim (the plural form of siddur, or prayer book). Over the past century, the rabbinical wings of different denominations have developed variations on these prayer books that include the Hebrew, English translations, transliterations, and interpretations from different sources. In addition, some congregations, particularly independent ones, draw on a variety of sources to create their own siddurim, as was the case at Or Hadash. All these books share the framework and themes that run throughout Jewish liturgy, but in each case the authors engage with and interpret Judaism differently.[30]

There are two distinct models for congregational Shabbat worship, which I describe as traditional and contemporary.[31] While both labels come with baggage, nonetheless they point to an overall mood created—intentionally or not—by each type of service. The traditional model consciously makes connections with past practice, whether real or imagined; the contemporary model uses current interpretation and music to connect to attendees. Jews who are used to one style or the other may notice only the differences between these models. Thus, a Jew who is used to the traditional service may feel that a contemporary service is nothing more than "Judaism lite," and one who is used to the contemporary service may feel that a traditional service is nothing more than rote repetition. Despite differences in presentation, the traditional and contemporary models share an overarching structure and liturgy, a central moment during which the Torah is read, and a sermon, or *d'var* Torah, that interprets the reading to the congregation.

Conservative and Orthodox congregations follow the traditional model, in which the congregation's primary service takes place Saturday morning. Services last for most of the morning and are almost entirely recited in Hebrew, with each section of prayer treated as a unit. Congregants daven—that is, they use a mode of prayer in which each individual chants the prayers quietly at his or her own pace, often accompanied by rhythmic rocking back and forth or side to side (this last is more common in Orthodox prayer), so that the service leader is responsible for leading a block of prayers, rather than only one or two. The service leader is responsible for keeping the congregation together, which is done by chanting the initial line of each prayer aloud, quietly and quickly reading the middle section, and then chanting the final line aloud. This mode of prayer requires considerable skill on the part of both leader and congregants. In the traditional model, the entire weekly Torah portion and associated Haftarah are chanted, while explanations and interpretations focus on issues raised by the texts. Orthodox rabbis use traditional commentaries to explicate the text and relate it to current issues, while Conservative rabbis may bring in other sources as well. In these congregations, it is common (although not universal) for congregants to lead the service and chant from the Torah; the rabbi's primary role is to teach.

Reform Judaism, along with most other types of Judaism found in the Bay Area, follow the contemporary model. In these congregations, the primary congregational service takes place on Friday night, and comparatively few congregants attend Saturday morning services. In some congregations, Saturday morning services take place only for bar or bat mitzvah services.[32] The contemporary model includes the same sections of the service as does the traditional model, though within that structure, it eliminates some prayers from the liturgy and abridges or modifies others. Additional English texts offer a variety of perspectives on the Hebrew prayers: these texts include both literal and interpretive translations, additional readings from Jewish and secular sources, and interpretations that filter Jewish values and practices through the lens of dominant American culture. In addition, the different sections are not treated as units led by one leader, but as individual prayers in a group. So while attendees at traditional services daven a set of prayers, attendees at contemporary services might read one prayer responsively, chant another in unison, and sing a third in a mixture of Hebrew and English accompanied by instrumental music. This type of service is usually led by a rabbi, sometimes accompanied by a cantor, rather than by congregants.

In both these models, the climax of the Shabbat morning service is the section when the Torah is read, commonly called the Torah service. Through the use of movement, touch, sight, and sound, the Torah service symbolically re-creates the central moment within Judaism: God's giving the Torah to the Jewish people.

The Torah is divided into fifty-four portions, one of which is read each Shabbat throughout the cycle of the Jewish calendar year.[33] Following this reading, a related section from the Haftarah is read. In the traditional model, the whole Torah portion is read, divided into seven sections, called *aliyot* (literally, "going up [to the Torah]"), along with the whole Haftarah.[34] In the contemporary model, the Torah reader chooses a section of Torah to chant, along with a section of the Haftarah. This can be divided into as few as one or as many as eight *aliyot*. Whether enacted in contemporary or traditional form, reading from and hearing the words from the scroll are a sacred obligation for Jews, and all denominations consider reading from the scroll itself a necessary part of the Shabbat service.

Finally, the *d'var* Torah is the interpretive moment. These talks vary greatly in length, language, type of references, and approach. For example, one guide to writing these talks gives seven approaches, from taking one line of text to reflecting on broader themes, and from mystical to historical explanations (Israel 1993, 40–58). However, most commonly, these talks address questions raised by the text, link the meanings of the text to concerns of American Jews, or use the text as a way to exhort listeners to action. The difference between the contemporary and traditional approaches appears primarily in the approach to sources, language, and textual references. These same differences shape students' bar or bat mitzvah speeches.

From Shabbat Morning Service to Bar or Bat Mitzvah Ritual

These three parts of the Shabbat morning service—leading different prayers or sections of the service, chanting all or part of the Torah and Haftarah portions, and delivering a modified *d'var* Torah—have been incorporated into the bar or bat mitzvah ritual, so that the bar or bat mitzvah service can appear to be another enactment of a Shabbat morning service. This is certainly the intent: even congregations that hold Shabbat morning services only when a bar or bat mitzvah ritual takes place follow the form of the Shabbat service. Despite the integration of the ritual into Shabbat morning services, it is a rite of passage. Thus, whether part of a traditional or contemporary Shabbat service, every bar or bat mitzvah ritual contains moments that deviate from that regular service, often incorporating family members or personal statements by the student and/or his or her parents. These might include:

- parents (or other relatives) presenting a prayer shawl (tallit) to the child;
- parents and grandparents handing the Torah scroll from one generation to the next;
- parents giving a speech or blessing to the child;
- in Orthodox settings, the father reciting the blessing that transfers the son's religious responsibilities from father to son (*sheptarani*);
- the student thanking guests for being present, teachers and rabbis for teaching him or her, and parents for support;
- congregational representatives presenting gifts to the student;
- rabbis' speaking to or blessing the child.

These moments are important, not only because they matter to the family, but also because their presence changes the nature of the Shabbat service. Yet these moments are simply markers of the ritual; the ritual itself is defined by the actions of the bar or bat mitzvah student. These actions almost always include chanting the blessings on reading from the Torah, and then reading and interpreting texts (Torah and Haftarah).[35] These three tasks (reciting the blessings, chanting texts, and delivering an interpretation) date from the early stages of the ritual and symbolically demonstrate the students' new Jewish status (Hilton 2014; Marcus 2005). Over the latter half of the twentieth century, having the student lead all or part of the service has become common, and the expectation that he or she will master the text has increased.[36] As with the regular Shabbat morning service, expectations for bar or bat mitzvah students are similar across denominations, but their enactment reflects different approaches to Judaism more generally.

Congregations following the traditional model consider themselves bound to greater or lesser degree by Jewish law and so expect the service structure to dictate what students do. For example, students chant at least the three or four verses that end the weekly Torah portion and lead into the Hafarah. The weekly portion is divided into seven sections, and students who chant additional verses must add a complete section, rather than—as would be the case with the contemporary model—simply adding a few extra verses. Similarly, many students lead the concluding Musaf section of the service. Students who lead more prayers must prepare the entire section, rather than adding just one or two individual prayers.

The contemporary model leads to an individual approach to the service. Congregations following this model usually ask students to choose 12–25 verses from the Torah portion and 6–12 verses from the Haftarah portion that raise questions or concerns. By making these choices, the reasoning goes, students will develop a connection to the texts and their own Jewish identity. These congregations also vary by the number and type of prayers students lead, with some expecting students to lead the entire service, while others expecting them to lead only one or two important prayers.[37]

Whether following contemporary or traditional models, rabbis and tutors in my study spoke in similar ways about encouraging students to take ownership of the material and engaging students through individual expression. The contemporary model explicitly encourages this individuality, as the rabbi of a large Reform congregation describes: "We meet with the kids nine months in advance. [We ask them] some questions, like: 'What are three main parts of the Torah portion that interest you, and why? Which one part would you choose to talk about? What interests you about it? What thoughts do you have about it?' I have them read the Torah portion with their parents and pick their twelve verses and talk about what it means."

But it is not only the contemporary model that encourages students to make individual choices so as to make Jewish tradition their own. Orthodox Rabbi Teitelbaum describes his philosophy as follows: "I explain to families [that their] child becomes a bat or bar mitzvah by waking up on their twelfth or thirteenth birthday, respectively. What are we going to do to make this transition into adulthood meaningful? That's when we talk: here are different things that can be done during services, here are different things that could be done teaching Torah, and let's look at it like a buffet. . . . I want them to take into account two things: their interests and what they're going to keep doing through their lives."

Rabbi Teitelbaum carefully preserves his understanding of the service's integrity, yet his philosophy quite closely mirrors that of the Reform rabbi with regard to forming Jewish identity through making Jewish choices. The Reform rabbi seems to offer more choices, but these are also within a carefully defined service structure—albeit one that includes a different set of choices. A similar balance between fixed structure and free choice takes place in developing the bar or bat mitzvah talk. While teachers share the desire for their students to think and to use logic, reason, and (sometimes) Jewish sources to develop an original speech, how they encourage students to do this varies.

From D'var Torah to Bar or Bat Mitzvah Talk

Bar or bat mitzvah students across the denominations give talks that largely mimic the d'var Torah of the Shabbat morning service, analyzing the text and often quoting commentaries or other texts to draw some moral lesson for the present. Yet there are also important differences.

Students often use personal anecdotes featuring school or sports as ways to relate the Torah portion to their lives, use the talk to formally commit to Jewish continuity or refer to their new status, and discuss their mitzvah projects.[38] As is appropriate at a life-cycle ritual—but not a congregational service—students have many people to thank for their accomplishment. Rabbis had remarkably strong and divided feelings about the place of these thank-yous. Some rabbis insisted that students must acknowledge those who helped them reach the ritual. Other rabbis distinguished between the private and public faces of the event, saying that thanking people should take place at the end of services or, preferably, at the celebration. As one Conservative rabbi said, "there are no thank-yous here. I explain to the child: you're introducing the Torah reading, background, and introduction for what we're about to read. Thank-yous are for the end of services." Though a minor point, these differences in approach illustrate how rabbis choose different ways to resolve the tension between the student's role as adult service leader and celebrant of a peak event.

Bar or bat mitzvah and Shabbat services roughly follow either the traditional or contemporary patterns of their synagogues. However, the style and length of bar or bat mitzvah talks are surprisingly diverse, representing the preferences of individual rabbis, rather than denominational norms.

Rabbi Doron of Sukkat Shalom expects short speeches from his students: "I always tell them it's not a long sermon, it's just three paragraphs long. [In] the first paragraph they take something of interest to them, either from their Haftarah or their Torah portion, and they describe it in their own words. [In] the second paragraph, they have to relate it to themselves in some way. The third paragraph is thanking everybody. So it's just a simple drash [synonym for d'var Torah]."

Other Reform rabbis require more complex speeches. For example, the rabbi of another Reform congregation of about five hundred families expects his students to use the speech "to learn, to teach, and to share a part of themselves. It's usually between four and eight pages double-spaced, fourteen-point type. They work on that with me. Some kids completely do it on their own, some kids need a lot of help. . . . It's a big writing project for them, and it's really how I connect with the kids." Not only does this rabbi expect substantial content from his students, but, unlike Rabbi Doron, he uses it as a teaching technique.[39]

Yet, while style and length vary with rabbis' individual opinions, how the text is interpreted follows distinct denominational patterns. Congregations following the traditional model tend to refer to the Jewish corpus of texts and draw conclusions based more on communal obligation. Congregations following the contemporary model incorporate secular texts and experience, in addition to Jewish source material, and draw conclusions that are more individual. The differences in approach represent, but also replicate, how the different branches approach modernity.

Both Rabbi Teitelbaum from Orthodox Adat Yitzhak and Rabbi Lerner, one of the rabbis at the large Reform Beth Jeshurun, expected substantial work and thought from their students, resulting in bar or bat mitzvah talks that summarize the text, expound on a question the text raises, then relate that question to their lives. Both rabbis meet weekly with their students over a period of several months, for around eight to ten sessions. Yet despite these similarities, the two rabbis teach their students using different sources and philosophical approaches that reflect denominational differences, and the students' speeches demonstrate both similarities in material and structure and differences in source material and conclusions.

Ethan, whose family belongs to Adat Yitzhak, referred to biblical characters in his speech using Hebrew, not English, pronunciation. He and Rabbi Teitelbaum used only Jewish sources in preparing for the speech, while the ending focused on Ethan's increased Jewish responsibility: "Being a bar mitzvah means a lot of the obvious things about becoming an adult in a community. But honestly, what it means most to me, is that I can be needed, and then I can fulfill that need . . . [to be] the last piece of the puzzle and hop in and fill that blank. I also look at my bar mitzvah as a base of a ladder so that I can climb higher in knowledge and might." This conclusion reflects the belief (stressed by all rabbis and teachers in my study) that the bar or bat mitzvah is not an end in itself. In the more intensive Orthodox environment, where daily services require a minimum of ten adult Jews, Ethan's absence could indeed make a difference.

Jeffrey, whose family belongs to Beth Jeshurun, referred to biblical characters using English pronunciation. His Torah portion included the episode of the golden calf, and his speech focused on Moses's leadership, concluding that Moses had taken responsibility for his own decisions and was thus a model for Jeffrey in the future. Jeffrey used this lesson to conclude: "If I have learned anything from my Torah portion, it is that in order to be able to make the right decisions, you have to know whether you are a leader or a follower. And if a leader, what type of leader you are. You can be somebody who makes decision[s] for the benefit of yourself, or someone who makes decisions for the best interest of others. This can sometimes mean that you take the most difficult route—up the mountain—and maybe twice!" Unlike Ethan, Jeffrey made no mention of Jewish communal obligation but instead used the text as a model for his individual decisions.

Though these speeches have similar forms and discuss similar types of questions, the different interpretations—here expressed by Ethan as responsibility to participate in Jewish community practice and by Jeffrey as a responsibility "to make the right decisions"—illustrate the importance of content and approach. Yet the results demonstrate how similar material seen from different viewpoints can lead to very different conclusions. Jeffrey's focus on an individual's responsibility to make good choices reflects the same sense of individuality that informs the contemporary service model. Ethan's focus on an obligation to God and community reflects the sense of God's ultimate authority that informs the traditional model service. Nevertheless, there is an underlying similarity: both pairs of rabbis and students took the speech seriously, as a time for engaging with Jewish thought, history, and values.

Reading and interpreting the Torah at Shabbat morning services remains the dominant pattern for bar or bat mitzvah. Attempts to change this, whether from leadership or laity, have met with minimal success in the Bay Area. In theory, bar and bat mitzvah rituals can take place whenever the Torah is read: not only on Shabbat morning, but on Shabbat afternoon, on a Monday or Thursday, or at the beginning of the month. In other regions, it is not uncommon for the bar or bat mitzvah ritual to take place as part of the afternoon service, followed immediately by a party. This pattern is rare in the Bay Area, taking place only for rituals held independently. Congregational rabbis uniformly rejected it, arguing that because these services are held only for bar or bat mitzvah rituals, the timing confirms the idea that the ritual is nothing but a performance. However, the Torah is read on Mondays and Thursdays, so some rabbis encouraged families to choose this time. Few obliged: weekdays are less convenient for both families and their guests.[40]

FROM CONTEXT TO CHARACTERS

It is easy to take both the congregation and service for granted. Both can seem to be part of the background, simply fields on which participants interact. Yet whether as concrete as a synagogue's location or as intangible as the customs related to reading from the Torah, both congregation and service have set characteristics that affect the limits of what is possible in a ritual. By making plain the set characteristics of both congregation and service, participants can understand the limitations of what they can do.

The realities of location, denomination, and size determine how congregants relate to each other, to religious practice, and to their place in the congregation.

The expectations for the bar or bat mitzvah service seem more mutable—and, indeed, some are. Yet the underlying assumptions of meaning and content can seem as difficult to change as relocating a synagogue.

In the next chapter, I turn to the participants. As with the congregation and service, many of their roles and perspectives are largely taken for granted both by themselves and others. As they negotiate the tensions that shape the relationships among congregation, ritual, and each other, these roles constrain the nature of that negotiation as well.

3 · STUDENTS AND PARENTS, RABBIS AND TEACHERS

Different Roles, Different Standpoints

Though the congregation and the bar or bat mitzvah service provide context and content, it is the participants who negotiate the tensions of the bar and bat mitzvah system. Congregational lay leaders, rabbis, teachers, parents, and children each have different roles and different relationships to Judaism and the congregation, which result in different visions of and for the ritual. As these different visions clash, it is not surprising that conflict is the result. Thus, before turning to these inherent tensions, it is important to delineate the different responsibilities, goals, and priorities that shape the participants' perspectives and determine their understanding of the ritual.[1]

Families—parents and children—understand bar and bat mitzvah through a personal lens: it is an individual event in family life, shaped by individual knowledge and circumstance. Students, obviously, are the focus and point of the ritual. They are hardly blank slates, coming to the ritual with attitudes, knowledge, and abilities that shape their response to their bar or bat mitzvah. Yet the consequences of the change of status implied by a rite of passage cannot be fully understood by those undergoing the ritual. This is especially the case with students preparing for bar or bat mitzvah, which holds so many expectations for adults in the family and Jewish community.[2] Parents determine if a bar or bat mitzvah event will take place, how children will prepare for it, and what kind of major family event will accompany it. More than that, they determine the family context in which Judaism is enacted (or not) in the home. While the student is the focus of the event, in fact, it is the parents who are key to its preparation and enactment.[3]

Leaders—rabbis and teachers—understand bar and bat mitzvah from a broader perspective of the congregation and community, bringing communal sensibility to the event. Rabbis bear the overall responsibility for the congregation, enact denominational policy as they see fit, and interpret Jewish thought and practice to their congregants. Bar and bat mitzvah rituals are only a piece, albeit an important one, of congregational life and the rabbi's responsibilities. Whether a rabbi works with each bar or bat mitzvah student, as happens at the smallest congregations, or supervises others who work with the students, rabbis have the final responsibility for the success of the ritual and its effect on the congregation. Education directors, teachers, and tutors have narrower standpoints: their roles are to teach children a specific curriculum or set of skills.

Finally, the congregants themselves shape the bar or bat mitzvah. Their view of the event; their presence or absence in the service; and their willingness to support the ritual all affect its place in the life of the congregation. While this group of participants often has strong opinions about the place of a seemingly private ritual in a public service, they have no formal role in bar or bat mitzvah preparation or enactment, so they make an appearance only in chapter 7, where I discuss the tensions between the different types of service.

Each group has a different view of the ritual and its place in the congregation and family: the student's role differs from that of the parents, and both of these roles differ from those of the rabbi or teacher. As I began to formulate this research, I conducted a pilot project in one congregation, to examine the premise that bar and bat mitzvah offered a way to mediate between American and Jewish society. While that premise was borne out (as, for example, the parental speeches discussed in chapter 4 demonstrate), it was simply a nonissue for those I interviewed. What was an issue was a complete lack of communication and understanding between families and leadership. It was not that I found overt conflict—quite the reverse: these were all well-meaning people who shared the goal of achieving a successful ritual. However, each side understood the meaning of the ritual and how it mattered in the lives of each family and for the congregation and Jewish community differently. Thus, as these leaders, parents, and children talked to me, they seemed to be talking about two entirely different events. Students and their parents share one perspective; rabbis and teachers share another. Yet students and parents have different roles and responsibilities, as do rabbis and teachers. In what follows, I present these different perspectives, roles, and responsibilities, so that the reasons for and consequences of the resulting tensions can be understood.

BAR AND BAT MITZVAH STUDENTS:
REPRESENTING THE FAMILY AND THE JEWISH FUTURE

When I met Zachary, a student at independent Or Hadash, I was prepared for a rather disengaged student, having been told that he was disruptive in class—and having observed that myself. Yet that was not Zachary's perception of himself or of his relationship to Judaism and the Jewish community:

> I started going to Hebrew school in kindergarten . . . and then in eighth grade it became more of a choice whether you wanted to or not. I decided I wanted to continue with Judaism in my life, just to continue with my friends, who I don't see that often, and just continuing to learn about it.
>
> There's a youth group at the synagogue. We just do like recreational activities or like volunteering, and fun stuff like that. It meets once a month. I go sometimes. I don't go to services all that much, but I guess now that I'm doing it, I'd like to continue. Being at the Jewish school [Zachary had begun attending the local Jewish day school at the beginning of the school year] brings out more Judaism in me, so I guess I'd like to go more. Before my class had all the bar or bat mitzvahs, we didn't go that much, like maybe once a month, and so I guess I'd like to continue going.

Like the other students I interviewed, Zachary's sense of self is developing. The way he saw himself was very different from the way his teachers saw him and might have differed from his self-perception on another day. His language reflected this uncertainty: "I guess I'd like to continue going." In this, he is typical: at twelve or thirteen, the twenty-eight students I interviewed are just beginning to develop their adult voices. All are being raised in comfortable (or even better off) homes, and their upbringings reflect a pattern of child rearing that Annette Lareau calls "concerted cultivation" (2003, 1–2). One consequence of this style of child rearing is that children expect to have opinions and express them—as these students did in interviews with me where their remarks ranged from terse to voluble, and from philosophical to concrete. Yet it was clear that, whether enthusiastic or indifferent to the event, they are being shaped by the adults in their lives. Adults provide the content and meaning of both preparation and performance; the students, as in other areas of their lives, are being taught to engage with that material, albeit imperfectly.

The students' role in the bar or bat mitzvah ritual is obvious: they are responsible for learning a given quantity of material and playing the adult by enacting it competently. It is not surprising that, for most, a successful ritual is one that is enacted competently, as Julia Orlansky of Conservative B'nai Aaron said: "I was worried about being pressured by everyone there, and messing up in front of everyone because there were like 300 people there, and all my friends were there. It would have been embarrassing."

Few children—even the most recalcitrant—truly want to embarrass their parents or appear foolish in front of people who have come to witness a significant ritual.[4] As students assume the mantle of adulthood, if only momentarily, parents have a glimpse of the adults their children may become. This image does not last—as one mother said, "the next day they go back to being thirteen, and they still have the dumb thirteen-year-old stuff that you have deal with."

Though adults, particularly the professionals, have a set of skills and knowledge that they expect students to master, the students bring their own attitudes, abilities, and knowledge to the process. Family context—including divorce or intermarriage—also matters to both the parents and the student. Like the teachers, students are most concerned with mastering the necessary material, which is the topic of chapter 5.

Though the students' role is easy to define, that does not mean it is easy to understand. As with many rites of passage, the ritual does not confer expertise but simply initiates the student into a new status. In the ritual, students are both filling an expected role—enacting a commitment to Judaism and the Jewish people—and doing so as an "adult," someone who is responsible for his or her own decisions. While the student's role is clearly defined, fulfilling that role takes on symbolic importance beyond the person him- or herself.[5] Adults, whether parents or teachers, assign meaning not only to what students do, but to what their attitudes are and how they prioritize bar or bat mitzvah—and Judaism more generally—with other aspects of their lives. A good student represents a vibrant, alive Judaism of the future; a bad student (or family) indicates the demise of Judaism. When rabbis discussed their experiences with students, several listed exceptional students, telling their stories to illustrate the ideal bar or bat mitzvah experience.

These stories confirm the difficulty that flesh-and-blood students have in living up to the symbolic weight that is placed on them. A rite of passage provides entry into a new role. Having a new baby inducts parents into a new role, which they learn; getting a driver's license enables a new driver to develop driving skills. Experienced parents and drivers understand the consequences of the new role in ways that the new initiate does not. Thus, it should be obvious that, regardless of training, these students undergo the ritual with little understanding of what it means or what it could mean. Nevertheless, they are well aware that it is important, and, like Zachary, they struggle to make sense of what it means for their future.

PARENTS: MANAGING THE CHILD, PLANNING AN EVENT

When Rosie Applebaum and her children moved to the Bay Area, she knew exactly what she wanted: religious education for her children at a congregation with a comfortable type of religious practice (in this case, Conservative) in a convenient location. B'nai Aaron fit her needs, so she joined: "I joined B'nai Aaron when we moved here. . . . My son was in the middle of second grade, and he had gone [to synagogue] since kindergarten; we start them all in kindergarten. My daughter was old for her year and they'd take her, so I figured it wouldn't hurt. We belonged to a Conservative synagogue on the East Coast, and I just wanted a consistent place, and it was close to where we lived, so that's the reason." The family had been members for more than a decade, and Ellen, the youngest of the three children, had recently become bat mitzvah. Like most of those I interviewed, Rosie's family joined their congregation for educational, religious, and communal reasons. Individual circumstances also affected family dynamics: Rosie and her husband divorced, and Rosie began to date a non-Jewish man. This fact, along with her children's changing interests and new job responsibilities, resulted in a decrease in the family's home religious practice. In this changing family context, each child responded differently to the new synagogue and religious school experience, and to the bar or bat mitzvah training. Ellen had a particularly difficult time, as Rosie recounted:

> She really didn't like religious school, and it was such a struggle, I thought, "What's the point?" . . . But she kept saying, "I really want to do this." I'm not sure why she wanted to do it, but I didn't want to bother with why, as long as she wanted it. . . . Then I did see a big difference in her and her attitude last year about it, and I think it made her feel really good to do it. She made a lot of friends, she had a lot of fun with the friends she had.

As with other areas of her children's lives, Rosie understood Jewish education and practice to be a matter of negotiation, with her role being to support and encourage, rather than to enforce attendance and practice. This attitude is similar to the way parents view other extracurricular activities such as sports or music, but Rosie wanted the bat mitzvah to communicate something more visceral to Ellen: "I wanted her to understand how proud I was of her, and to attach her to where she came from, and the people she's named for, and that she's part of a continuation, and that she embraced it and did what she set out to do."

While other extracurricular activities are part of cultivating a well-rounded adult, Ellen's bat mitzvah served a deeper purpose: a connection to a people and history. Developing this sense of Jewish identity is one of the central meanings that parents attribute to bar or bat mitzvah.

While Ellen prepared to lead the service, Rosie was responsible for all that goes into planning a life event—clothes, invitations and announcements, and the celebration:

> It was a disaster! It just feels like you're on a treadmill. . . . I had another life event at the same time, and work, and it just feels like you can't pull the whole thing off. Whether it's making your speech, or reading your Torah portion, and making sure everyone has their clothes, and people call and they're not coming, and you have to shift it around, it's just crazy. For us everything was really last minute each time, and I'm not really a last-minute person. . . . I got to the party, and Ellen had a problem with her dress, and then her sister was upset with where I sat her. Once we got through that part, it was pretty fun.

Rosie's family is no more or less typical than any other family: the variation across families was striking. Each parent brings a different set of experiences and knowledge to family life and to their participation in Jewish communal life.[6] Yet regardless of these differences, parental roles and responsibilities are similar. Parents establish the family's Jewish practice and culture—often negotiating within the family on whether to attend Shabbat services or play soccer, whether to eat or abstain from shrimp, and whether and how to observe Jewish holidays. In addition to establishing the relationship to Judaism and Jewish practice, parents decide if, when, and where to join a congregation, to what degree children participate in congregational life and religious school, and how engaged the family will be with the rabbi and community. Although parents often defer to their children's wishes or the synagogue's rules, ultimately they are the ones who determine if a bar or bat mitzvah ritual will take place and the nature of the following celebration.

There are two requirements to joining a synagogue: being Jewish or being related to someone Jewish (often non-Jewish spouses are included in an intermarried family's membership) and supporting the congregation financially.[7] Both of these requirements can be barriers to membership: intermarried families often wonder if they will be welcome, and unless families have a prior sense of communal obligation, the financial commitment can seem overwhelming and unfair. Nevertheless, congregations require that families be members for two to five years prior to a bar or bat mitzvah, so that the children can learn about Judaism and Hebrew and so that families can become integrated into the congregation. Joining a congregation thus requires that the parents invest substantial time, money, and effort over a number of years.[8] During this time, children attend supplementary religious school one to three times a week during the school year. In the Bay Area, few can walk to synagogue, so parents must arrange transportation, often carpooling. Students are assigned Hebrew homework, and parents may be expected to monitor it (if they have the ability). And finally, some congregations expect parents to attend family education programs as part of their children's education.[9]

Of course, transporting and monitoring children are part of what parents do. Driving children to Hebrew school is not so different from driving them to soccer practice or violin lessons. Monitoring Hebrew homework or planning a Purim party is not so different from checking math problems or helping with the school picnic. Nevertheless, the bar or bat mitzvah represents something more. Like Rosie, other parents expressed the sense that bar or bat mitzvah represents something above and beyond soccer practice. Furthermore, particularly in the Bay Area where rates of affiliation with a congregation are low, choosing to affiliate and enroll children in religious school is evidence of some level of commitment to Judaism, while preparing for the peak event that bar or bat mitzvah is for most families raises parental responsibility well beyond that of monitoring piano practice.

During the bar or bat mitzvah year, parents drive children to lessons with tutors or meetings with rabbis to develop the talk the children will give. Parents supervise the mitzvah project and may monitor practice sessions (or fight with their children about them). These tasks can be enacted with a greater or lesser degree of consistency and/or conflict (many rabbis complained about families that were inconsistent, while both parents and children rolled their eyes as they described family arguments about practicing), but ensuring that the work gets done falls within the parents' set of responsibilities.

Finally and not insignificantly, parents plan and execute the celebration following the bar or bat mitzvah. Though observing these celebrations fell outside the parameters of my research, parents all discussed the stress of planning these celebrations. While their children were responsible for enacting the ritual with competence, the parents faced a similarly daunting task in ensuring both the comfort of their guests and the party's success. Their responsibilities included everything from the guest list to accommodations, and from managing different needs of family and friends to planning the number and type of events surrounding the ritual. Furthermore, while the congregational leadership sets the parameters around bar or bat mitzvah preparation and performance, there was no consistency in if or how congregations approached the celebrations, leaving most parents to rely on congregational culture, other families' shared experiences, and copious online material.

All parents have these responsibilities in common, but three factors determine the manner in which they fulfill them. First, individual family circumstances determine what is possible within the family structure, while family culture and priorities determine what families are willing to do. In particular, divorce and children with special needs create challenges for students and their families, while extracurricular activities (most commonly sports, but also dance, music, and theater) compete with supplementary religious school for time.[10] Second, each family member's relationship with Judaism affects how different aspects of Judaism infuse the house. Parents' past history, current knowledge, and areas of interest become children's models for how they approach Judaism. At the same time, children's response to Judaism affects the household Jewish culture, which is a matter of negotiation between family members, rather than an average of individual approaches. Third, each family's participation in congregational life and connection to congregational leaders and other members influence their engagement in bar and bat mitzvah preparation.

Family Circumstances: Challenges and Culture

When family circumstances and culture are healthy and aligned with congregational expectations, problems are minor. In these cases, children attend religious school regularly, families and congregational practice complement each other, and the progress to both a successful bar or bat mitzvah event and the family's continued Jewish engagement is smooth. Needless to say, this is the ideal, although not uncommon, scenario. However, some families in every congregation I studied—whether Orthodox or Reform, large or small—had problems that resulted in students' frequent absences from the congregation and school, and a consequent effect on Jewish engagement, including preparation for and enactment of the bar or bat mitzvah ritual. Whether these absences were due to missed lessons, the need for special attention, or conflict between hostile parents, the consequence was the same: less engagement in the life of the congregation and with Judaism itself.

Of all family circumstances, congregational leaders singled out divorce as creating the most serious disruptions for students and their families. Problems resulting from divorce often began with the children of divorce having difficulties attending religious school and bar or bat mitzvah training regularly, but tensions or conflict between parents could spill over into the ritual itself. One meaning of bar or bat mitzvah is that of continuing Judaism from one generation to the next. Divorce calls that neat continuity into question, requiring substantial work to repair the breach in the symbolic family. The work takes place during preparation for the ritual, during the service itself, and into the celebration.

When parents see religious engagement differently, those differences are exacerbated by divorce. And when those differences include different religious backgrounds, as is the case with marriages between Jews and gentiles, the non-Jewish parent may not view participation in religious school as important, resulting in inconsistent religious school attendance. For example, one divorced father described his son's experience: "It wasn't easy for anybody. It was a struggle and was a big demand on Isaac to have to put in the time. . . . Isaac had more of a challenge because he didn't have the same foundation in Hebrew that a lot of the other students had, because . . . he hadn't attended the midweek Hebrew that they began in third or fourth grade. That was primarily because he was living with his mom."

The child as a pawn in the battle between divorced parents is a modern cliché. Isaac's mother did not attend his bar mitzvah, nor did he expect her to. This was not the case for Dina, as her tutor described: "She came in crying one day because her father wouldn't invite her non-Jewish mother to the bat mitzvah. He was angry because the mother hadn't brought the children to religious school—this was payback. But Dina really wanted her mother to be there. I don't know what the rabbi did, but in the end, Dina's mother did show up. Dina was so happy!"

Most parents attempt to present a symbolic front during the ritual itself, but that front is often maintained, as in Dina's case, due to efforts by the rabbi using the authority of that role to manage parents' rancor for the sake of the child. Yet even when both parents are committed to their child's Jewish education and bar or bat mitzvah, problems can arise: parents disagree over who pays for what, which honors are given to whom during the service itself, and how to manage the following celebration.

Zachary, whose words introduced the section on students above, is the child of an acrimonious divorce. He has two committed Jewish parents, both of whom wanted to shield him from their conflicts, which included "whether or not to serve alcohol at the lunch, whom to invite, who would pay for what." As his father, Jesse, optimistically noted: "I'm really glad Zachary didn't bring it [the divorce] up [during my interview with him] because that means that whatever issues [Zachary's mother] and I had were completely invisible to him, and that's always my goal. Divorce isn't his fault, and he shouldn't be in the middle of any of that." That quote sums up both the goals of most divorced families and the reality that the heightened emotional and symbolic nature of the bar or bat mitzvah may lead to a reprise of past disputes.

Though not as involving as much conflict as divorce, students' special needs—be they emotional, learning-related, or physical—affect how or if a student can attend religious school and what level of learning and participation in the service is possible. As with divorce, these challenges are common; in a cohort of twenty students, it is not uncommon for three or four to face a challenge of one kind or another. These issues often result in extra demands on time or emotional resources. As parents advocate for their children's needs in congregations, congregations may provide special programs or individual tutoring.

Only rarely do congregational schools—or Jewish day schools—have programs that address these students' individual needs (as with any private school, funding is an issue).[11] Two of the schools in my study had developed programs of which their education directors were justly proud. While enabling participation for people with all kinds of special needs is a growing issue in American Judaism more broadly, the range of responses varies from full-day programs to ignoring the different needs of these children. Here I simply point out that the nature of the special needs and the congregation's response affects the ability of families to participate.[12]

One common solution for bar or bat mitzvah students is extended tutoring. While this assumes that the family is able to pay for the extra lessons, the result can be effective for developing individual relationships with an adult mentor. For example, at Conservative B'nai Aaron, Mindy Simon's learning and emotional issues challenged her family and her teachers. She had been adopted at a young age, and in addition to struggling with learning issues, she wrestled with her identity as both American and Jew. Around two years before her bat mitzvah, she began to work with the congregation's tutor to solidify her Hebrew, and then she spent extra time on bat mitzvah material. This individual attention enabled her to work through both identity and learning issues. Her mother explained: "She started out very anxious about her ability to learn Hebrew, work with her tutor. They had some friction in the past, but it bloomed into a gorgeous friendship. And she needed more tutoring, but then she blossomed. She gained confidence, and . . . wanted to do more."

Divorce and special needs are quite different in cause and in their effect on individuals and family dynamics. Yet in both cases, families and congregations are faced with situations to which they need to respond, and the consequences for families' relationships with congregations and for bar or bat mitzvah preparation and enactment are similar. In contrast, the ways that the relationship between minority Jewish and dominant American cultures affect Jewish families is less obvious.

The Jewish Cultural Tool Kit in Community and Family

The contradiction between Jewish and American values is played out within families as they make choices about how to spend limited time and resources. Unlike in many other regions with similar Jewish populations, the Bay Area has no real Jewish enclaves, so Jewish families are well integrated into the rest of the population.[13] Thus, whatever its inclination toward Judaism, each family has to contend with the realities of the American context, which includes the concerted cultivation approach to child rearing mentioned above (Lareau 2003). This model includes developing each child's unique abilities. As a result, Jewish practice and education compete with other activities: sports, and soccer in particular, are ubiquitous across the Bay Area, and these teams cut children who miss practice or games. One of Reform Beth Jeshurun's rabbis commented: "The challenge with Saturday morning services in the modern era is that the god of youth soccer is a powerful and vengeful god."[14] Though fewer students enroll in dance, music, and drama, these programs have similar participation requirements.

As a result, attendance at religious school and services suffers: many education directors and some rabbis commented on the difficulty of enforcing attendance requirements for either supplementary school or religious services.[15] There are fewer obvious consequences for students when they miss school or services: disapproval from their religious school teachers is less threatening than being cut from a soccer team or doing school make-up work for attending holiday services.[16] The conflict between secular and religious activities also presents an implicit choice between Jewish and American values. Extracurricular activities have well-rehearsed instrumental benefits: physical, social, academic, and career-related.[17] Jewish values are less easily expressed by families. When asked to name the most important characteristic of Judaism, the most common answer given by participants in my study had to do with pride. Zachary's father, Jesse, remains engaged in Jewish life and gave a typical answer: "I think just ensuring the continuity of the Jewish people, being visibly Jewish, and not being afraid to be Jewish in public. People at work and all my friends know that I'm Jewish."

The concept of a cultural tool kit of "symbols, stories, rituals, and world-views" (Swidler 1986, 273) used strategically to navigate cultural contexts helps explain why Jews have trouble articulating Jewish values. The parents I interviewed are comfortable with a wide range of American cultural tools, which enable them to negotiate—with great success—the American milieu.[18] However, they are much less familiar with the Jewish tool kit. Thus, while leaders and those immersed in Jewish life are conversant with Jewish values and practices, parents and children in congregations often are not—and acquiring knowledge of those values and practices requires time and the willingness to learn. One father noted the conflict between Jewish practice and other activities: "I think we were supposed to go to eighteen services [as part of bar or bat mitzvah preparation], and I enjoy going—but it was always hard to get the kids to go because they had their soccer and other Saturday stuff." It did not occur to this father to press his children to attend the services: it was taken for granted that their secular activities took precedence.[19]

Negotiating cultural differences takes place within the home as well. Judaism itself is multifaceted, so even when two parents have strong Jewish feelings and knowledge, they may have two very different Jewish tool kits. One person might focus on Jewish practice and text study; another on the cultural dimension of art, music, and food; and a third on historical connections.

This was the case for Judy and Josh Small, members of independent Or Hadash. Josh had no interest in Jewish practice but read extensively about Jewish history. Judy found great meaning in Jewish practice and community as ways to express more universal ethics: "[Judaism] gives you a code of ethics to live by and to be involved in your community and to help people. . . . I think helping to make the world a better place is the most important thing in the end." Nathan, their son, took these different approaches and blended them: "I believe that Jewish ethics are the best. . . . Judaism is not just a religion but is also a culture, and . . . it's very important to be part of that culture." While Nathan had absorbed both parents' attitudes, the family practice was established by Judy's sensibilities, with Josh participating as necessary.[20]

Josh's and Judy's different approaches to Judaism extend back to their childhoods: Josh was raised in a relatively secular home, while Judy was raised in a moderately observant home surrounded by Jewish culture. Yet both had similar American upbringings. This was not the case for Gabriel and Aziza Orlansky, whose family belongs to B'nai Aaron.

The Orlanskys both feel strongly about their Judaism, and their comfortable home is filled with Judaica. When I visited, their youngest daughter was ensconced in front of a Hebrew children's program on television, while their son wandered in and out of the kitchen as he prepared to leave for a Jewish youth event. Yet within this committed and loving Jewish home, Judaism itself is the source of conflict that results from the parents' very different backgrounds and Jewish tools.

As is the case with many other Jews of European ancestry, members of Gabriel's family perished in the Holocaust, which continues to loom large in his thinking. Like Judy, Gabriel was raised in a moderately observant home and continues to find his primary connection to Judaism through prayer and learning. He attends both services and classes at B'nai Aaron regularly.

Aziza grew up in Gibraltar in an Orthodox family with Moroccan roots, in which the gendered nature of Orthodoxy, particularly in that time and at that place, excluded girls from religious practice and study. That gendered practice— which excluded her and, in her eyes, diminished her worth—left her feeling angry at Jewish law and has continued to define her relationship with formal Jewish practice. While Gabriel expresses his Jewish identity largely through religious observance at the synagogue, Aziza expresses hers through food, language, and holiday celebrations. In an animated voice, she described the way she prepares for holidays: "I do the cooking, the hosting, everything. It's very important for me that the kids appreciate the holidays and the traditions and they know the stories, you know, for Passover and Sukkot and apples and honey on Rosh Hashanah." Ironically, her anger at being excluded prevents her from claiming the practice she strongly desired for her daughters. At the same time, the bat mitzvah of Julia, her oldest daughter, enabled Aziza to see another path, which Gabriel felt "created a common ground" and allowed the couple to better understand each other's point of view.

As is the case with marriages between two Jews, a Jew and a gentile who are married bring their personal histories and attitudes toward Judaism and religion in general, which are integrated into family life. According to the rabbis and education directors I interviewed, while interfaith marriages complicated the ritual (due to the need to include non-Jews in a Jewish ritual), such a marriage was not a factor in determining the nature of bar or bat mitzvah preparation. Rather, what mattered most in all cases was the family's level of engagement in the congregation and the process. Nevertheless, intermarried families face a set of challenges that are qualitatively different from those of families without non-Jewish members. These challenges stem as much from the matter of Jewish identity as from lack of knowledge. Though Aziza Orlansky declined to participate in religious services, she criticized Judaism from the inside. The non-Jewish parents I interviewed—regardless of whatever knowledge of Judaism they had acquired—expressed the viewpoint of supportive outsider. Because of the complexity of the issues, this subject is examined in some detail in chapter 6.

Vern Bengston (2013, 186), in his longitudinal study of religious transmission through generations, finds that religious transmission is successful when families take their religions seriously and when the parental approach to religious engagement is affirming. Whether or not they include a non-Jewish spouse, whether they are negotiating religious issues inside or outside the family, these families confirm the importance of family dynamics in creating a context of Jewish knowledge and connection. However, Judaism does not stop at the family's door; for these families, it also takes place within the congregation, and it is to the relationship between family and congregation that I now turn.

Connection and Community: The Family and the Congregation

A family's relationship with the congregation begins when parents join the congregation. While most parents listed their children's Jewish education and the congregation's support in raising Jewish children as their primary reasons for joining, many gave other reasons as well: a personal relationship with the rabbi, comfort with denominational practice, the congregation's location and convenience, past family history, community feeling, and the congregation's social action goals as reasons.[21] Though families join as units, each parent or child develops an individual sense of connection—or not—based on different areas of engagement and interest.

Some of these areas are particular to individuals or individual families. Gabriel Orlansky explained: "I stay principally because of the rabbi . . . our social circle is outside the congregation. I like the religious observance. The kids' education is good, but if my rabbi moved to another shul down the street, I'd probably follow him. If he stayed and everyone else left; I'd stay."

In contrast, Leslie Moses said: "We stick around [large Reform Beth Jeshurun] because of the sense of community we feel. We just had our twentieth wedding anniversary. I contacted one of the rabbis and I just said, we don't want a big party, we just want some sort of blessing or something, and he . . . gave such a beautiful tribute to us . . . it just made me feel, wow, we really are part of this temple." Leslie's husband, Jason, is Jewish but she is not; however, Leslie was the one who contacted the rabbi. It is indicative of the nature of the family's relationship with the congregation that she felt comfortable making the call. Furthermore, in her mind, the rabbi acted as the congregation's representative, so rather than feeling directly connected to the rabbi, she felt connected to the whole congregation.

These larger relationships affect the resources—both knowledge and assistance—that families can draw on as they plan and enact the bar or bat mitzvah. A child raised in a family that knows the rabbi well, is engaged in leadership (for example, when one parent has a position on the board or a committee), and participates in congregational activities regularly will likely have a bar or bat mitzvah event with a larger congregational attendance, more support in planning food and festivities, and more Jewish knowledge on which to draw than will a child raised in a family with minimal engagement. Though each kind of family is likely to consider its event a success, the planning process, the service, and the number and type of attendees will differ substantially.

In addition, families' engagement with the congregation shapes their experience of planning and enacting the event. Having connections to others in the congregation has very real consequences for the parental role of arranging luncheons and parties. Thus, a family with an individual relationship with a rabbi and little integration into the congregational community will have fewer resources to draw on than better integrated families. Rabbis are responsible only for content and delivery of the service; their role does not include event logistics. As a result, family concerns outside the service may not be addressed—as was the case for the Orlansky family above: Aziza and Gabriel managed the expected luncheon and party largely with help from their relatives.

Even when congregations have intensive bar and bat mitzvah preparation programs, as at Beth Jeshurun and Or Hadash, parents can feel alone in the process. Beth Jeshurun's program teaches parents and children about prayer and study and ideally connects families with the congregation as a whole. While the intent is to meet each family's individual schedule, the effect can be isolating, as Tina Aronson reflects: "Sometimes I felt like—are we just another number? Or is there a personal thing going on here? In the end I did feel that there was. And the rabbi is very busy, very busy, but we would have liked her to stay a little more in touch." By contrast, at Or Hadash, the bar and bat mitzvah program requires families to support each other in planning and enacting the service and in setting up the lunch following the service. Regardless of a family's personal connection to the institution or leadership, during the bar or bat mitzvah year, the cohort of bar and bat mitzvah families were required to work together.

These three factors—individual family circumstances, relationship to Judaism, and connection to the congregation and leadership—all shape the context in which parents accomplish their role. Within that context, they manage their children's preparation for bar or bat mitzvah and plan and enact the celebrations surrounding the event. Although their children are the focus of the ritual, parents are the ones who initiate the process and support their children as they progress through the different steps along the way. As parents are immersed in the individual nature of the event, it is not surprising that often their focus contrasts with the broader view of the rabbis and teachers.

RABBIS AND TEACHERS: PREPARING STUDENTS, MANAGING THE CONGREGATION

Laurie Goodstein writes: "Children and their families go through . . . an 'assembly line' that produces Jews schooled in little more than 'pediatric Judaism,' an immature understanding of the faith, its values and spirituality. Most students deliver a short speech about the meaning of the Torah passage they were assigned to read, but they never really learn to understand or speak Hebrew, only to decode the text" (2013). The quote exemplifies the attitude that bar or bat mitzvah as it currently exists is an empty ritual.[22] The "B'nai Mitzvah Revolution," a program developed by the Reform movement, aims to return meaning to the ritual by empowering "synagogues to return depth and meaning to Jewish learning and reduce the staggering rates of post-b'nai mitzvah dropout." As with many leaders, the rabbis and educators who founded and administer the program believe "that a root cause of these challenges is the perception that b'nai mitzvah celebrations are like graduation ceremonies."[23] The B'nai Mitzvah Revolution is only the most recent attempt by leaders to control and use the bar and bat mitzvah ritual to further the larger goal of increasing Jewish knowledge and building Jewish continuity—an effort that has arguably shaped the ritual from its inception (Hilton 2014). While parents, however knowledgeable, see the ritual through individual eyes, the natural direction of the leaders is communal: to see the ritual as integrated into congregational life as well as the life of each child.

Rabbis, education directors, teachers, and tutors are the experts who interpret and teach Judaism, uphold standards of Jewish practice, and determine levels of competence—that is, they determine what is learned, how it is learned, and who has learned and may enact it. Each of them has a different set of responsibilities and a different sphere of influence: rabbis are responsible for balancing the needs of an entire congregation, education directors are responsible for managing the religious school (of which bar or bat mitzvah preparation is only a part), teachers for their classroom, and tutors for the progress of individual students. All share a view of the ritual as a repeated event within the institutional framework, which gives them a very different perspective from that of families preparing for an individual peak event. Yet their different roles, scope of knowledge, and levels of engagement with families result in different approaches to the bar or bat mitzvah, family, and congregation.

By definition, rabbis are leaders of congregations. Though the meaning of the role can vary with the size and culture, the rabbi sets the direction and tone of the congregation. As part of fulfilling that role, they embody Judaism and Jewish practice to the congregation, interpret denominational policy for the congregation (instituting change from the top down), address the needs of different groups within the congregation (instituting change from the bottom up), and balance the needs of different congregational groups. While rabbis have different styles that range from directive to inclusive, when the rabbi either withdraws from the role of leader or enters into a congregational conflict, those actions spell trouble for the congregation.[24] My intent here is not to delve into those conflicts but to point out that the rabbi's role is both crucial and difficult. Because preparation and enactment of the ritual intersect with so many areas of congregational life, managing the bar or bat mitzvah is particularly delicate—so it is no wonder that many rabbis find the whole subject troubling.

Rabbis are responsible for determining the relationship of the ritual to the congregation: the content of preparation and bar or bat mitzvah prerequisites, and the nature of the bar or bat mitzvah service itself, including its effect on the regular congregational service and who participates, and the role of the congregation in the service.[25] Ideally, these responsibilities entail assimilating and integrating new ideas and policy from denominations (such as material from the B'nai Mitzvah Revolution), understanding and integrating issues from the congregation (for example, integrating Jewish members' non-Jewish spouses into the congregation), and negotiating between different groups in the congregation. Though rabbis may choose to delegate pieces of the process (such as entrusting the school curriculum to education directors or discussions of participation in the bar or bat mitzvah service to the religious practices committee), ultimately the responsibility for the ritual rests with them.

Rabbis vary considerably in how they approach the different responsibilities related to bar and bat mitzvah. Some, like Rabbi Melmed of independent Or Hadash, saw bar and bat mitzvah preparation and enactment as being very important to students and the congregation. As the number of students grew, so did the amount of time he spent with them and their families. During the time I observed Or Hadash, he and the congregation were trying to find ways to minimize the scope of these responsibilities, so that other areas would not suffer. Others, like Rabbi Rosen at Conservative B'nai Aaron, spend little one-on-one time with a given family or student. At B'nai Aaron, students work with the congregation's b'nai mitzvah tutor and one of a number of speech coaches. Rabbi Rosen prefers to interact with students through classroom teaching: "They typically meet with me at the end, and I review the product [speech] and schmooze with them and the family a little bit and answer questions. But I also go in and teach two units to the sixth and seventh grade, so I'm not like a remote stranger to them."

Size introduces another complication. While both Rabbi Melmed and Rabbi Rosen have individual control of the bar or bat mitzvah, large congregations, like Reform Beth Jeshurun, bring the expert leadership—including rabbis, cantors, and educators—together to negotiate policy. Not surprisingly, disagreements about content, training, and other issues arise. At Beth Jeshurun there is a disagreement over which parts of the service students should lead. Some rabbis in the congregation believe that a student's ability to lead services is fundamental. Rabbi Ben-Ami told me: "I'm not as interested [as the other rabbis] in the kids learning so much Torah. I think it's nice, but it doesn't give them much Jewish knowledge after it [the ritual]. I would like to see the kids more actively engaged in actually leading the entire Shabbat morning service." Others want to ensure the student's ability to understand and interpret texts: "They are conversing with sacred Torah and Torah study. It's a pretty amazing accomplishment."

Throughout the rest of this book, I will show that it is the rabbis who carry much of the weight of negotiating the different tensions: for interpreting and symbolically enacting meaning, ensuring competent preparation and enactment, determining the level of inclusion, and managing the degree to which the ritual is part of the public congregational service. No matter what the issue, the rabbi is a primary force in determining the scope and success of the negotiation.

Whereas the rabbis and parents negotiate the several tensions that shape the bar or bat mitzvah, education directors, teachers, and tutors are responsible for only one area: the children's education. This is by no means inconsequential—determining the scope of Jewish education as opposed to bar or bat mitzvah preparation is an area of substantial conflict. While I take up that conflict in chapter 5, what follows here serves to introduce the different roles each educator holds.

Rather than overseeing and leading the entire institution as do rabbis, education directors direct a subset of the congregation through their formal (and sometimes informal) Jewish education. Whether the school's focus leaned toward or away from bar or bat mitzvah training, all congregations in my study had some means of educating children within the congregation.

In the most common model, supplementary religious schools enroll students from kindergarten through seventh grade, with programs usually including bar or bat mitzvah preparation.[26] These supplementary schools serve the large population of students who do not attend Jewish day school. Even in the Orthodox case, where most children do attend day school, some education is provided. For example, at Adat Yitzhak, junior rabbis supervised children during Shabbat services with some low-key instruction, as well as leading classes during some Shabbat afternoons.

Whatever the model, education directors are responsible for creating and carrying out the curricula, finding and supervising teachers for both Hebrew and Jewish studies, managing the necessary administrative tasks related to finances and personnel, and evaluating students. In public schools, principals have substantial training; this is not necessarily the case for the education directors. In some Bay Area congregations, education directors may be rabbi educators, working in conjunction with other rabbis, as was the case in a number of large Reform congregations and one of the Conservative synagogues. In other congregations, these directors may have degrees in Jewish studies but no formal training in education—or the reverse.

Though religious school curricula rarely state explicit connections to bar or bat mitzvah preparation, because the ritual requires specific knowledge, education directors must either include that knowledge or be held responsible for the students' lack of preparedness. This is a real problem: at two of the congregations I observed, parents were angry due to their perception that students were unprepared to begin bar or bat mitzvah training and, fairly or unfairly, blamed the education director.

As is the case with the congregations' schools, no single description applies in all cases to the education director's role with regard to bar or bat mitzvah. Some congregations have separate programs and coordinators (such as the elaborate program at large Reform Beth Jeshurun); many do not. Some congregations include family preparation within the religious school curriculum; some do not. As a result, the education director's role with regard to bar or bat mitzvah varies from complete responsibility for ensuring that students are prepared to simply coordinating the education program with rabbis and bar and bat mitzvah administrators. In either case, as with the rabbis, bar and bat mitzvah preparation and enactment are only part of the directors' responsibility.

Teachers have an even narrower focus than the directors: teaching a group of students material that, depending on grade, may have everything or nothing to do with the bar or bat mitzvah. My observations included only teachers in fifth grade and above for precisely this reason; prior to that grade, the curricula have little or no bar or bat mitzvah content. Though the teacher's role matters in preparing students for bar or bat mitzvah training, he or she is not directly involved in the process. Nevertheless, the teacher's knowledge of Judaism, ability to transmit that knowledge to often unruly students, and relationship with those students affects how students approach the bar or bat mitzvah.

The tutors and cantors who train students work with individual students and, in some sense, have the narrowest role, but that role is key. Most obviously, these teachers are responsible for ensuring that students have mastered the material necessary to enact the ritual competently. In that role, they also choose how to approach both material and students—how much to individualize, and whether to focus on music or meaning. However, they have an equally important, though unstated role: to mediate between the different participants in the ritual. Because these teachers spend several months meeting with students, they develop relationships with the students and, often, their families. As tutors gain experience, they are able to bring that history to the families, placing the individual event, which almost always feels overwhelming to each family, into context. Tutors see students' progress or lack thereof in mastering the material. They can calm worried parents or make overly confident students worry. They can also communicate potential problems to rabbis before the ritual performance itself, giving both tutors and rabbis the ability to rescue the ritual if the need arises. When tutors are unable to fulfill this role effectively, students can suffer, rabbis can look foolish, and the ritual can be compromised.

Whether rabbi or tutor, whether responsible for the whole institution or an individual event, these professionals share the broad perspective that bar and bat mitzvah rituals are regular events (however meaningful and individualized) in the life of a congregation, events that must be managed—ideally with care and attention—but not treated as the unique peak moments that they are for families. Furthermore, they tend to share the perspective that the event, however meaningful, is not itself an end but the means to the greater end of ensuring Jewish continuity.

THE PARTICIPANTS AND THE BAR AND BAT MITZVAH SYSTEM

While the ritual, congregation, and participants interact through the tensions that comprise the bar and bat mitzvah system, in fact, rituals and congregations do not act—people do. People attribute different meanings to the ritual, give the ritual form based on those meanings, and transform both form and meaning over time. Congregations are composed of people, and it is through those people's actions that congregational change takes place. This is not to claim that social facts and context are irrelevant; they are the social reality that shapes the possibilities. For example, though Reform leaders in the late nineteenth and early twentieth centuries tried to replace the individual bar mitzvah, held at age thirteen, with a group confirmation, held around age sixteen, that attempt failed: bar mitzvah mattered to families in a way that confirmation did not.[27] Important though it was, the ritual itself did not act. Instead, the conflict over the eventual place of bar mitzvah was between leaders and the laity. Though congregations have characteristics that affect their members and determine who will and will not join; and though the ritual, however conceived, will influence students, parents, and the leaders who teach them, it is important to recognize that it is the people who act. It is through their interactions that the tensions discussed in the coming pages are negotiated.

Chapter 4 categorizes the different meanings attributed to bar and bat mitzvah. Though it is likely that every Jew—and a fair number of non-Jews—will attribute meaning to the ritual, in congregations these meanings are primarily negotiated between parents and rabbis, while students are given and interpret the meanings. Finally, other congregants also attribute meaning to the bar or bat mitzvah service, particularly as it affects the congregational service.

Chapter 5 considers the relationship between the process of inculcating Jewish knowledge and identity and the needs of a successful ritual performance. Students, parents, teachers, and rabbis all take part in negotiating this tension. Because the stakes for both the ritual performance and Jewish continuity are high, it is this issue that can generate the most heat and conflict as rabbis and teachers set standards and goals—based, at least in part, on the ritual's requirements—as students comply or not, and as parents worry about the result.

Chapter 6 examines the tension that results from the desire to include previously excluded groups while still protecting the sacred quality of the ritual. This tension has developed from the bottom up—that is, from the changing expectations of families—and is managed by rabbis (in some cases, with participation by the laity). Rabbis are bound—however stringently or loosely—by denominational rulings. Their task here is to interpret those rulings while respecting individuals.

Chapter 7 concludes the section on inherent tensions by showing how the public and private dimensions of the bar or bat mitzvah service are manifested in two very different patterns, each of which is negotiated differently. The size of the congregation and the type of congregation service set the parameters within which rabbis, families, and other congregants negotiate their different needs and expectations. As these needs are negotiated, the content of the service, its participants, and its attendees all change.

A different set of parameters exists for each of these tensions, and participants interact in different ways, so that it is entirely possible to take each tension separately. This, in fact, is often what happens: Jewish educators tend to look at the tension between process and performance, while other congregants and many rabbis tend to see only the tension between public service and private ritual. Yet by looking at the system as a whole, the different perspectives and problems of other participants come into focus, as do the parameters that limit change. Through this knowledge, participants—the laity and leaders alike—can gain a better understanding of the ritual, each other, and future possibilities.

4 · VARIATIONS ON A THEME
Different Meanings and Motives

The bar mitzvah was a disaster. Nimrod refused to study, and as the weeks went by, unlearned verses piled up. His mother, Gail, nagged and shouted, which only increased his resistance. The rabbi discussed postponing or even canceling the service. Gail refused. She insisted that the bar mitzvah was necessary for Nimrod to truly feel part of the Jewish people. The rabbi conceded and cut the number of lines of text Nimrod would have to read.

Too soon, the day of the ritual arrived. Nimrod appeared with combed hair and scrubbed face. Despite having hardly spoken a civil word to him in six months, Gail draped his new tallit over his new suit with tears and words of love. This did not miraculously confer competence: Nimrod stumbled through the prayers with the rabbi's help. When it came time for the Torah reading, he chanted the few verses he knew, then hesitated. His tutor quietly fed him each phrase, which he repeated until he completed his allotted number. His speech was short and disjointed.

And then, mercifully, it was over. Nimrod's mother embraced him and offered her congratulations with obvious joy and pride as the tutor and rabbi looked at each other with relief.[1]

Nimrod's performance exemplifies the negative stereotype of the American bar or bat mitzvah: an unwilling child who has been compelled to memorize and recite meaningless Hebrew makes a mockery of an already empty ritual. Yet what appeared to be hypocrisy to the rabbi and tutor brought Nimrod's mother to tears of joy. For her, all that mattered for the success of the bar mitzvah was that her son stand up in front of witnesses and, in so doing, become an adult member of the Jewish people.

This example complicates the story presented in the first chapter, in which I argued that bar or bat mitzvah ritual bridges the gap between American and Jewish values by allowing American Jewish parents to show they have raised children who are both American and Jewish. Gail had no interest in Nimrod's free choice: he was Jewish, and that was that. Rather, by insisting that he enact the service, she claimed the ritual as a moment of Jewish identity: bar mitzvah was simply a sign of belonging, willy-nilly, to a particular people. Therefore neither Nimrod's competence nor his choice mattered. Instead, the act itself was what mattered.

The rabbi and tutor saw it differently: Nimrod's ability—or lack thereof—to enact the ritual competently placed the ritual in jeopardy and called its meaning into question. Though a Jewish child becomes a Jewish adult with the turning of the calendar, to many Jewish professionals, an authentic bar or bat mitzvah incorporates Jewish learning or growth. To one educator, the ritual represents moral development, and a ritual without evidence of good character and moral virtue is a sham: "Perhaps part of Bar/Bat Mitzvah preparation should be letters of recommendation, in which the recommenders needed [sic] to answer some pointed questions about the student's behavior and character. These recommendations could come from teachers, peers, community members. We could ask the Bar/Bat Mitzvah candidates to answer questions in an essay that describes their character and intentions" (Stern 2013).

To one rabbi, the ritual is evidence of full adult maturity and should be categorized with other secular rites of passage, rather than being appropriate for a new teenager: "If we're not going to deal with kids' physical and psychic development at Bar Mitzvah, we might be wise to wait until the next, more politically correct milestone, maybe getting a driver's license, or high school graduation. And if we want to hold onto the golden 'today you are a man' line, might I suggest waiting till age 25" (Lev 2011). Whether through demonstrating good moral values, mature conduct, or Jewish knowledge, these and other Jewish professionals felt that an authentic bar or bat mitzvah ritual should mark some accomplishment, with the ritual becoming the means to a greater Jewish end.

It is not surprising that bar or bat mitzvah gives rise to different and contradictory meanings: this is what significant rituals do (Turner 1967). Yet these different meanings have consequences for both participants and the ritual. If a child simply becomes a Jewish adult on turning thirteen,[2] expectations for preparation and enactment of the ritual become less important than the simple acknowledgment of that change of status. But if the ritual represents moral behavior, maturity, and Jewish knowledge, participants will focus on preparing the student correctly, while the ritual itself will demonstrate the students' accomplishments. In either case, the ritual's efficacy depends on its ability to express multiple meanings to and for the participants and the community.

Four ways of understanding bar or bat mitzvah emerged from my research. First and most literally, participants defined bar or bat mitzvah as a status change that occurs when a child turns thirteen. The child does not have a bar or bat mitzvah but becomes one. Unlike passing medical boards or getting a driver's license, this status does not depend on competence or competition, but simply on age and being considered a Jew. Second, participants understood bar or bat mitzvah to be that formal moment when the child chooses to affirm a Jewish identity publicly, often incorporating the characteristic American value of self-definition through choice. While many parents often explicitly offer their children a choice, even where parents insist on the ritual, choice is part of the preparation: for example, Nimrod chose the verses he read. Third, participants understood the ritual to be the successful accomplishment of a difficult Jewish task that can be framed as one of developing Jewish skills, of mastering Jewish learning, or, more universally, of developing discipline and moral values. Fourth and finally, participants understood the ritual to be a moment for family, friends, and sometimes the community to celebrate the child's accomplishments and new status.

It would be difficult to trace the genesis and continued importance of each meaning. Even if it were the case that change of status, for example, developed out of early rabbinic teaching, participants use those teachings only as they apply to current cultural issues. Like the other meanings, change of status is invoked when it serves current needs: either an etiological explanation for the ritual or a desire (usually on the part of the leadership) to minimize the performance aspect. What can be said is that these four meanings persist through filling various cultural needs and, as participants negotiate their relative importance, result in shaping both preparation and bar or bat mitzvah service.

BECOMING A BAR OR BAT MITZVAH: A NEW STATUS BRINGS NEW RESPONSIBILITIES

Turning thirteen both defines a Jewish adult (a bar or bat mitzvah) and is necessary for the actions that symbolically demonstrate Jewish adulthood. No matter how competently performed, a bat mitzvah ritual enacted by an eleven-year-old would not be considered real. So when I asked what makes a successful bat mitzvah, Shoshana Pinsker, a bat mitzvah student from Orthodox Adat Yitzhak, replied: "Don't mess up! I mean, you can mess up. Really, there's no successful or nonsuccessful, all you do is wake up and you're bat mitzvah, congratulations." This is a telling statement: Shoshana's first impulse was to express the concern shared by all students that they will "mess up" through not knowing the material. But she had also learned the "right" answer: that bat mitzvah is a matter of age, rather than performance, and she quickly corrected herself. She was not alone; all of the students I interviewed were worried about performing competently.

At the same time, these students also explained that their teachers and rabbis had emphasized that the ritual merely marks the change of status: a Jewish child becomes a bar or bat mitzvah, a Jewish adult, at age thirteen, and with that change of status comes responsibility for observing the mitzvahs, or commandments.[3]

By emphasizing the change of status, rabbis and teachers focus on new roles and responsibilities to address their ongoing concern that the ritual means little in and of itself. This definition of the ritual speaks to the students as well. At thirteen, American teenagers are looking ahead to other age-related responsibilities: driving at sixteen and starting college and voting (for many) at eighteen. Yet with the exception of Orthodox and some Conservative congregations, the Jewish character of this change of status is difficult to demonstrate, as there are few regular times and places where Jewish practice can be enacted.[4] Rather, students from all denominations took the idea that some kind of change should occur and then identified that change as an increased sense of responsibility for themselves and their own behavior. As Denise Shore, of Reform Sukkat Shalom, put it, "it's going to symbolize you *being an adult in your synagogue*. The rabbi said that I'm going to have to start *taking on more responsibilities*, help my family out more, help my friends out more. When other kids turn thirteen, they don't realize how much they're growing up and that you take on more responsibilities. But a bat mitzvah shows you that" (emphasis added). These students were well aware that Jewish adulthood did not mean the same thing as turning twenty-one, but they interpreted becoming bar or bat mitzvah as a moment to take stock in the process of becoming an adult.[5] Sasha Kasinsky, of Orthodox Adat Yitzhak, captured this feeling by saying: "I'm responsible, and not responsible at the same time. Like the training wheels came off, but I . . . have one training wheel left. The other falls off when I turn eighteen."

Most students expressed this newfound sense of responsibility in universal terms. Bill Wolfson, also from Adat Yitzhak, was one of the few who mentioned specific Jewish responsibilities: "Now I've become more involved in the community. I put my tefillin on every day. I'll get to help my brothers and sisters, teach them and help get them ready for their time."

For most students, preparing for the ritual heightened the importance of the new status. Without the intense preparation and the ritual, the larger message of becoming adult would not have had the same power. Again Denise Shore speaks to the issue: "When I started, I didn't really think it was a big deal. But as I [got] closer to my bat mitzvah, I realized, 'Wow, this is a really big deal. *If it wasn't a big deal, I wouldn't be taking this much time to prepare for it.*' And I realized that after this, people are going to expect more of me. I'm going to need to be more mature, I'm going to need to help out more and be more responsible" (emphasis added). Despite the efforts of the leadership, simply turning thirteen was not sufficient to create the sense of meaning. Rather, it was through the effort of preparing for and performing the ritual that Denise and others felt the significance of that expected new maturity.

For parents, part of the power of the ritual was observing their children's growth. Sometimes parents noticed differences in their relationship with their children and in their children's behavior following bar or bat mitzvah. For example, Jim and Georgia Spector, members of Reform Sukkat Shalom, saw their formerly disengaged son, Kevin, behaving in a new way:

GEORGIA: I have a little bit of a different feeling when I go to temple with him now. He's a participant, he knows the prayers better than I do. I have a different expectation of him, not that he's fully involved, but when he's there he knows what he's doing. And I think he does.

JIM: That's probably true. It's like he's now a young man in the eyes of the temple.

GEORGIA: He's not the kid who just sits in the back and never wants to be part of anything. I think he is more comfortable with himself and more comfortable when he's at synagogue and he can recite the prayers.

Whether the ritual changed Kevin or not—and Kevin was one of the few who denied that it had—the ritual changed the way his parents saw him and his role in the synagogue. The change of status was important, but so was the preparation and performance: one gave him the skills to participate, and the other highlighted his new role. In this way, the two meanings reinforce each other, linking the change of status with responsibility, competence, and community.

"Now you're a 'Jewish adult,' meaning that now . . . you're responsible for your actions officially. You've inched towards that when you were younger, and now there's an official demarcation. There's no mistake about it, it was publicly announced, right? It was in front of lots of people. Now you can be officially counted in a minyan," mused a parent from independent Or Hadash.

The definition is a central part of the meaning: invoking it can relieve anxiety created by leading the service (as with Shoshana), be reinterpreted to allow for a more universal sense of adult responsibility, or simply act as the prerequisite necessary for other approaches to feeling authentic. Understanding the change of status as a consequence of turning thirteen is necessary, but it is not sufficient to support the weight the ritual carries in American Jewish life.

CREATING JEWISH BONDS TO FAMILY AND PEOPLE

The rabbi of a Conservative congregation told me: "The ultimate goal of a bar/bat mitzvah moment is that the child feels empowered and engaged with the community that they [sic] have grown up in. . . . If the child goes through the training and is excited and proud and has the skills and confidence to be part of a Jewish community elsewhere in the world, then we've done a good job because the measure of success of a bar/bat mitzvah is actually the continued Jewish identification of the child. I feel very strongly about the question of identity versus skill." The change of status simply provides the possibility of a ritual; the ritual then offers a chance for adults to instill in the child a sense of Jewish identity and connection to the Jewish people, as this quote illustrates. Rabbis and teachers see inculcating that Jewish identity as central to the bar or bat mitzvah process and want each student to feel a sense of belonging, with the overarching goal being the continuity of the Jewish people.

Jewish identity and peoplehood are central to Judaism; Judaism has always been an ethnic religion, although that element has long remained in tension with the American value of choice (Eisen 1983; Kaplan [1934] 1994). Like the Conservative rabbi quoted above, almost all rabbis expressed the desire for their students to develop strong Jewish identities. Fewer of the parents felt so strongly about this, although it was also one of their concerns. Yet even with strong agreement that Jewish identity was a central element of the ritual, there was little agreement on how to define it, express it, or infuse it into the ritual.

In its strongest form, Jewish identity informs every aspect of the individual's life. Rena Seuss, of Orthodox Adat Yitzhak, told me: "I don't see a distinction between my daily life and my Jewish life. Some of these [interview] questions imply that certain things you're doing are Jewish, and some are not Jewish. . . . Even when I'm going to the grocery store, I'm getting kosher food. Much of my day, whether it's dealing with the kids' homework, planning what I'm going to make for Shabbat—much of my day is structured or somehow affected by my religious life. It's not like there's a divide." As a Modern Orthodox Jew, Rena lives in both secular and Jewish worlds simultaneously, worlds which can exist in parallel, collide (as when she missed a conference that took place on Shabbat), or coincide. The Seuss family's tradition for both observing Shabbat evening while celebrating the Fourth of July exemplifies how the family combines the religious and secular aspects of their lives. Rena described celebrating both the Shabbat evening meal and the Fourth of July fireworks with a group of nearby friends. To do this, on Friday afternoon before Shabbat began (and restrictions regarding driving and carrying came into effect), she delivered a potluck contribution to her neighbor's home. That evening, the family walked to their friends' home for Shabbat dinner, then hiked up a nearby hill to watch fireworks. In contrast, in its weakest form, Jewish identity is a form of "symbolic ethnicity" (Gans 1979), a nostalgic feeling toward family or people backed by little knowledge, belief, or practice. This is frequently called gastronomic Judaism, eating symbolic foods in the same way that other ethnic groups retain special dishes: corned beef and cabbage, lox and bagels, and tamales all fall into this category.

Most of the families participating in this research had moderately strong Jewish identities, as expressed through attachment to Jewish ethics and values, history, arts, Israel, texts, and religious practice, with each path favored by different families.[6] Not surprisingly (given their choice of profession), rabbis and teachers focused largely, though not exclusively, on ritual practice as a primary mode of expression. At the same time, leaders recognized the different ways to engage with Judaism and, above and beyond any level of competence, wanted the bar or bat mitzvah ritual to be a means of connecting their students to ongoing Jewish identity.

For the Conservative rabbi whose quote begins this section, a student who performed a bar or bat mitzvah service with skill but did not feel a connection to the Jewish people would not have accomplished the real goal of the ritual. One of the rabbis from Beth Jeshurun expressed similar goals: "I'd rather have a kid that sees a bar or bat mitzvah as a means toward a positive Jewish identity. I'd rather a kid have a positive identity and not have a bar or bat mitzvah than have a kid who has a bar or bat mitzvah and sees it as the establishment of a religion that they resent and they never want to be part of again."

That sense of Jewish peoplehood encompassed both past and future. Georgia Spector, from Reform Sukkat Shalom, saw it as a powerful connection to family history: "My mother spoke loud and clear in my head . . . my grandmother and my mother were just coming through me." Her husband, Jim, felt the ritual was a necessary symbol for future Jewish identity: "If he [Kevin, their son] didn't get bar mitzvahed, I would have felt like I robbed him of the chance of at least going through the rite of passage as being Jewish."

Students understood it in more concrete terms, seeing the ritual in terms of family togetherness. A student from Conservative B'nai Aaron explained that a successful bar or bat mitzvah included "people being there with you. Your family and people you care about being with you when you become a bar or bat mitzvah," while a boy from independent Or Hadash said that the best moment of the day was "hanging out with my relatives."

Within all but Orthodox congregations, bar and bat mitzvah preparation and enactment are egalitarian.[7] This is not to say that gender differences are completely absent, but those differences are—with few exceptions, such as markedly different styles of tallits for boys and girls—not specific to Judaism, but rather to American gender roles more generally. Some rabbis noted that girls and boys behaved differently: they saw boys as louder and more physically expressive, and girls as more careful in their approaches to the material. This matches general cultural expectations.[8] Most rabbis and teachers found their students responded similarly to the material, while boys and girls voiced similar opinions about preparation and performance.[9]

Parents of girls were a distinct exception to this egalitarian mode. To them, bat mitzvah represented their daughters' full membership in the Jewish people, unlike the partial membership they or their sisters experienced. They illustrate both how much liberal denominations have normalized egalitarian practice and how the experiences of one generation affect those of the next.

Both mothers and fathers felt their daughters' bat mitzvahs were as much about preventing their daughters from feeling "not Jewish enough" as about simply belonging to the Jewish people. As they grew up, around half of the mothers had understood that, while bar mitzvah was required, bat mitzvah was a choice and therefore less important. Those who had not enacted the ritual through choice or circumstance often felt that they lacked a critical piece of Jewish knowledge or identity.

Jamie Kemach, from Reform Sukkat Shalom, felt this alienation particularly strongly: "When it came time for the preparation for my own daughter, I felt a little bit of the otherness of what it must feel like to be a non-Jewish parent going through this with your child. . . . I think it's interesting [that] for me, it brought up a certain—it was like, 'I'm part of this tribe,' but there is an otherness about me within this tribe." Jamie felt her own lack more strongly than most, but the desire to give their daughters what they had missed was common among women I interviewed: "I could have had one" [a bat mitzvah], said Lani Danziger, of Conservative B'nai Aaron. "I just wasn't enamored of religious school, and what it meant. There was always a piece of me that regretted not having done that. It was important for me that she [Lani's daughter] could prove to herself that she's capable of going through that process and achieving something."

Aziza Orlansky, with her Orthodox Moroccan upbringing, felt this even more strongly: "In Morocco and Israel you don't do bat mitzvah. The only thing you do for girls is a party . . . like, 'Okay, let's do something for the girls so they don't feel bad that the boy has all this big attention and he's a boy and more important than the girls.' So it was very important to do bat mitzvah for Julia exactly like we did for Daniel [Julia's older brother] because boys and girls have same abilities, right?" For Aziza, Jewish identity is not sufficient if that means taking on a lesser identity. Bat mitzvah as a ritual represented a way of rectifying gender inequity within Judaism, while Julia's bat mitzvah was a concrete demonstration of gender equality.

Parents of girls did not express concerns that were qualitatively different from those of parents of boys: parents of both girls and boys wanted to ensure their children felt part of the Jewish people. Nevertheless, many parents framed these common concerns through their individual childhood experiences of the less egalitarian Judaism of the mid- to late twentieth century.

Instilling an amorphous feeling of Jewish identity was not sufficient for either leadership or laity. Both groups have introduced into the bar or bat mitzvah service explicit moments that symbolically connect students to their families and/or to the Jewish people.[10] When parents present a tallit to their child or pass the Torah to their child, they are symbolically connecting the child with his or her Jewish family. When rabbis introduce statements of Jewish allegiance into the service, they are creating moments for students to explicitly identify with the Jewish people.

An example of this expression takes place at Reform Sukkat Shalom, where Rabbi Doron emphasizes the student's "bond to the Torah." As the central narrative within Judaism, the Torah thus acts to connect the student to all Jews throughout history:

> Every kid starts with the same sentence: "This is my bond to the Torah" . . . their connection or pledge to the Torah, past, present, and future. They write something about what their memories were when they first saw a Torah. . . . Then they talk about what they know is in the Torah now, and then I also ask them: "Why would we read the Torah over and over again every year?" That plants the seed in their mind, but it also gives them a chance to say: "Yes, when I was five years old, I understood Abraham on a very childish level, now I understand Abraham, and in the future when I look at it again, I'll see other dimensions." Then I ask them to think back to what they've learned over the years. . . . And I ask: "Which of those areas of study would you like to return to in the future?" I think it's a powerful moment for the families to see their kid making a public pledge.

Students memorize this piece of writing and recite it while holding the Torah. Both the process of making an explicit connection between the student's past, present, and future and the act of saying the words aloud to a group of witnesses increase their importance to the student, in this case, linking Jewish identity with the Torah. One student made this connection very literally: "Becoming an adult in the Jewish community, you really have to understand yourself and how you're connected to your Jewish identity. I think through your Torah portion you can really understand that."

Rabbi Doron separated the "bond to Torah" from the bar or bat mitzvah talk on the Torah portion, but it is more common for the personal connection to be part of the talk, as this Orthodox rabbi expected: "There's usually three sections to the speech: there's a theme of the Torah portion or Haftarah, and its connection to the day. The middle section would be 'what being bar [or] bat mitzvah means to me as an individual,' and I have them spend time writing it themselves. The third section is the acknowledgment, thank-yous, and the recollection of childhood leading up to this point."

These moments were developed from rabbis' deliberate attempts to infuse a Jewish connection into the service. The tallit presentation and Torah passing have evolved through folk custom, and these moments use symbolic gestures, rather than statements of loyalty. They serve family needs by connecting bar and bat mitzvah students to individual family history but do little to address leaders' primary concern of connecting students to the Jewish people and its history. These personal moments also intrude on the public nature of the service. As a result, rabbis have responded in two ways: by moving personal moments to private spaces, as when parents present the tallit to their child in private before the service, and by modifying the moment so that it becomes both personal and communal.

This latter approach is how Rabbi Melmed of independent Or Hadash incorporates Jewish history and peoplehood into passing the Torah. In one typical case, as the Torah service began, he called Talia Jacobs's parents and grandparents to join her in front of the Ark. Holding the Torah, he recited the opening sentences of Pirkei Avot (Ethics of the fathers) that establish the authority of the leaders of the early rabbinic period: "Moses received Torah at Sinai and passed it on to Joshua, and Joshua to the elders, and the elders to the prophets, and the prophets passed it on to the men of the great assembly." As he completed the quote, Rabbi Melmed handed the Torah to one of Talia's grandfathers. As family members passed it to Talia, Rabbi Melmed declared: "And they to the grandparents and to the parents and to the sons and the daughters up to this very day." Holding the Torah confidently, Talia stepped forward to lead the congregation in the Shema, the sentence that encapsulates Jewish belief. Words and actions combined to connect Talia to her family's history and to the Jewish people.

The Torah represents Jewish history, law, and relationship to God, so it is not surprising that the physical act of passing the Torah became a moment that symbolically connects one generation of a Jewish family to the next, with the implicit statement that the child holding the Torah also holds the family's Jewish future. By adding the words of the early rabbis to this custom, Rabbi Melmed explicitly connects the family, the Jewish people, and the broader context of Jewish history. Whether the ritual connects students with family history, the Jewish people, or both, the student demonstrates that connection through competently displaying some level of Jewish knowledge and character development.

DEVELOPING JEWISH KNOWLEDGE AND MATURITY

Isaac Levitats writes: "The Bar-Mitzvah ceremony should serve as a certification of the fact that the child is eligible to enter the adult Jewish community as a person who knows and feels what it means to be a Jew. It is for this reason that Jewish educators have within the past decade sought to promulgate minimum requirements for the Bar-Mitzvah ceremony" (1949, 154). It is not enough for students to simply change status or identify with people: for the ritual to be real, students must demonstrate their maturity through their behavior (including a competent performance). Thus, since the beginning of the twentieth century, Jewish leaders have worked to associate the bar and bat mitzvah with basic Jewish knowledge and practice. This serves two goals. Levitats articulates the first: that the student is someone "who knows and feels what it means to be a Jew." In addition, a ritual that requires a substantial amount of time, effort, and knowledge gains greater symbolic weight and importance than one that does not.[11] Therefore, teachers—rabbis, cantors, and tutors—turn from teaching basic Jewish knowledge to helping students develop and demonstrate maturity and understanding intended to develop some or all of four themes:

1. An ongoing relationship with God.
2. Familiarity with Jewish texts and knowledge that may lead to ongoing Jewish practice (including the specific tasks necessary to accomplish the ritual).
3. Discipline and a set of universal work habits that can be applied to other areas of life (school, for example).
4. Morality and good character in behavior toward other people, other living things, and the world.

These themes can be taught from a universal or Jewish perspective, and—as one might expect—Reform rabbis tend to take a more universal approach, while Orthodox rabbis tend to take a more particularistic one. These are only tendencies: teachers in my study across the religious spectrum incorporated both approaches into their teaching. Some rabbis focused on one theme, while others saw them as inextricably interrelated. Regardless of perspective, it is through teaching knowledge and ensuring ritual competence that rabbis invest the ritual with substance and power.

Although Orthodox and liberal rabbis teach a different understanding of the concept, both groups attempt to connect their students to God, making an "appeal to ultimate authority" (Eisen 1998, 260).[12]

Rabbi Teitelbaum of Orthodox Adat Yitzhak emphasized the correct enactment of Jewish law, given by God and therefore binding on Jews: "The child needs to be able to successfully do whatever they're doing in a way that fulfills their obligations—if the child cannot say their blessing or read Torah properly, it would be a problem because everyone is depending on this person to say the blessing and read Torah properly." Although Rabbi Teitelbaum discusses competent performance, competence is not a virtue in and of itself. Rather, competent performance is a means of connecting to God through fulfilling sacred communal obligations. The connection to God is not made explicit, but it underlies the ritual.

Rabbis from more liberal denominations made more direct connections to God with less emphasis on God's commandments. The rabbi of a large Reform congregation wanted his students to learn that "the Torah can be made relevant. This is not a performance. The way in which they lead the service with dignity, they are helping the congregation draw closer to God and sharing their words of Torah." Liberal congregants are less likely to feel commanded by God's authority. Rather, liberal rabbis use bar or bat mitzvah preparation as an opportunity to connect students with a more nebulous sense of awe.

Other teachers emphasize prayer competence or textual interpretation as a way to demonstrate Jewish identity and build Jewish skills for future participation in the Jewish community. Developing these skills takes time, and, particularly in congregations where students attend supplementary religious school only a few hours a week, rabbis choose to focus on one or another area.

At Reform Beth Jeshurun, students have only a small role in the service but put substantial effort into developing their speeches. As noted in chapter 3, the congregation's several rabbis disagreed on this decision, with some rabbis wanting more attention paid to learning the Shabbat morning service, as Rabbi Ben-Ami expressed above. For Rabbi Ben-Ami, the issue was not one of values but rather practicality: determining which knowledge would better lead to future Jewish engagement and identity.

Other rabbis with similar concerns made the opposite decision and emphasized a connection to reading or interpreting the Torah. Thus, the rabbi of a Conservative congregation wanted his students "to see in Torah a way of beginning to think about and answer some of the questions that they're dealing with in their own life and . . . see for themselves both the moral responsibility they have both spiritually and to the world around them and the tremendous agency that they have toward that world. So Torah becomes a way of uncovering for themselves what that agency could look like and who they are as people."

This approach places the ability to use the Torah to interpret the world at the heart of being Jewish. Moral behavior, interpretation of the text, and Jewish knowledge are all integral to Torah and therefore, difficult to separate from each other. Most often, the student's attitude was important: whatever the subject, rabbis expected their students to take the material seriously. One Conservative rabbi noted that he would not allow a bar or bat mitzvah ritual for a student who "showed disregard for teachers and learning. There's no perfunctory bar/bat mitzvah. We would not allow an insincere celebration."

In other words, diligent and respectful preparation shows respect for the ritual and its role as a symbol of Jewish commitment. If the ritual is a symbolic declaration of allegiance, then taking that commitment lightly undermines both the declaration and the ritual. Rabbi Melmed of independent Or Hadash stated this expectation most strongly: "I won't allow a bar mitzvah if they don't do what they're supposed to do. I've called two families in all these thirteen years and said: 'Your child hasn't been to services enough, and we're going to have to reschedule.' . . . If you've got rules, you've got to use them, otherwise you might as well not have them." Rabbi Melmed established these strong expectations as part of his bar and bat mitzvah process, but he is the exception: rabbis rarely tell students, no matter how recalcitrant, that the ritual will not take place. From a practical standpoint, doing so would alienate families from the congregation.[13] It can also send the symbolic message that the child has failed at being Jewish, even alienating the family from Judaism and the Jewish people. While knowledge and respect are important, the consequences of a failed bar or bat mitzvah are high enough that all parties work to ensure that, no matter how difficult, the event happens—as was the case with Nimrod.

A third approach emphasized the discipline and skill set necessary to learn the material for the bar or bat mitzvah, which can also be applied to learning other subjects. Some rabbis made an explicit connection between Jewish and secular learning. Rabbi Melmed noted: "They all develop a great sense of poise at the bimah. . . . [Later on] parents say their teachers don't know how . . . [the students] can understand texts and ask the text questions and feel confident exploring different aspects. I'll tell them that's what I'm trying to do. It's the first time they're giving a text a close reading."

Both parents and students recognize the generalizability of these skills as well. At Orthodox Adat Yitzhak, where bar mitzvah ushers in real changes in adult Jewish responsibilities, one student noted both Jewish and universal skills that he is employing more often: "I've started showing up to shul more, and being a community member rather than being seen as a child. . . . I've stepped up a lot of the rules." However, he also sees the preparation and event as changing him in more general ways: "I think it also changed my life in other ways: how I look at my life and how I can say that I achieved something. I think I can achieve other things if I really try. I think it gives me a boost of confidence."

Building the universal skills of analysis, discipline, and presentation is an indirect result of preparing for the ritual. More directly, rabbis and teachers tie the bar or bat mitzvah to moral behavior. Almost all congregations expected their students to participate in a mitzvah project, defined as some form of social action.[14] Reform Beth Jeshurun is an example of a congregation with an elaborate introduction to social action: students are expected to participate in several types of projects that include helping in a congregational garden plot and then donating the food grown there to food kitchens, serving in those food kitchens, and caring for Jewish cemeteries. Whether framed using Hebrew words and Jewish references (for example, the plot of land is the pe'ah garden, a reference to the commandment to leave corners of a field of grain for the poor to glean) or

English words for similar values, these projects are intended to build character. Despite their ubiquity, the projects enter into the service itself only peripherally (if at all), in a section of the bar or bat mitzvah talk.

Students are trained for and demonstrate competence in ritual practice within the service: prayers, texts, and talk. That competence is important so the student can enact the service in the moment, signal the potential for future Jewish practice and identity, and demonstrate a set of general skills. Achieving this competence is, not surprisingly, the primary concern of almost all of the students. While teachers and parents work to ensure that students are prepared and feel supported, the pressure is quite intense, as Julia Orlansky reflects: "[I was worried about] messing up, because my Haftarah was two and a half pages long, or forgetting how to do something. When I'm nervous, my voice shakes. . . . I was worried about being pressured by everyone there . . . because there were like 300 people there and all my friends were there."

Students also understood the performance as representing the hard work of preparation and a serious attitude. One of Julia's classmates said: "If people watching feel like the person who was the bar or bat mitzvah worked really hard until this day, and they took what they were doing seriously, even if they didn't do a lot or their voice wasn't perfect—if they practiced a lot and they knew what they were doing, I think that's a success."

As they do in other contexts, students attempt to make sense of what the performance itself means. Shoshana, whose immediate response to the meaning of the ritual was "don't mess up," exemplifies this split. While she understands that she simply becomes a bat mitzvah on her twelfth birthday, she also believes that the enactment of the ritual is important, and "messing up"—as she believes she did—means the ritual lacks something essential.

Although rabbis and teachers would certainly agree with Shoshana, others place less importance on knowledge, focusing on celebrating the child with their community—although that community is often the individual family's relatives and friends, rather than the congregational community. The ostentatious party, long the subject of derision, is the most obvious, but by no means the best, illustration of this.

CELEBRATING THE CHILD
THROUGH SPEECHES AND PARTIES

One boy at Orthodox Adat Yitzhak told me: "I don't like to think of bar mitzvah as succeeding or failing because I think everyone succeeds. . . . I think that no matter how good or bad you do [sic], it's not success or failure. It's having the people around you and celebrating with other people that makes it special." As is the case with other life-cycle events, part of the bar or bat mitzvah ritual is a celebration of the change of status. While celebrations are considered a usual part of most life-cycle events, this is not the case for bar or bat mitzvah: parental speeches and parties alike are routinely derided. Online media sites make it easy to find the extremes of bad taste, and these are discussed with delicious enjoyment. These extreme examples are notable for their shock value, but the attempt by leaders to control even tamer celebrations extends back to the early development of the ritual.[15] So, although leadership and laity have common expectations for the first three ways of understanding bar or bat mitzvah mentioned above (albeit with differences in interpretation and emphasis), the celebration of the child, both in parental speeches and through parties, creates substantial conflict, with leaders attempting to educate families and regulate their behavior and parents resisting that regulation.

The heart of the conflict lies in the different perspectives held by families and leaders. Families (particularly the parents) see the ritual as the peak event that Gabriel and Aziza Orlansky described in the previous chapter, a moment when children take their place in family tradition—as passing the Torah demonstrates so concretely. In addition, bar or bat mitzvah gives parents a rare moment to reflect publicly on their child's new phase of life—whether that be new Jewish responsibility or looming puberty. Thus, more than two-thirds of the parents interviewed understood the bar or bat mitzvah as being "a time to celebrate the child and build his or her self-esteem," and around half saw it as "a statement on the part of family about continuing Judaism in the next generation."[16]

Rabbis and education directors, in contrast, most often understand the ritual as a means of furthering the education and continuity of the Jewish people. Many present the bar or bat mitzvah, in the words of one Reform education director, as "a Jewish journey, and the bar or bat mitzvah is not a stop sign or red light. It's just another passage, a taking stock point as we move into the next dimension." From this point of view, the family celebration becomes a distraction from the overall flow of Jewish life, both communal and individual. Yet these leaders are caught in a dilemma. If they do not act to inform parents of their knowledge and perspective, parents' views will be shaped by the surrounding culture. However, the very act of preparing the students and (sometimes) educating parents creates a contradiction: the more time leaders spend preparing students and parents for the ritual, the more the ritual takes on an aura of importance.[17] The conflict that shapes this negotiation can be seen particularly clearly in the case of parental speeches or blessings.

Before turning to that subject, I would be remiss if I did not first mention the famous—or infamous—party as the primary means of celebrating the bar or bat mitzvah student. Because, for the most part, these parties take place outside the auspices of the congregation, they were only peripherally included in this research. In fact, almost all rabbis emphatically declared that these celebrations were outside their purview. Yet congregational bar and bat mitzvah handbooks often include planning and etiquette advice that congregational families were expected to heed. And while evening celebrations are virtually always private affairs, in congregations where kiddush lunches are expected, anyone who attends the service may attend.

Parents felt that the party was necessary to celebrate the child but not sufficient to define the event—a party without the service would simply be another birthday party. As one Reform parent put it: "The party is the least of it. We had big exciting parties [following the services], but that's not why we did it. We can have big exciting parties without that."[18] While the party certainly attracts everyone's attention, in fact, more can be learned from the speeches, and it is to them that I turn now.

The earliest form of what became the parental speech can be found in the blessing still recited in Orthodox congregations: "Blessed is the One who has relieved me from the responsibility due to this one" (Genesis Rabbah 63:10),[19] commonly referred to as the *sheptarani*. This blessing refers to the fact that a parent (father) is responsible for his child's behavior, and any rules that the child breaks would result in the father being punished.[20] When a child reaches thirteen, he becomes responsible for his own actions and would receive any punishment that resulted from violating Jewish law. The blessing formally marks the change of status, as well as reflecting the changing relationship between parent and child, something made explicit in modern speeches from parents to children.[21] Parents address their children during the bar or bat mitzvah service in all but Orthodox congregations, where that parental address takes place at some time following the service (either during the kiddush luncheon or at the evening celebration).[22]

While the adult *d'var* Torah provides the model for the bar or bat mitzvah speech, with the exception of the *sheptarani* blessing, there is no Jewish model for a parental speech to the child. Yet a peak family event demands some acknowledgment, and over time the parental speech has become a cultural norm for American Judaism.

Some of these speeches make connections between Judaism or Jewish identity and contemporary culture, connections that the leadership encourages. For example, David Abrams from independent Or Hadash referred to the Torah portion his daughter had just read and interpreted, using that to link her Torah reading and Judaism to his hopes for her future:

Today's Torah reading was, without a doubt, the hardest *parashah* I've ever had the pleasure of reading. As we stood side by side—with me recounting God's words to Abraham as he was instructed to take his only child, whom he loved, and offer him up as a sacrifice, and you, our only child, whom we love, replying "but Father, where is the lamb for the offering?"—it sent chills up my spine. . . . Your mother and I, like so many before us, chose to bind you to our tradition, so that you might make it your own and find within it a unique way of seeing the world and navigating its narrow straits.

David begins with a crucial moment in the Jewish narrative, and uses it to offer direction for the future. As a liberal Jew married to a gentile, he uses Torah to connect the particularly American circumstance of intermarried families raising Jewish children with the American value of voluntary affiliation to arrive at a Jewish conclusion. David's affinity for Jewish learning enables him to refer to traditional Jewish learning styles while still approaching the material with a distinctly liberal approach that assumes Jewish tradition offers guidance, rather than commands.

Liberal Jews are not alone in connecting Jewish and American values. An Orthodox mother offered a blessing at the kiddush luncheon that, after referring to her daughter's work for a food bank, hoped she would "continue [to value] both aspects of water—helping provide physical sustenance for those who lack and growing spiritually by drinking of the water of the Torah."

Neither of these parents focused on the child's character or accomplishments; instead, they offered their children paths toward the future that connect Jewish and American values. It is not surprising that leaders approved of this type of speech. More often, as parents discuss their hopes for their children, they frame them in secular American terms, giving the Jewish ritual a universal meaning.[23] One parent's carefully crafted speech provides a good example: "My hope for you is that you move through life as gracefully as you move on the field or in the snow coming down a bump run at Alpine or Squaw. And that you keep on bombing down hills. And that you keep on discovering and creating new moves. And that when you fall, you remember to roll as only you can. And that you remember this moment that we have now." The analogy to skiing explicitly demonstrates the family's love for that sport and indirectly identifies the family with a high socioeconomic status. Although the values the parent mentioned—grace, accomplishment through speed, creativity, and recovery—exemplify American individualism, there is nothing in this speech that identifies either the Jewish character of the ritual or engagement in Judaism beyond the bar or bat mitzvah.

Parents also use the speech to describe their child's particular strengths in glowing terms. Some focus on academic brilliance: "We know that you have worked very hard for this day, the same way you worked very hard in school, to get straight As in your honors classes and to learn to play the violin." Others describe the child's sterling character: "From the moment you arrived . . . you captivated my heart . . . with your kindness, sensitivity, generosity, polite manners, and thoughtfulness." Anyone who has raised teenagers would have trouble imagining that these parents truly believe that their children are the remarkable people presented in these speeches, yet these sentiments are, in fact, common ways of celebrating the individual.

Jewish leaders frown on this "adoration of the child": "Rabbis, cantors, educators and presidents all told me how painful it is to sit in a service where the child is the star and the theme is 'Steven Schwartz, King for a Day' or 'Sarah Goldstein, Queen for a Day.' Inevitably, this leads to speeches in which every boy or girl is smarter than Einstein, a better soccer player than Mia Hamm, more of a computer whiz than Bill Gates and more of an activist than Bono" (Yoffie 2007).

Yet changing the nature of these speeches is not easy: in some congregations, these speeches are looked on as acts of love. One parent told me she had told her daughter: "You know we aren't planning to talk about you and how wonderful you are, but just to quickly draw some lesson from the Torah portion." The daughter responded, "But you have to!" She went on explain that she would be humiliated if she was the only student whose parents did not praise her.

Though some rabbis simply assumed that parents would make inappropriate speeches, others worked to change the culture surrounding what they see as inappropriate speeches by educating parents or by providing guidelines. These rabbis tried one or more of three interventions: moving the speech to a different place in the service, providing specific guidelines for the speech's content and length, and reframing the speech as a blessing.

Moving the speech within the service is a subtle and not necessarily effective strategy. One Reform rabbi explained: "We moved the speech to when the Torah is passed down because the kid is holding it, and if they have any sense, they'll make it shorter. Also it's more of a religious moment, so we get more emphasis on Jewish values."

This indirect approach assumes that parents will understand that holding the Torah points to a short speech that includes Jewish content because the Torah weighs a lot and represents Judaism. This is not necessarily the case—many parents need these instructions made plain—so some congregations provide directions that detail both length and content. These can include sets of instruction, templates, or examples. After years of frustration, one rabbi developed an explicit set of directions detailing both word limits and content: "The worst parents embarrass their child . . . by telling some event that you never wanted them to share. . . . Now they do their 400 words with us. . . . Over time, this has been the most difficult part of the experience for me. But sometimes it's also the most moving." This rabbi's comments reflect an ongoing struggle to manage the parents. The stakes are high: while much effort is spent to ensure that the student does not embarrass him or herself, the expectation that parents need similar guidance is not the norm, and not surprisingly parents receive this guidance with mixed feelings.

One large Reform congregation worked to develop community support through a class website that included templates and model speeches. Families were required to attend a family retreat at which speeches were discussed. Through the year, some parents developed their speech through an elective family class. The rabbi explained: "We talk a lot throughout the year about the blessings. And they [parents] e-mail them [speeches] back and forth so they're really in the form of the blessing."

Calling the speech a blessing or a charge enables rabbis to reframe it so that parents focus on their hopes for their child's future, rather than cataloging the child's present virtues. For example, one parent from Beth Jeshurun wrote: "Like the people who worshiped the golden calf, your failures won't be someone else's fault. You will have to take responsibility for your decisions. But at the same time you will get the credit for your achievements. . . . May you continue to explore and experience new things and places by wandering down paths you have not traveled. . . . May you always be able to look in the mirror and smile at what you see. . . . May your dreams and goals be as big as this sanctuary." This speech is a good example of how a Jewish narrative (in this case, that of the golden calf) is used to make a universal point (taking responsibility for one's own actions) while also including family values (exploring the world and trying new experiences). It demonstrates how the speech can reconcile the peak individual family event with the communal demands desired by leaders. By connecting the child to Judaism and Jewish identity—a basic concern of leaders and of most parents—with language specific to both family and child, the child is both acknowledged and celebrated within the community. The conflict and negotiation around the parents' speeches demonstrates that not only can each meaning attributed to bar or bat mitzvah be given more or less validity depending on whose perspective is taken, but that content and enactment also matter in creating the desired meaning.

FROM NEGOTIATING TO ENACTING MEANINGS

The meanings that different participants ascribe to bar or bat mitzvah determine the nature of preparation, the content and direction of the service, and its meaning for the students and their families. If the ritual represents a change of status that occurs with the turn of the calendar, rather than the performance of a ritual, then the content of the ritual might minimize service participation, emphasizing new responsibilities instead (as is imagined in some liberal congregations and enacted in some Orthodox congregations). If the ritual represents passing tradition from one generation to another through establishing Jewish identity, then preparation may include activities that explicitly build connections to the Jewish people, while families are likely to insist that symbolic words and actions be inserted in the ritual. If the ritual represents an important Jewish task, then preparation will include activities and material that attempt to teach knowledge and build character, while the service will include opportunities for the student to display that knowledge and character. Finally, if the ritual is primarily a moment for celebrating the student, then the service will contain opportunities for that celebration.

These different interpretations interact with each other, with different stakeholders placing greater or lesser emphasis on each. Although parents, students, and leaders all mentioned these four meanings, the fundamental differences between the goals and perspectives of the three groups lead to different emphases. Leaders, whose goal is the protection of Jewish practice and reproduction of Jewish community, primarily emphasized Jewish identity and knowledge. Students, whose goal is to complete the expected task successfully, emphasized the performance of the ritual (that is, demonstrating some degree of Jewish knowledge) and, as they had been taught, their status change. Parents, whose goal is to celebrate their child's peak Jewish moment, emphasized Jewish identity and celebration of their child, often (but not always) accompanied by celebrating the child's new Jewish status.

As a result, participants often engage in unspoken negotiations based on assumed meanings with variable results. Some negotiations result in confusion or wildly different perceptions of the same event—as with Nimrod's bar mitzvah above. Some differences are reconciled through broadening the ritual to accommodate multiple viewpoints—as Rabbi Melmed did with the Torah passing. And sometimes, as in the case of parental speeches, rabbis manage those differences through enacting rules or developing parent education programs. Yet even if everyone agrees on the meaning, enacting the ritual competently matters for the service itself. In the next chapter, I turn to the tension of balancing that competent performance with the process of inculcating Judaism.

5 · WHAT IF I DROP THE TORAH?

From Learning to Doing Judaism

Everyone at independent Or Hadash agreed: though the congregation was proud of its demanding bar or bat mitzvah service, preparation was a problem. Cynthia Rosenthal, the chair of the bar and bat mitzvah committee, described the families' concerns: "The kids are there for their rehearsal on Thursday before the bar or bat mitzvah and they're not ready, and that's way too late to be able to do anything about it. That's the worst-case scenario. The best-case scenario is that the kids are more able to read, but they aren't familiar enough with the prayers, and so they are spending time with their tutors when they hopefully should be just spending time learning their trope [melody] and their portion."

It is not surprising that, as the bar or bat mitzvah year approaches, all parties worry about whether the students have the necessary skills to begin training for the service itself. Whether the service is considered primarily to be a Shabbat or a bar or bat mitzvah service, a stuttering, uncertain leader undermines the reality created by the ritual, so enacting the ritual competently has inherent value—irrespective of the leader's underlying Jewish knowledge, commitment, or identity. That competence is not sufficient: a stellar performance without basic knowledge becomes the hollow event decried by the leaders, and if the student, however knowledgeable, performs the service in a halting manner, neither bar or bat mitzvah ritual nor Shabbat service feels real.

Yet the concern with ensuring a competent performance is in tension with instilling Jewish knowledge and identity. Learning to "do Jewish"[1]—like developing any identity—is an ongoing process of both formal study and practice to develop a worldview consonant with that identity and acquire cultural patterns of behavior.[2] Jewish educators work to teach basic Jewish knowledge to, model

Jewish behavior for, and instill a sense of Jewish identity in their students. These educators, whether teaching at full-day schools or congregational supplementary schools, are first and foremost concerned with developing a foundation for future Jewish engagement.[3] However, because the bar or bat mitzvah service requires students to use specific skills, Jewish educators—whether they be rabbis, education directors, or classroom teachers—are also responsible for preparing their students for a performance.

The tension between the process of learning to "do Jewish" and preparing for a performance exists throughout the students' education, although it manifests itself differently at each stage. In religious school classes, rabbis and education directors balance teaching basic Jewish knowledge with teaching the specific skills students need to begin bar or bat mitzvah training. As students learn the material for their bar or bat mitzvah service, rabbis and tutors balance inculcating a general approach to prayer and text study beyond the event itself with ensuring that students are prepared to perform the ritual competently. During the service, rabbis balance the student's enactment of a rite of passage with the role of a worship leader whose goal is to ensure the satisfactory experience of others. Adam Miller's story illustrates these different points of tension throughout preparation and service.

A BUMPY RIDE: ADAM MILLER'S BAR MITZVAH

Harvey and Karen Miller initially joined independent Or Hadash for common reasons: children's education, friends, cost, and previous experience with Rabbi Melmed. "[He] was a good teacher and a good rabbi, and that was a draw for us," explained Harvey. "We also had another couple of close friends [in the congregation] . . . so the rabbi and friend connections and also a lower overhead because it [the congregation] didn't have a building at the time, so it was more reasonable [financially]."

Adam, the younger of the Millers' two children, began religious school in kindergarten, attending first once and then twice a week. Or Hadash's supplementary school, like most, spends about equal time teaching general Jewish knowledge and teaching Hebrew. Carla Twersky, the education director, had separate goals for each area. The congregation has a strong intellectual bent, and both Rabbi Melmed's and Carla's educational emphasis reflected this. She also believed students should be able to navigate Jewish texts—Hebrew biblical and ethical texts—as well as have a "personal picture of Jewish history." She is proud that the congregation's students "have an appreciation for the fact that there are lots of Jewish answers . . . so they understand the facets and the scope of Jewish thinking."

Her goals for acquiring Hebrew are more limited: learning a language effectively requires consistent and frequent practice, something not possible at this type of school. Carla simply wants her students to be able "to read Hebrew with comfort . . . so that we don't have them going to the service and being really afraid because they don't know what's going on, but they can read it and see where we are."[4] Yet she is proud of the fact that "when we graduate kids . . . , we can throw them into any service and they know what's going on, what it means, and they could probably lead some of the service, adjusting for different liturgy and melody."

While some students gain this knowledge, others do not—as was the case with Adam. About a year before his bar mitzvah, his parents were unpleasantly surprised to discover that he knew little or no Hebrew and would need extra time to learn the skills necessary for bar mitzvah training.[5] Or Hadash recommends several independent bar or bat mitzvah tutors, all of whom are expected to follow a program laid out by Rabbi Melmed. From this list, the Millers chose Gilbert Gershman.

"We started nine months before instead of six months," Harvey explained. "Gilbert just went back to the basics like flash cards and showing him [Adam] how to read, but Hebrew is not the kind of thing that comes easily to him. We'd pick him up after tutoring, and we'd get eye rolls . . . and sometimes tears."

During the first few months, Adam and Gilbert met often—for an hour twice a week. As Adam's knowledge grew, they met less frequently, around once a week. "Gilbert really knew my learning process and . . . when I should be done, so he planned out my whole calendar," Adam told me. "I learned how to speak slowly but still get the Hebrew solid. . . . I learned a lot of trope[s] [melodies]. I learned to read without the vowels from the Torah. I also learned the Haftarah and how to memorize: going little by little, repeating words, and then going further."

Adam had found religious school difficult: "Sometimes it seems like the teachers can't handle all the kids, and before they learn about the stuff they are going to be teaching, they have to learn about the kids and how to deal with them. They know their material, but they don't know how to handle us." In contrast, Gilbert inspired Adam's confidence through careful organization and teaching methodology, which moved smoothly from learning the mechanics of the language to learning the material necessary to perform the bar mitzvah service: knowing how to recite the Hebrew, understanding how to memorize it, and learning the chanting schema.

Over the nine months of tutoring, Adam and Gilbert developed a relationship through Adam's study and growing knowledge of basic Hebrew, as well as its place in Judaism. Part of that preparation included translating the texts, so that Adam could clearly connect the Hebrew with its English translation. Nevertheless, as the bar mitzvah loomed, Gilbert focused on performance. "I think it went really well," Adam said with pride. "I only remember messing up one small time, and my tutor . . . whispered it [the correction] to me, so I fixed it right away."

One common narrative in American Jewish culture is that teaching students a bit of Hebrew and then using that bit to recite prayers and texts that are only minimally understood is a waste of students' time and contributes to the ersatz reputation of the bar or bat mitzvah ritual. Better, this argument goes, to spend the time learning something that is both more easily understood and more relevant. Yet despite his difficulties, Adam had received the message that both the words and the language mattered: "I think it was important for people to hear what came out of the Torah word for word, so I did a little translation."

Developing the talk required a different set of skills, including the ability to understand the texts in their historical context. At twelve, Adam did not have that background, and he and his family relied on Rabbi Melmed to provide it. During several hour-long sessions with Rabbi Melmed, Adam chose the verses he would read, discussed the questions those verses raised for him, and developed one question on which his talk and the subsequent discussion would focus: "When do you think you have a connection with God?" With Jewish source material provided by Rabbi Melmed, Adam asked his parents, brother, and other relatives for their answers to the question and then used those responses to prepare his talk. It was a topic that fit him well, and he was pleased with the result: "My final draft was really good, and I was really proud of it. I feel like I got my ideas into it."

Yet preparation was not fun for either Adam or his parents. "There are so many balls to juggle, and, fortunately, we started early enough on the Hebrew, and that was the bumpy part of the ride, and even doing the d'var Torah, it was hard," said Harvey. He added that Adam "wanted to do this but just found it hard and was frustrated."

Nevertheless, a few weeks before the service, everything came together. Adam "was a caterpillar for nine months, miserable, and then on the weekend or the two weeks before, you could see him become this amazing butterfly. All of the sudden he just sort of got it," Karen explained, still amazed at the recollection. "I can't speak for Harvey, but I was very apprehensive for Adam with his sermon and stuff, and he just exceeded my expectations by far. He was so confident up there. He was exceptional that day."

Adam's story exemplifies the tensions that run through this chapter and the whole book. The bar and bat mitzvah program and the school were, as several leaders explained to me, "two sides of a river." The school focused on the process of learning about Judaism, though some Hebrew was part of that program. The bar and bat mitzvah program was demanding. Some of its requirements included attending and commenting on eighteen services over two years, developing booklets of their own commentary, and attending family classes.

These requirements were intended to engage students and parents in the process of Jewish practice. At the same time, the performance requirements were relatively high, requiring a knowledge of Hebrew that the school simply did not provide. As a result, when students began tutoring, the needs of the upcoming service took precedence. Though the primary goal of tutoring is to ensure a competent performance, the tutors I interviewed felt strongly that students should take more from the experience than the cliché that a bar or bat mitzvah is simply about memorizing meaningless words and melodies. However, for Adam, simply ensuring that the seemingly insurmountable task could be mastered competently was enough. And at the service, because of the time he had spent on ensuring that his performance would be competent, he was able to feel confident and comfortable, which led him not only to perform well, but to feel that he was doing the real Jewish work of leading and teaching the congregation. At each stage, the process of learning and the need for a competent performance were in tension; in each case, the results of that balance affected the next stage.

SUPPLEMENTARY SCHOOL: TEACHING THE BASICS

"I joined the year that Leah went into kindergarten," one mother who belonged to independent Or Hadash told me. "I was definitely looking for a congregation because I knew I couldn't do the do-it-yourself Jewish education that my parents did. [Or Hadash] had a parent-child program that met loosely every other week. . . . It was [an] enormously welcoming and wonderful experience for me. I found people that I liked, I found a community that was supportive, I found education that I enjoyed—all those things." Like Leah's mother, most of the families I interviewed had enrolled their children in Jewish preschool or kindergarten to give their children an adequate Jewish education and to fill their own needs for Jewish community. In these early grades, learning bar or bat mitzvah skills does not enter into the conversation, and parents and leaders have common goals for Jewish education: it should impart basic Jewish knowledge and practices, provide a Jewish space and community for the children, and develop their Jewish identity.[6]

Supplementary schools meet through the school year, for a total of around thirty weeks.[7] In the early grades, children spend a few hours weekly covering a few core topics each year: time-bound practices (Shabbat, holidays, and life-cycle events); values, including ethics and social action; texts and liturgy; Jewish history, including that of Israel; and the nature of prayer and God. Young students are often exposed to Hebrew, but formal study of the language begins in the third or fourth grade, generally with its own program that effectively doubles the time spent each week in religious school from two or three hours to four or five.[8] These topics have remained remarkably stable since the beginning of the twentieth century. For example, the 1938 standards for bar mitzvah of Chicago's Jewish community included: "(a) Understanding of the Hebrew language.... (b) Ability to read the prayers with a reasonable degree of fluency.... (c) Understanding of the customs and ceremonies of Jewish life. (d) Knowledge and understanding of the major events, personalities and movements of Jewish history" (Levitats 1949, 155). These same subjects are still covered today, as the education director of a large Reform congregation described: "The five big ideas that we want kids to look at in every year are God, Torah, Am Yisrael [peoplehood], Eretz Yisrael [the land of Israel], and Tikkun Olam [repairing the world, or social action]. Then they also do a Hebrew component, and they do Jewish holidays."[9]

While there is continuity of subject matter, the descriptions also reflect contemporary language and issues, as this example from another Reform congregation shows: "My goal is for children to love the Jewish side of themselves. Because they come from intermarried backgrounds . . . embracing Judaism as a religion and a culture in a very positive and wonderful way is how Judaism continues." Though this rabbi focuses on intermarried families, identifying as Jewish and practicing Judaism is increasingly a matter of choice for all American Jews, as recent data from the Pew Research Center suggest (Lugo et al. 2013). As a result, schools and congregations now need to make a compelling case for children— and often their families—to make Jewish choices.

The families I interviewed represent one pattern of joining congregations and enrolling children in religious school. Other families wait until their children are entering the third to fifth grades, when Hebrew teaching begins. Around this time membership requirements for bar or bat mitzvah begin to apply: families are expected to join synagogues and students to attend religious school for between two and four years prior to the ritual, with congregational leaders arguing that bar or bat mitzvah is not an end in and of itself but is embedded in community life, and becoming part of that community requires time.

Supplementary schools face a number of problems. They meet for a very limited time, during which teachers are expected to teach a broad range of subjects—any one of which has generated an entire literature for adults. Teachers are hired to work only a few hours each week and often lack formal training in teaching methodology and classroom management. Students enter these programs at different ages and with a wide range of skills and knowledge. They attend these schools after school or on weekends, when they are tired and/or when other activities compete for their attention. Many of the subjects taught— history, language, and theology—require the same academic skills as do secular academics, and thus they compete for students' intellectual attention. While success or failure in secular subjects has the real consequences of poor grades, there are few or no external consequences for not knowing, for example, that the names of the three patriarchs are Abraham, Isaac, and Jacob. This litany of woes is well known: the field of Jewish education devotes substantial effort to examining these problems and implementing potential solutions.[10] The need to teach skills necessary to enact a bar or bat mitzvah service—familiarity with Hebrew, liturgy, and texts—complicates this already difficult situation, as an education director at a large Reform congregation summarized: "For me, [the goal is] to keep the kids engaged in Jewish learning and experiencing living Jewishly, seeing the world through a Jewish lens. However, . . . many parents have a goal for their children to become b'nai mitzvah. As for the students, . . . some say, 'I want to have a bar mitzvah,' and some say, 'I want to learn Hebrew because I want to go to Israel.'"

These different goals lead to the perception that there is a clear division between acquiring bar or bat mitzvah skills and developing Jewish identity and knowledge. That is part of the premise behind the B'nai Mitzvah Revolution, a research and policy program developed by the Reform Movement that aims to change the place of bar or bat mitzvah in the lives of families and congregations. Part of the goal is to reduce the effect of the bar or bat mitzvah on the school curriculum: "We share with many synagogues a growing unease about . . . the fact that b'nai mitzvah preparation has, in many cases, supplanted other goals of synagogue educational endeavors" (B'nai Mitzvah Revolution n.d.). Yet the tools necessary for bar or bat mitzvah ritual also serve the goals of Jewish competence, which include understanding a relationship to God, the Jewish narrative, and the meaning of prayer. The tension among the different participants in bar or bat mitzvah is at least as much about meaning—does the subject matter have intrinsic or instrumental value?—as about content.

It would be difficult to overstate the role of Hebrew in this conflict. Hebrew is an important component of Jewish identity: the common language of a people's history and current nationality, acting—as do languages in general—as a means of establishing group cohesion and boundary distinctions.[11] Jewish texts, from the ancient to the modern era, are written in Hebrew, while it is also the modern language of a nation and people. In addition, it has deep symbolic meaning: as Arabic does for Muslims and Latin did for Catholics,[12] it serves as a sacred language for both study and prayer. Thus, Hebrew is deeply embedded in the process of "doing Judaism," and irrespective of its effect on bar or bat mitzvah, most educators agreed that learning some Hebrew was part of acquiring Jewish identity—although they did not agree on which aspects of the language should be taught.

One educator emphasized biblical Hebrew because it enables students to study Torah; another felt that most American students experience their Jewish identity through religious practice and, therefore, needed liturgical Hebrew. Some teachers want to incorporate conversational Hebrew, but as students approached bar or bat mitzvah age, the biblical and liturgical Hebrew skills required for the ritual made teaching modern Hebrew more difficult. "If bar or bat mitzvah was not a factor," explained a teacher at Conservative B'nai Aaron, "we would scale back on the amount of *t'fillot* [prayers] we teach, so we could devote more time to conversational Hebrew."

The skills students need to perform the ritual overlap with those needed to enact Jewish ritual practice: the ability to read Hebrew, to lead and follow some or all of the Shabbat liturgy, to use appropriate sources to develop a speech, and usually to chant the different Torah and Haftarah melodies. Within these general categories, the expected level of expertise varies: for example, students at Orthodox Adat Yitzhak could read and translate the Hebrew texts (with some assistance), while some students at Beth Jeshurun had difficulty simply sounding out words. This difference reflects denominational expectations and those of the individual congregation. Beth Jeshurun expected students to lead one or two prayers and chant around twelve verses from the Torah portion and four or five from the Haftarah. At Sukkat Shalom, Rabbi Doron expected students to translate their Torah portions with him, going so far as to give vocabulary tests. Without some basic knowledge, students—whether expected to simply decode the Hebrew or to be able to translate it—will, like Adam, be unable to proceed.

Educational materials reflect concerns for ensuring students have acquired this knowledge. For example, Behrman House, a publisher of Jewish educational material, produces six different Hebrew programs, four that primarily teach liturgy and two that teach conversational Hebrew (Behrman House n.d., 91–106).[13] In one typical program, *Hebrew through Prayer 1*, fourth- or fifth-grade students are introduced to the themes and meanings of several blessings and prayers, the first few prayers of the Shabbat morning service, and several grammatical concepts and some basic vocabulary (Trager 1996). As is necessary with the study of any language, students are expected to practice the material, take tests, and be evaluated. It is a highly structured approach, very different from the more experiential approach taken toward other topics.[14]

The approach of the bar or bat mitzvah ritual shapes the concerns of families, so the ability to perform the Hebrew correctly can seem more important than the goals of the great majority of education directors and rabbis: the inculcation of regular practice and broader Jewish knowledge. Yet Hebrew has a crucial role in shaping Jewish life and identity; its role in the ritual is not accidental. Though the tension between performance and process manifests itself through the place of Hebrew in the curriculum and classroom, the tension is a result of the high stakes inherent in the ritual.

In supplementary schools, the tension between process and performance manifests itself largely in the development of the Hebrew curriculum and its implementation in the classroom, as educators and rabbis determine what and how to teach a classroom of students. As students and families begin bar or bat mitzvah training, individual relationships between student and tutor or rabbi become central. It is to that situation that I turn next.

THE BAR OR BAT MITZVAH YEAR: PREPARING PARENTS AND STUDENTS

Somewhere between two years and six months before the date, families begin formal preparation for the bar or bat mitzvah. This preparation can be as simple as choosing or being assigned a date and being given a list of tutors for complicated programs in which both families and students participate. While the student's competent performance is a necessary goal, rabbis, educators, and tutors all see this period as a chance to deepen his or her understanding of and connection to Judaism. In religious school, students learn a set curriculum as a group. As they prepare for bar or bat mitzvah, the mode becomes more individual, with learning tailored to the students' needs and abilities. Thus, the possibilities for engaging in the Jewish process increase—but so do the stakes for the approaching performance.

In the mid-twentieth century, when the bar mitzvah bargain began, congregations focused on teaching the students, assuming that parents were knowledgeable. However, with the dissolution of ethnic enclaves and increasing intermarriage between Jews and gentiles, that assumption no longer holds (if it ever did). As a result, supplementary religious schools often hold family education classes. These programs serve two purposes. They can provide general Jewish knowledge, albeit knowledge related to the service—as at Beth Jeshurun, where the family program includes learning key prayer vocabulary, which is both part of basic Jewish literacy and directly related to the ritual. They can also be a direct response to the parents' focus on performance, framing bar or bat mitzvah in the context of ongoing Jewish life.

Tutoring is virtually universal, but some congregations—particularly those where students attend day schools or in congregations with small cohorts of bar or bat mitzvah students—have no family program. Congregations with small cohorts and individualized preparation can informally include the family and often the congregation in this preparation.[15] Congregations, mostly Orthodox ones, with students who attend day school usually have no additional school. As a result, there is no organization within the congregation to take responsibility for these programs, and planning for the ritual depends on the individual skills, knowledge, and communal network of each family. This was the case at Orthodox Adat Yitzhak where, though congregants attended the service and luncheon following the bar or bat mitzvah, each family prepared individually. Though this approach implicitly minimizes the place of the ritual, it also reduces the control that leaders have over the nature of the event. Thus, another Orthodox congregation had recently instituted a bar and bat mitzvah program to ensure that families approached the ritual with some standard knowledge.

Both student tutoring and family programs (where they exist) are part of bar or bat mitzvah preparation, and both must balance the twin goals of inculcating process and ensuring a competent performance. Because they are very different in form, content, and intent, I discuss each separately.

Family Education: Bar or Bat Mitzvah Is Not Just for Students

Unlike supplementary school programs and individual student tutoring, family programs vary widely in content, organization, and methodology. Some programs focus only on preparing families for the bar or bat mitzvah event, placing it in a Jewish context and/or providing specific information about parents' responsibilities for managing guests and celebrations. Other programs use the opportunity to set the Jewish context through teaching basic Jewish knowledge and skills. Still others incorporate activities that build community cohesion for families, students, or both. These programs also vary in their place in the curriculum. Some, as at Beth Jeshurun, replace the entire seventh grade year. Others supplement the school program, adding a family or parental component. Regardless of content and form, when these programs exist, they are shaped by the tension between teaching parents and their children the skills necessary to ensure a competent performance and engaging them in the process of Jewish living.

For example, at large Reform Beth Jeshurun, a two-year bar and bat mitzvah program addressed topics of general Jewish knowledge while also introducing skills necessary for the ritual. In one component of the program, students and parents attended a set of six Saturday morning classes that addressed the specific prayers and themes in the Shabbat morning service but also introduced the underlying concepts of prayer, peoplehood, and practice. Though this class is part of bar or bat mitzvah preparation, the focus remains on the service, with the ritual hardly mentioned.

Beth Jeshurun's bar and bat mitzvah program requires substantial effort from leaders: both education directors and an administrator, as well as several of the rabbis, participate. Programs that require such an intensive commitment of resources are found primarily (though not exclusively) in large congregations. It is more common for bar and bat mitzvah programs to take place concurrently with supplementary school. Independent Or Hadash expects parents and students to attend a nine-session program that, as at Beth Jeshurun, includes both basic Jewish knowledge and skills for the ritual.

In one session that focused on skill building, students and their parents progressed through a set of stations in which families practiced these skills: putting on a prayer shawl correctly, locating a verse in the Torah, reciting blessings correctly, and passing the Torah safely. Each station addressed the need for a competent performance, having families practice the key places where service attendees could notice a mistake and where that mistake could embarrass the individual or damage the ritual.

Another session focused on how Jews create knowledge and teach it to successive generations. The topic has both general relevance (developing a mode of thinking about transmitting Jewish knowledge) and relevance to the bar or bat mitzvah (creating a larger context to frame the passing of Judaism from generation to generation). The following example I observed illustrates the dual goals.

Before the session, each family submitted two mottos that meant something special to that family. These included: "Chew with your mouth closed." "People are more important than things." "Don't find problems, find solutions." and "No whining!" As families entered the room where the session was held, they received the collected mottos along with sayings from Jewish tradition. To begin the session, each family chose one motto and one saying that represented that family's values.

Rabbi Melmed then situated the exercise in Jewish tradition: "Around 200 C.E. the rabbis put together the Mishnah . . . [which] means 'repetition.' So what are you going to repeat? They shared what they knew. Everyone asked everyone else: 'What do you do? What happens if . . . ?' . . . Even now, that's what rabbis do—someone asks a new question, then a rabbi will apply what he knows." Making the moment personal, he called on Joel Steinberg to explain one of the phrases that his family had chosen.

"Laugh and live longer," answered Joel.

But Rabbi Melmed wanted more. The lesson was about the transmission of knowledge, which required not only repeating the phrase but also citing the source. As Joel and his family frantically searched for the answer, the rabbi taught the group the Hebrew phrase used when citing someone—*b'shem omro* (in the name of)—along with the rationale for using it: "That's their immortality. That's what keeps them alive. When you are adults, you will be quoting each other and keeping each other alive that way."

By the time Rabbi Melmed had finished this explanation, Joel and his parents had found the answer, which Joel gave correctly: "We chose 'laugh and live longer,' *b'shem omro* the Stern family, because we like to have fun."

Through using Jewish texts along with family sayings, Rabbi Melmed integrated Jewish past and present, giving families a way to interpret their behavior—creating individual family cultures—through a Jewish lens, thus linking current experience to the heritage rooted in rabbinic Judaism.

What all these examples have in common is that in developing programs that fill the perceived need to build the families' skills and knowledge, rabbis and education directors are also providing a way to link these skills to more general Jewish knowledge. That is, rather than being in tension, ensuring a smooth performance was congruent with the process of learning context and history. For the students, working to master the material for the ritual, the situation was different.

Preparing for the Service: Chanting the Texts, Developing the Talk

Like Adam Miller, Henry Eisenheim began bar mitzvah tutoring around a year and a half before the ritual. In his case, his parents attributed his weak Hebrew skills to learning problems and lack of interest in the language and hoped that a tutor would inspire him. While Lisa Mendeloff, the tutor, and Henry worked well together, their lessons were often spent discussing the moral issues raised by the texts. A few months before the bar mitzvah date, Lisa had a previously scheduled commitment and, as had been planned, Henry switched tutors. As Gilbert did with Adam, this tutor pressed Henry to stay on task, so that he could learn the material necessary for the performance. Even so, the bar mitzvah date was too close for Henry to learn everything.

"I don't think Henry was as far along as he should have been when Lisa left," Henry's mother, Linda, reflected. "In the end we had to cut lines from Henry's Haftarah. . . . I would have liked the tutor to be proactive about where we should be at certain points. . . . The rehearsal on Thursday was very rocky, and Friday was very stressful because we didn't know how it was going to go. It went well, but it was stressful."

Despite enjoying his discussions with Lisa, Henry also found the experience difficult: "If I'm going to read Torah again, I want to know what I'm reading about a month and a half ahead of time . . . because I don't want to be in a situation where I'm pressured. . . . We had so many fights in our household based on that."

The difference between Henry's and Adam's experiences illustrates the importance of preparation for a performance, irrespective of how interesting other subjects may be. Both boys began tutoring with relatively weak Hebrew skills. However, while Henry and his family became more stressed at the performance approached, Adam and his family were able to relax. Most rabbis and tutors want their students to develop the ability to appreciate Jewish narratives and values and to find ways to connect these ancient texts to the present. However, when the process of engaging with the material overwhelms the needs of the performance, the result can be difficult for everyone. Henry retained his interest in debating Jewish issues, but his feelings about the event itself were decidedly mixed.

Like Adam and Henry, almost all bar or bat mitzvah students work individually with tutors to learn their Torah and Haftarah material and to review and rehearse the service, particularly the prayers they will lead.[16] These lessons have much in common with other kinds of individualized learning—music lessons or personal sports coaching, for example—in which teachers with expert knowledge in a given field work with individual students, taking into account their skills, knowledge, and tastes. Through the process of learning and teaching the subject matter, these teachers ideally develop relationships with their students that lead the students to develop a love for and competence in the given subject. This ideal student-teacher relationship is the stuff of dedications in which successful students credit former teachers for inspiring them to continue. Based on the passion with which rabbis and tutors discussed working with students, that ideal is also what these teachers strive for. At the same time, as with these other subjects where a performance (be it a ball game or a music recital) structures the lessons, so does the looming bar or bat mitzvah service structure these lessons. But where there is always another ball game or piano recital, bar or bat mitzvah tutoring has a distinct beginning and end, with the consequence that teachers have limited time to train their students and to inculcate a deep understanding of the material. So while individual training for the ritual has much in common with other forms of tutoring, the finite duration and focus on a one-time peak performance intensifies both aspects of tutoring.

Six months to a year prior to the bar or bat mitzvah service, students begin working with tutors on texts and prayers. Chapter 2 discussed similarities and differences between congregational and bar or bat mitzvah services, as well as differences in how congregations approach the bar or bat mitzvah material. This section builds on that material to understand how students learn texts and prayers from tutors and develop their speeches with the rabbis. Both rabbis and tutors take the available time, expected content, and individual variation of the students into account, and most of them work to balance the process of learning to wrestle with Jewish narratives and values with the need to ensure a competent performance.

Though both rabbis and tutors take process and performance into account, how the two groups balance process and performance is very different. On the one hand, tutors are primarily responsible for ensuring that students are prepared to competently perform the texts and prayers. This is no light matter: that enactment does not merely show off the student's ability; it also creates something real. A stuttering performance damages the ritual, the attendees, and the leader, as was almost the case with Henry. Because he and his tutor were engrossed in textual analysis, Henry's ability to lead the prayers and chant the Hebrew suffered. On the other hand, rabbis are primarily responsible for helping students develop their speeches, which means teaching Jewish interpretation and patterns of analysis. The speech represents the students' engagement with that process, so a perfunctory speech, no matter how well delivered, does not demonstrate the expected competence. Because of these differences in orientation, I discuss each experience separately.

Developing the Bar or Bat Mitzvah Talk: Rabbis and Students

At most Bay Area congregations, rabbis work with students on their speeches.[17] Through working with individual students to analyze and interpret specific texts, these rabbis attempt to communicate their vision of Judaism and Jewish identity. Rabbis hope and believe that these brief relationships can affect students' views of the ritual and Judaism, or their relationship with the world. Rabbis shared success stories with me: the student who regularly returns to lead services or chant from the Torah; the student who brilliantly analyzed a difficult text; the student who became inspired to use the bar or bat mitzvah ritual for good rather than gain. These stories have a mythic flavor, speaking to the potential these meetings have to transform students. Students and parents also have expectations of these meetings. As they recalled childhood or recent experiences of bar or bat mitzvah students, both adults and children recalled relationships with their rabbis, sometimes positively and sometimes not. In either case, they hoped for an inspiring relationship.

The relationship is built around teaching students to develop a modified *d'var Torah*.[18] These talks are based on material—themes, verses, and questions—found in the week's texts. However the bar or bat mitzvah date is chosen, that choice fixes the portion that will be read. Some weeks are full of stories, others full of laws. Some deal with sex and violence, others with acts of revelation. Whatever the portion, students struggle to make sense of the material, although a student trying to relate to the sibling rivalry of Jacob and Esau will have an easier time than one trying to relate to the laws governing sacrifice or leprosy. Their interpretations become the speeches that they develop during their meetings with rabbis.

Students begin meeting with rabbis somewhere between three and six months prior to the event to develop these talks. Like the adult *d'var Torah*, they usually include a summary of the text, a problem or question raised by the text, and an interpretation of the text—to which students often add a discussion of their new status as Jewish adults. The two examples below demonstrate the variation in approach. Rabbi Doron of Sukkat Shalom, who comes from a Reform perspective, expects a short speech that incorporates the student's response to the subject, and his students typically have minimal Jewish knowledge. Rabbi Teitelbaum of Adat Yitzhak takes an Orthodox approach to the texts and expects a much longer exposition supported by Jewish sources, while his students typically have some knowledge of Hebrew and Jewish texts. Not surprisingly, the different contexts and expectations on the one hand and the different levels of knowledge and practice on the other hand result in two different kinds of talks. However, these obvious differences mask similarities in the ways the two rabbis work with students to communicate a vision of what Judaism is and can be, and how they lead each student to an individual interpretation of the texts.

Unlike most rabbis, Rabbi Doron sees developing the students' speeches as inseparable from translation and interpretation of the text. Therefore, he works with all students to translate that text and expects them to read—not chant—from the Torah. This decision is not made lightly: in having students translate and read, he is emphasizing that the text has meaning, rather than simply being sounds and a melody to memorize. Rabbi Doron meets with each student ten times, during which, in addition to translating the text, the student develops his or her speech and writes an individual statement of Jewish commitment. Rabbi Doron sees himself as mediating the students' move to a more adult place in their family and the world, striving to make the bar or bat mitzvah "a positive emotional experience. I want them to have a sense that they're going to go on. . . . I use the *yad* [pointer for reading Torah] as the central symbol of the service, implying a grasp and a competency of what they're doing, but the goal is really more for the family, to have a sense of respect for their growing teenager."

I observed Rabbi Doron as he met with Denise Shore around six weeks prior to her bat mitzvah. Denise's portion fell in the Book of Numbers, and from it she had chosen to read and discuss the ending verses about one of the Israelites' rebellions against the leadership of Moses and Aaron. In these verses, God causes Aaron's staff to sprout, blossom, and produce almonds overnight. As she has learned to translate and recite the text, she has also worked to interpret the event so it makes sense to her.

Rabbi Doron began by reading the draft and then corrected some basic facts before turning to the interpretation, asking Denise why she thought the staff bloomed. Hesitantly, she replied, "Because God wants to show that Aaron is the one who's in charge . . ."

"Good, but tell me more about what happens," Rabbi Doron said.

Denise summarized the rebellion, ending with the description of Aaron's staff: "First there was a bud, then there was a flower, then an almond. So that shows that Aaron deserves his high position."

Rabbi Doron pressed her to connect the text with her own life: "You have to talk about three stages . . . something like 'My bat mitzvah happened in three stages.' Why is the first stage like a flower?"

"Because it's pretty," Denise said. "I didn't think about the hard work—it was just pretty to think about. The bud is next—it has a hard shell and isn't pretty—that's the hard work. You have [to] sit and do the hard stuff to get to the next stage."

"And the end is the almond?" asked Rabbi Doron.

"Yeah, the last stage is the almond. . . . Maybe the almond is what I've been working for all this time, and now I get to pop it into my mouth," Denise answered.

Through this gentle prompting, Rabbi Doron ensured accuracy and clarity, only then pressing Denise to link the text with her life. In keeping with both his philosophy of a simple talk and the knowledge base of his congregation, his primary goal is not to bring other commentary, whether Jewish or secular, into the discussion but simply to encourage students to relate to the text.

While Rabbi Doron's expectations for student mastery are quite different from those of Rabbi Teitelbaum, both rabbis strive to connect students with these texts and what they represent.

Rabbi Teitelbaum gives students substantial flexibility in how they demonstrate their adult Jewish status. Some students give bar or bat mitzvah speeches that follow the d'var Torah model; others deliver extended lessons on topics of Jewish interest, often explicating Jewish law relating to that topic. Bill Wolfson took the latter path, choosing to study the laws of the Cohanim, a traditional ancient priestly class.[19] Becoming bar mitzvah gave Bill real motivation to learn these laws: he is a part of this class and, as an adult Jew in a traditional community, would be subject to both the rights and privileges of this status.

Rabbis vary in how much they integrate Jewish texts into their lessons. Rabbi Doron rarely used them, wanting to focus on the students' individual connections to the text. On the other hand, Rabbi Berel, of Reform Beth Jeshurun, expected students to incorporate these texts into their speeches. Rabbi Teitelbaum not only used Jewish texts, but he saw them as authoritative. Thus, Bill's responsibility was to understand and interpret these laws, rather than questioning them.[20] To understand the laws of the Cohanim, Rabbi Teitelbaum relied on the Shulchan Aruch, a sixteenth-century compilation of rabbinic law that assumes a substantial knowledge of traditional Jewish texts. Rabbi Teitelbaum's role in these lessons was to help Bill fill in the gaps in his knowledge.

I observed the two during Bill's early stages of learning the material, when Rabbi Teitelbaum was simply ensuring that Bill understood the text—as the following example shows.

Bill read from a Hebrew text and then translated it: "As it is written: 'You will make him holy. Rabbis receive the tradition, for everything this holy, to open [the Torah reading] first.'"

Bill understood the plain meaning of the text: that the Cohanim had the honor of being called up to recite the first blessing upon chanting from the Torah. Rabbi Teitelbaum then explained that the text generalizes that honor to other situations in which Cohans are given the first opportunity.

Bill wrote the information down and then continued: "But with regard to Torah reading in shul, the sages made a rule 'darchei noam' [paths of peace] to encourage peace."

The meaning of this sentence was opaque to Bill (and me), but Rabbi Teitel-baum explained: "This means that you can't give away the spot; the Torah reading has to be in that order. Why? Because if Cohanim could give it away, people would fight over it."

They continued to work through the text, with Bill translating it and—where he could—giving a simple interpretation, while the rabbi clarified difficult passages. Toward the end of the hour, they moved to the rabbi's computer. Bill reviewed the lines they had covered, as Rabbi Teitelbaum checked his understanding and, at some points, extended the discussion to different applications of the rules covered.

The differences between the content, the student's knowledge, and the rabbi's goals in the two cases are substantial. Bill is mastering detailed material that he will explain and use as an adult Jew, while Denise is using broad metaphors to connect a Jewish narrative to her own life. Bill's knowledge of Jewish writing and his ability to read and translate Hebrew enables him to engage with material that Denise does not even know exists. However, in both cases, the rabbis are working to build a deeper sense of the material with which the student is engaged and to connect Jewish knowledge to their students' lives. The quantity and depth of material differ, as do the use to which the knowledge will be put, but the process of engaging the student is quite similar.

Language, Melody, and Performance: Tutors and Students

No matter how students arrive at the verses from their Torah and Haftarah portions that they are expected to master, learning to read and chant these Hebrew texts is a relatively structured exercise, and across denominations there was striking similarity in how tutors approached learning the texts and chanting melodies. Learning to chant from the Torah requires three steps: reading printed Hebrew without melody (trope); then chanting it with melody; and finally transferring that chanting from the scroll itself, which is written in a more ornate alphabet and lacks vowels and trope marks. Though tutors and congregations vary a bit in how these tasks are accomplished, each task is well-defined and necessary for a competent performance. The steps for learning the Haftarah portion are similar, although it is read with vowels and requires a second set of melodies. In most cases, tutors also check (but do not necessarily teach) prayers for which the student is responsible and rehearse the student, sometimes with the rabbi, prior to the bar or bat mitzvah. If these tasks are not accomplished, the performance is at risk. Nevertheless, tutors vary in their approaches, depending on their own interests, a given student's ability and motivation, and the length of the lesson. As result, despite the underlying similarities, tutors varied substantially in how they balanced process and performance. Two examples from the opposite ends of the spectrum—one from Orthodox Adat Yitzhak, the other from large Reform Beth Jeshurun—illustrate these differences.

About a month before his bar mitzvah, I observed Bill, whom we met above, as he began to work with his tutor, Simcha Solomon, on his Haftarah portion. The text, taken from Ezekiel, discusses the reunion of the Northern and Southern Kingdoms, a parallel to the Torah portion which tells of Joseph's reunion with his brothers in Egypt.

Unlike most of his fellow students, Bill does not attend day school. Nevertheless, he had learned enough Hebrew to translate it with moderate skill and, through regular service attendance, knew the extensive Shabbat morning liturgy. Bill has a particular affinity for chanting. In addition to chanting the Haftarah, he chose to master the entire weekly portion—an unusually large amount of Hebrew even at Adat Yitzhak. Because of the length of the material, he began hour-long weekly lessons with Simcha a year prior to his bar mitzvah.

One lesson took place at Simcha's home, around a table stacked high with Hebrew books. Simcha began by ensuring that Bill could chant and translate the first few verses. Then he started working with Bill on their interpretation. He began by asking Bill to make the connection between his Torah and Haftarah portions, which Bill did with ease, explaining that the reunion between Joseph and his brothers was like the reunion between the Northern and Southern Kingdoms.

Simcha then gave that statement a broader context: "The Haftarot have a general sense of movement from one prophet to the next. They have a sad side—we've been beaten down—but the hopeful side is bringing people back together. . . ."

This pattern of chanting, translating, and interpreting continued throughout the hour-long lesson, at the end of which they had completed the Haftarah reading. Simcha summed up the interpretation: "We saw three dualities: [first,] sadness in the destruction of the Beit haMikdash[21] and happiness in the joining of the two halves of one people. Then there is the duality in God, between 'Elohim' and 'Adonai,' or King and Master. And finally the promise of a covenant with Yaacov's children of peace (shalom) and land (Olam)."

For each section of Hebrew, Simcha confirmed first the accuracy of text and melody, and then the accuracy of translation and simple meaning. Only after that foundation had been established did he turn to deeper interpretation, extending the plain meaning to a symbolic interpretation that encompassed the entire text. The kind of in-depth lesson Bill and Simcha shared results from the community's shared values and narratives, the student's Jewish knowledge and motivation, and time spent both in individual lessons and other synagogue and home participation.

A very different kind of lesson takes place at large Reform Beth Jeshurun. To keep track of the very large cohort of bar or bat mitzvah students, the religious school supplies them with brightly colored notebooks containing everything from bar or bat mitzvah program schedules to photocopies of the texts. Following a six-session program to ensure that their Hebrew reading (decoding) skills are adequate, students meet weekly with either the cantor or one of the cantorial soloists for twenty-minute sessions over a six-month period. During that time, they learn twelve to eighteen verses from the week's Torah portion and four to six verses from the Haftarah reading.[22] Tutors meet their students during religious school, using the synagogue library, where glass doors reduce privacy. Students are not expected to know much Hebrew, although many are familiar with some key root words and rudimentary Hebrew grammar. Tutors use a color coding system to teach students to chant. However, unlike Bill, students at Beth Jeshurun do not formally learn the trope markings. Judith's experience with Mira, one of the cantorial soloists, illustrates the process.

About three months before Judith's bat mitzvah, I observed Judith and Mira working on the Torah portion. Because Judith was one of the few students at Beth Jeshurun who attended Jewish day school, her knowledge of Hebrew was substantially better than that of her classmates, and she found the tutoring relatively easy. Though Judith had been absent the week before, Mira had e-mailed her audiofiles, which had enabled her to master the three verses she had been assigned. Using an enlarged photocopy of the text, highlighted with different colors to identify the different melodies, Judith chanted it confidently and correctly.

With little discussion, Mira began to color code and label the next set of verses, as Judith practiced fitting melody and words together. With only five minutes remaining, Mira checked Judith's prayers. Judith recited them accurately but very quietly, so Mira asked her to stand up, saying: "You need to be louder. The sound isn't good in the sanctuary, so you'll have to belt it out to be heard." Judith complied, standing and chanting the three prayers loudly. Mira had just enough time to write the next week's assignment in Judith's binder book before it was time for the next student.

The contrast between the two lessons is striking. Like Simcha, Mira also proceeds by step-by-step checking for accuracy. But where Simcha checked at several levels—reading and melody, translation, simple interpretation—Mira checked only for words and melody. With less time in each lesson and students who are, for the most part, less knowledgeable, tutors at Beth Jeshurun—by necessity—focus primarily on these basic elements. Because of her day school experience, Judith knew more Hebrew than the typical Beth Jeshurun student and could read the text with ease. Nevertheless, the lesson was not long enough for her to translate the texts, let alone interpret them. Beth Jeshurun does not teach the trope system for chanting from the Torah, so though Judith had begun to figure it out on her own, she was not able to combine melody and text without help. Furthermore, Simcha chose to work with only a few students and, as an independent tutor, controlled the communication with parents. In contrast, Mira was assigned students and time slots, with communication happening through notes kept in the bar or bat mitzvah notebook or with the congregation's administrative staff members acting as intermediaries. Though the comparison here happens to be between Orthodox and Reform, the differences are emphatically not denominational. Rather, the differences are related to time, number of students, and how much knowledge students bring to the lessons.[23] The shorter lessons, the greater number of students, and the need to teach basic material constrained how much time could be spent on either the relationship between Judith and Mira or that between Judith and the text.

The Big Day: Managing the Service

For Joel Green of independent Or Hadash, the service was a success and a worthy conclusion to a year of study. He told me: "It kind of just went by and boom! I was done. I didn't really realize it was my bar mitzvah. I just . . . sang with them [the congregation] like it was a regular service. . . . When I read Torah, I felt exhilarated and I felt some adrenalin, but nothing crazy. . . . Leading the discussion was my favorite part and was [sic] what I remember most." Throughout the service, however, both Rabbi Melmed and Joel's tutor acted unobtrusively to make sure the service proceeded smoothly. When Joel chanted from the Torah, the tutor quietly corrected his pronunciation a few times. As Joel led the prayers, Rabbi Melmed added his voice for clarity. While Joel conducted the discussion on his Torah portion, Rabbi Melmed occasionally repeated comments from attendees or clarified Joel's answers. For the leaders, the correct question is not "What might go wrong?" but "How can I rescue the ritual when the inevitable problems arise?"

Any religious service demands a competent leader to ensure the "aura of factuality" (Geertz 1973, 90) that rituals of all kinds create. This is particularly the case when the service includes a bar or bat mitzvah ritual, in which students are both the focus of the ritual and the expected leaders of the service.[24] Yet no matter how well prepared students are, by definition they are inexperienced: they are becoming adults and being introduced to new adult responsibilities. Therefore, part of the leaders' role is to anticipate and manage difficulties that may arise during these services. Some problems are clear well before the service, and rabbis or tutors may intervene before or during the service.[25] In Henry Eisenheim's case, verses were cut from his Haftarah reading; in Adam Miller's case, his tutor corrected a few words during the service.[26] However they choose to manage the service, the professional leaders are expected to ensure a competent enactment, and when all goes well, students feel successful, as Joel did.

Thus, as the bar or bat mitzvah date nears, focus necessarily shifts from the process of inculcating meaning and understanding to ensuring a successful performance. When used to refer to bar or bat mitzvah, the term "performance" has acquired a derogatory connotation, implying mere rote recitation. Yet in other contexts performance means quite the opposite. Storytelling, dance, plays, and music all are diminished when the performance is merely rote. The act of performance includes not only a deep understanding of the material but also the ability to use content (whether words, movement, or music) to create a shared meaning in which all participate.[27] The same is the case for bar or bat mitzvah: as with any performance, students rehearse their service shortly before the day itself. These rehearsals both ensure that the student knows the details of leading the service and is prepared for the upcoming role as service leader. Rehearsals also alert the tutors and rabbis to any remaining problem spots. Both aspects can be seen in Mindy Simon's bat mitzvah rehearsal.

Mindy, who was introduced in chapter 3, had been an ambivalent student who struggled with learning issues. She had worked with Shelley Weinstein, the tutor at Conservative B'nai Aaron, for over a year, and though she had become engaged in the process of learning, she still lacked confidence in her ability to successfully fulfill her bat mitzvah service responsibilities. The rehearsal was intended to give her that confidence and alert Shelley to any unexpected glitches.

Mindy began with the Torah service but lost her place after only a few verses. Before she had time to start crying, Shelley insisted that she try again: "Come on! Sing it out to the back wall!"

This time, Shelley sang too, softly, and Mindy was more successful. As they continued through the choreography of the service, Mindy's voice grew louder and more confident.

Before Mindy read from the Torah, she and Shelley practiced the associated choreography. Mindy's first attempt at reading was shaky, but she improved over time. As she read, Shelley noted the places where Mindy would probably need prompting. When they reached the Haftarah, Mindy was feeling quite comfortable. She chanted flawlessly and concluded with a huge grin.

This fairly typical rehearsal shows how much effort goes into protecting both ritual and participants. First, Shelley made the details of the service explicit, including not only the choreography but even when to drink some water and take a bathroom break. Second, the rehearsal enabled Mindy to experience the event ahead of time and imagine herself in the unfamiliar role of congregational leader. Third, the rehearsal revealed weak spots in Mindy's knowledge of the prayers and Torah reading. Shelley both encouraged her so that she gained confidence as the rehearsal proceeded and assisted her through the rough patches by prompting her or singing with her. In doing so, Shelley practiced for her own role in the service: ensuring that her student could enact the ritual successfully. All three of these aspects of the rehearsal helped ensure a smooth enactment.

During the service, Mindy appeared poised and confident, while Shelley prompted her where necessary.

Joel's and Mindy's experiences represent the usual case: students are well prepared, although not perfect, and enact the service with some degree of prompting. But sometimes there are unavoidable problems, with illness, injury, or weather being the most common.[28] These circumstances are usually managed in one way or another. The student who faints is revived; the student who has the flu takes aspirin, sips chicken soup, and pulls through before collapsing after the service; and the student with a broken arm asks a sibling to help carry the Torah around the sanctuary. While memorable, these incidents say nothing about the student's knowledge or ability to enact the ritual but simply pass into family and congregational lore.

However, problems that are (or are judged to be) within the participants' control—involving errors, inexperience, or ignorance—are another matter, as one student reflected: "I just couldn't do . . . the whole Hebrew thing, because I wasn't very fluent. I tried to read the English, but . . . I read really fast [and finished more quickly than expected] and I wasn't sure what to do. [My tutor] never told me how many seconds to count [before beginning the next prayer], and I didn't realize she wasn't up [on the bimah] with me until I turned around, and she's sitting on the bench! And someone else started it for me! It was really horrible."[29]

None of the adults saw this mistake as anything more than a minor glitch; in fact, both parents were quite proud of their daughter's accomplishment. Yet because she was both uncertain of the material and unprepared for the choreography, her mortification was obvious even several months after the event and illustrates why leaders place such importance on preparing for the performance aspect of the ritual.

The students' feelings are not all that is at risk: mistakes can jeopardize the integrity of the service, and the tension between preserving dignity and guarding the ritual runs throughout the service. Because of the role of Torah in Jewish life and its symbolic role for the bar or bat mitzvah, how rabbis correct the mistakes made during a student's chanting from the Torah provides a particularly good example of the ways this tension is negotiated. The Torah reader performs the important role of enabling attendees to hear the sacred text chanted accurately, and to ensure that happens, a reading assistant, called a *gabbai*, stands by to prompt or correct as needed. The decision about when to correct the reader has to do with precisely this balance between protecting the individual and the sacred nature of the reading.

During a lesson close to one student's bat mitzvah, her tutor explained his philosophy: "The text is most important. If you can't get all that right, get the consonants. The vowels can change a bit, depending on meaning, but the trope [melody] is to serve the words." This order places the meaning of the words first, while the melody is there only to guide the reader and amplify the meaning of the words. This tutor will correct words, but not melody. Another approach was taken by a Reform rabbi who rarely corrects students aloud, but quietly repeats the correct pronunciation: "So long as the word is pronounced correctly by someone, that's okay. But I don't like to rattle the kids and it's embarrassing for them." In this case, the rabbi prioritized the students' feelings over the text.[30]

A competent performance is necessary to protect both the student and the ritual. These goals are congruent with each other: a well-prepared student will perform capably, fulfilling the needs of the bar or bat mitzvah and the service. Preparation for this kind of performance has much in common with other performances, up to and including rehearsals before the service and prompting during it. When the necessary preparation does not take place, both student and service are put at risk. At the same time, unlike a musical or dramatic performance, the sacred quality of the service—particularly the Torah reading—introduces a tension between ensuring textual accuracy and protecting the feelings of the student.[31]

FROM LEARNING TO PERFORMANCE: SUMMING UP

The tension between learning for its own sake and performing has deep roots in Judaism. Traditional Jewish texts instruct Jews to do both: Pirkei Avot 6:1, recorded in the second century C.E., praises a person who studies Torah *lishma* (Torah for its own sake). Yet the person who leads services is the *shaliach tzibbur* (the community's messenger), so the acts of leading services and chanting from the Torah also carry a sacred quality, as the Shulchan Arukh, from the sixteenth century, notes. Ideally the process of learning leads to a competent performance, yet the skills necessary for performance and the emotions evoked by performance are not the same as those involved in learning.

There is an additional tension. On the one hand, the diffuse nature of Jewish life in the Bay Area—and throughout American Judaism—results in leaders trying, in very limited time, to teach children (and sometimes parents) the process of engaging in Judaism—of "doing Jewish." On the other hand, bar or bat mitzvah is a one-time event for the student. Though the act of leading services and chanting from the Torah has real and symbolic consequences for the regular leaders, those are heightened substantially for the subject of the rite of passage. From supplementary school to bar or bat mitzvah training and the service, leaders balance these tensions, striking a different balance at each stage. When children are young, the process of learning about Judaism is all that matters; by the week of the bar or bat mitzvah, the focus is entirely on the performance, with bar or bat mitzvah training providing the bridge from process to performance. It is through this relatively brief but intense period that students can move from uncertain or terrified to competent and comfortable, taking ownership of the moment and material. Progressing from one stage to another happens through the relationship among the students, their teachers, and the material.

6 · WHAT ARE *THEY* DOING ON THE BIMAH?

Setting Boundaries around Bar or Bat Mitzvah Participation

This chapter begins with the Torah being passed through the generations of Deborah Berkowitz's family until it is handed to her. Though a quick and seemingly simple moment, it illustrates the problems that arise as rabbis balance the desire to include participants with the need to protect the Jewish nature of the service.

As the Torah service began, Rabbi Doron calls Deborah's parents, Jacob and Christine, and Jacob's parents to join Deborah on the bimah. Jacob's father takes the Torah and hands it to his wife, who passes it to Jacob, who gives it to Christine to place in Deborah's arms. After Deborah has carried the Torah through the attendees, she readies herself to chant several sections from the weekly Torah portion.

As Deborah chants each section in Hebrew, family and friends participate by reciting the first three sets of blessings before and after reading Torah or read English translations. For the fourth reading, Rabbi Doron asks Jacob and Christine to come forward, saying: "We call Yaacov ben Herzl v'Leah, accompanied by Christine Berkowitz, for the fourth *aliyah*." Jacob recites the blessing, while Christine stands beside him. Deborah chants from Torah, then Christine reads the English translation, after which Jacob recites the next blessing. Jacob and Christine remain on the bimah as Deborah is called for her first *aliyah*. As she completes the final reading and blessing, her parents hug her with pride and delight.

This moment goes by so smoothly that it is difficult to notice how Rabbi Doron has resolved—for Sukkat Shalom at that time—three questions regarding who is permitted to participate in the service and in what capacity. First, and most taken for granted, Deborah's bat mitzvah looks precisely like the bar mitzvahs of her male classmates. In non-Orthodox American congregations, egalitarian practice is the norm. But even in these congregations, egalitarian practice dates back only several decades, and the debate over egalitarian practice is ongoing within the Orthodox community.

Second, Deborah is being raised as a Jew although her mother is not Jewish (her father is). The Reform movement considers her Jewish. Conservative and Orthodox movements adhere to an older definition: a Jew is the child of a Jewish mother, regardless of how the child is raised.[1] In that case, without a formal conversion, Deborah would not be considered Jewish and would not be allowed to have a bat mitzvah service.

Third, Christine is not Jewish, but she is part of a Jewish family, the mother of the bat mitzvah student, and a participant in the life of the congregation. In determining whether and how she could participate in the bat mitzvah service, Rabbi Doron balanced her status as a non-Jew with her role as a community member and the parent of a Jew. He explicitly acknowledges Christine's part in raising a Jewish child by having her pass the Torah to her daughter. However, the blessing on reading Torah includes a phrase that is specifically said by Jews and has no meaning for non-Jews, so Jacob recites this blessing alone (although Christine reads the translation). Rabbi Doron also is mindful of Christine's non-Jewish parents, who are not community members and have not actively raised a Jewish child, but who are Deborah's grandparents. There is no role for them in the Torah service, but later in the service, they read a section of English from the siddur.

Both the inclusion of a non-Jewish parent in the bar or bat mitzvah service and the participation of Orthodox girls in the Shabbat service raise the difficult issue of how to draw appropriate boundaries around the service. Including non-Jews, especially parents, in a Jewish ritual raises twin questions: To what degree can a non-Jew participate in a Jewish ritual before that ritual loses its meaning? And to what degree can or should supportive parents—though not Jewish—be excluded from their children's ritual? There is no question that Orthodox girls are Jewish, but the strict division of gender roles in Orthodox Judaism raises a similar question: To what degree can girls or women lead Orthodox services before they lose their meaning?

Rabbis, congregants, and families struggle with the same underlying tension: that of reconciling the desire for an inclusive service with the need to maintain coherent religious boundaries. In the end, rabbis, sometimes with input from congregational leaders, find ways to allow girls in Orthodox settings and non-Jews across the denominational spectrum some, but not full, participation in the bar or bat mitzvah service.

This chapter looks at how participants negotiate those decisions, asking the following questions: How do rabbis and lay leaders do the cultural work of reconstructing or defending the boundaries of Jewishness? Where in the service do the boundary issues arise, and what decisions are made about who is inside and who is outside them—about who may participate and how? How do leaders balance the strictures of Jewish law, the desires of the individual family, and the expectations of other congregants? What are the meanings and consequences of these decisions for leaders, families, and congregants?

This is not primarily a Jewish question or even a congregational question, but part of the broader sociological inquiry into how groups wrestle with the fundamental problem of setting and maintaining group boundaries. Because boundaries and roles are determined by rules tied to a group's history and symbolic group narratives and to its values and practices, when these boundaries are challenged—whether by changing norms (as happened to spur egalitarian practice) or by changing membership (as happened with intermarriage)—so too is the group's self-definition.[2]

Examples of these changes surround us, with different consequences for both groups and individuals. Rather than choosing one race or ethnicity, Americans filling out census forms can now check multiple boxes; rather than the mass being entirely in Latin, Vatican II encouraged Catholic priests to say mass in the vernacular; and rather than marriage being defined as a relationship between a man and woman, it has recently been redefined as one between two people, regardless of gender. These are all examples that challenge accepted norms and lead to redefining boundaries—as both non-Jewish and egalitarian participation in the bar or bat mitzvah service do. In so doing, they present existential challenges not only to a ritual's meaning, but also to the group and group values. Thus, getting these boundaries right matters to everyone concerned.

Considering how group boundaries change is a question of general sociological interest, but recent and ongoing changes in the American Jewish community make it very much a question of how American Judaism is changing. Both the norms of egalitarianism and rising rates of intermarriage between Jews and non-Jews raise questions of who is a Jew, how non-Jews can participate in congregational life and Jewish ritual practice, and in what capacity women (and girls) can lead the service. Throughout the 1970s and 1980s, pressure for gender equality in religious life led to changes throughout Judaism.[3] In non-Orthodox congregations, egalitarian practice is the norm: girls and boys are expected to fulfill the same responsibilities in the services, while rabbis and educators noted few, if any, differences between genders. This is not the case in the Orthodox congregations, where rabbis are negotiating in various ways how to accommodate women on the bimah—a subject that particularly affects bat mitzvah.[4] However, because there are few intermarried families in Orthodox congregations, rabbis face little pressure to change congregational rules. On the other hand, Reform and, to a lesser degree, Conservative congregations see increasing numbers of intermarried families joining, and both these denominations have had to find ways to manage the issues that result not only from how they define the role of the non-Jewish parent, but also how they answer the basic question of who is a Jew.[5]

These changes reconcile general cultural shifts with Jewish practice but also call into question group beliefs and narratives. If men have specific religious obligations imposed by Jewish law—that is, by God—then allowing women to participate equally can be seen as challenging the relationship between God and Jew. Similarly, if Jews have specific obligations imposed by Jewish law, allowing non-Jews to participate challenges that relationship. And if Judaism is passed from mother to child, then expanding that definition changes the definition of Jewishness from one that is above all ethnic or racial to one that relies more on practice and belief.

Denominations set broad policies regarding these issues, but the policies are enacted by people in congregations. The 1983 Reform ruling on intermarriage set a new policy but did not address how it would be enacted or what consequences the decision might have for congregations and congregants. Orthodox Judaism retains different roles for each gender but does not account for the broader cultural changes that result in egalitarian roles outside the congregation. These societal norms result in many congregants wanting similar (if not identical) participation by their daughters in a Shabbat service to acknowledge their daughters' new adult Jewish status. With intermarriage, rabbis are faced with interpreting general policy; with gender roles, rabbis must reconcile denominational strictures and family expectations.

However, these decisions do not rest with rabbis and families alone. Many congregants belong to a particular denomination to practice that mode of Judaism, so a decision that pushes the boundaries too far—for example, allowing a non-Jew to wear a tallit—is likely to result in outraged congregants. As rabbis set limits around who may participate in bar or bat mitzvah services and in what roles, they must juggle denominational regulations, the congregation's sensibilities, the family's expectations and/or needs, and their own philosophies. Thus, the ritual is shaped by the different expectations and needs of the participants in tension with the denominational policy as enacted in the congregation.

Although both issues are matters of determining boundaries, they differ in one important way. Non-Jewish parents who raise Jewish children do not claim to be part of the Jewish people. Though they are the cause of negotiations about group boundaries, they have a liminal status in the community and congregation. However, as noted above, Orthodox girls are certainly Jewish. In this case, it is a question of assigning roles within the group. To give each situation due consideration, I consider them separately.

INTERMARRIAGE IN CONTEMPORARY AMERICAN JUDAISM

As intermarriage between Jews and non-Jews increased during the twentieth century, the debate concerning its effect on American Judaism both intensified and changed. For much of the twentieth century, intermarriage represented Jewish assimilation and disappearance; however, until the 1960s, only a small percentage of Jews intermarried. Marshall Sklare (1964) first heralded the changes to come, predicting that the low 7.2 percent intermarriage rate would soar as third- and fourth-generation of Jews born in the United States married. During the 1960s, social scientists, rabbis, and Jewish educators all discussed the issue. However, it was not until the 1980s that the changes resulting from intermarriage began to be studied in detail—notably by Egon Mayer, whose sociological analyses moved the discussion of intermarriage's effect on Jewish continuity from a focus on heritage alone to the nature of practice. Mayer, Calvin Goldscheider, Bruce Phillips, and Steven Cohen bring both quantitative and qualitative tools to the debate about whether intermarriage represents the salvation or downfall of American Judaism.[6] As intermarriage has become increasingly normalized, others have examined the reality of what happens in intermarriages, looking at how the gender of the non-Jewish parent affects the Jewishness of the whole family, the ongoing tension between individualism and particularism, and how intermarried families negotiate Jewish identity and practice in their marriages and through interactions with institutions by adopting "universal individualist" and "ethnic familialist" (Thompson 2014, 17) approaches.[7]

In the 1970s, the share of Jews who married non-Jews began to grow from just a few percent to the current rate of around 50 percent (Association of Statisticians of American Religious Bodies 2010). The rabbinic arm of the Reform movement responded by declaring that "the child of one Jewish parent is under the presumption of Jewish descent" and by making a second and no less radical change: deciding that Jewishness could not be transmitted by heritage alone, but required "appropriate and timely public and formal acts of identification with the Jewish faith and people." These "public and formal acts" included several life-cycle rituals, bar or bat mitzvah among them (Central Conference of American Rabbis 1983). Since the adoption of the resolution, the North American Reform movement has actively encouraged intermarried families to join congregations, and these congregations have found ways to integrate non-Jews into congregational life. Enabling or limiting non-Jewish participation in religious rituals generally and in the bar or bat mitzvah service in particular is part of this larger issue for Reform congregations.

Both Orthodox and Conservative Judaism adhere to the matrilineal definition of a Jew. However, Conservative congregations have also encouraged intermarried families to join, although less actively than is the case at Reform congregations, as Rabbi Josephson of Conservative B'nai Aaron describes: "We are starting to tell people, 'Hey, this is a new Conservative movement. If you marry somebody who isn't Jewish and we couldn't officiate at your wedding, and if you want to raise Jewish children but the partner didn't convert, we are happy to try to help as much as we can.'" Rabbi Josephson's statement reflects the ambivalence that remains in the Conservative movement. On the one hand, some rabbis and others see intermarriage as less than ideal, and the Conservative movement's policy does not allow rabbis to officiate at the weddings (although this is being debated within the rabbinate). On the other hand, the rabbis recognize the current reality of intermarriage. Although Rabbi Josephson attempts to balance the boundaries of the community with an inclusive approach, his words reflect uncertainty about the place of these families in the Conservative congregation.

Orthodox Judaism strongly discourages intermarriage and, not surprisingly, few intermarried Jews affiliate themselves with Orthodox congregations. Even so, all Orthodox congregations that participated in my study included a few intermarried families, and these congregations, too, face the problems that result from setting boundaries around non-Jewish participation in the congregation.[8] Rabbi Teitelbaum explained that "a majority [of people attending] tend to be on a path where they are actively engaging their Judaism or else they wouldn't join an Orthodox synagogue. Others are here for a social family reason—'I grew up in the synagogue.' But far more likely: 'I am not Orthodox in practice or belief, but I'm enjoying the sense of learning and community.'"

While everyone, including Christians, are welcome to attend Adat Yitzhak, only those who are Jewish according to Jewish law (Halakhah) may join the congregation. "Sometimes we have someone Halakhically Jewish married to someone who isn't, so the Halakhically Jewish member joins, and the non-Halakhically Jewish member comes along," the rabbi told me. That is, at Adat Yitzhak, people with non-Jewish mothers or who have had non-Orthodox conversions to Judaism would not be considered full members.

Congregational demographics, not surprisingly, reflect these different approaches to non-Jews in the congregation. In the Bay Area, Reform congregations' intermarriage rates were 30–70 percent, Conservative congregations' rates were 5–15 percent, and there were only a handful of intermarried families in even the most liberal and welcoming Orthodox congregations.[9] Like other member families, intermarried families join congregations where they feel comfortable, so the different denominational approaches that result in these different demographics lead to very different congregational contexts. A congregation with only a few intermarried families faces a different set of problems from one in which 50 percent of the families are intermarried. In addition to denominational norms, these contexts affect the decisions rabbis make about when, how, and which non-Jews could participate in the bar or bat mitzvah service. These decisions affect three categories: the words non-Jews on the bimah may say, the objects they can use, and the actions they may perform.

SETTING LIMITS AROUND THE SHABBAT SERVICE: THE NON-JEW ON THE BIMAH

Decisions about the content of and participation in bar and bat mitzvah services ultimately rest with the rabbi, and these decisions begin with determining appropriate participation in the regular Shabbat services. These rules are often modified in the bar or bat mitzvah service to account for the special role of the non-Jewish parent. In either case, the rabbi—sometimes with the guidance of a lay religious practices committee—balances the need to protect the Jewishness of the rituals with the desire to include community members.

At one extreme, the rabbi of a very small Orthodox congregation set very strict limits on participation. This rabbi allows intermarried Jews to participate only minimally and the non-Jewish partner not at all, saying: "We want them to realize their situation is not perfect. If the spouse can convert . . . that's good. [And] we want to stay a role model. Orthodoxy as a whole has a very low intermarriage rate. . . . So while we encourage everyone to come, we discourage intermarriage." Intermarriage falls into a category that includes other offenses against Jewish law: "We wouldn't give an *aliyah* to someone . . . who wouldn't give [his wife] a *get* [divorce document] [or who performed] any serious public breaking of Jewish law. . . . [On the] East Coast where the standards are higher, if you transgress the Sabbath they wouldn't give you an *aliyah*." Jewish law is as immutable as gravity for this rabbi: "We [Orthodox Jews] really view Jewish law as a reality, and not just they're nice things or persuasive or easy." Thus, regardless of his relationships with either Jews or non-Jews, the rules remain fixed.

At the other extreme, the rabbi of a small independent congregation describes one of most lenient policies: "I'm really for Isaiah: 'my house shall be a house for all peoples.'" She illustrated this viewpoint with the story of a bar mitzvah family in which the supportive and active non-Jewish stepfather asked that his non-Jewish children (the bar mitzvah's stepsiblings) participate in the *aliyah* as part of the whole family. In the end, the stepfather's children did not participate because more strictly observant family members objected, but the rabbi would have allowed it: "I didn't mind if a non-Jewish person stood up there, so long as there was someone Jewish in that group who was going to say the blessing."

Whether firm or flexible, rabbis determined boundaries to participation in three categories: words, ritual objects, and performance. That is, they ruled on who says which words in what language, who uses which ritual objects, and who performs which actions at what time.

Rabbis limited language and words to Jews in two ways: imposing limits both on who led part of the service and/or recited Hebrew, whether leading prayers or reading sacred texts, and on who was allowed to recite prayers incumbent on Jews alone. While no rabbi explicitly stated that Hebrew was to be treated as a sacred language, in only one exceptional case, discussed below, did a non-Jew lead a Hebrew prayer. This distinction applied to leading prayers, rather than participating from the pews. A number of Reform rabbis noted with pride that some of their non-Jewish congregants chant the Hebrew prayers along with (and as fluently as) their Jewish families.

The differences between the traditional and contemporary service models affected participation as well. The fact that each prayer is treated independently in the contemporary model left room for English-language participation. Though only Jews led the central prayers, some congregations substituted interpretive reading or English translation for less central prayers. These interpretations were treated much less stringently. This option was not possible practically or theologically in the traditional model: the sections of the services are treated as units led in Hebrew by a single person without interruption.

As noted above, rabbis almost universally set a key boundary around blessings that included the phrase "asher kidshanu b'mitzvotav vitsivanu" (Who has sanctified us with His commandments and commanded us), with the rationale being simply that the words being spoken must have meaning for the person speaking them. Non-Jews, by definition, are not bound by obligations incumbent on Jews, and therefore speaking these words that imply obligation is a misrepresentation of the non-Jew's status.[10] This boundary was stretched in some congregations, with rabbis saying that as long as a Jew represented the congregation, non-Jews could be present. So, for example, a non-Jewish spouse could stand next to a Jewish spouse reciting an *aliyah*.

Rabbis also limited who was allowed to handle or wear specifically Jewish objects, in particular, who could wear a tallit or hold the Torah. The same rationale that applied to the blessings also relates to ritual objects: boundaries are drawn around objects that are sacred to Jews or that represent the special relationship between Jews and God, separating those objects from what all attendees can wear or touch. Thus siddurim and Hebrew Bibles are expected to be used by all attendees, and every congregation made them available. In contrast, all congregations reserved the tallit for Jews alone. Because the knotted fringes represent commandments, as with reciting the blessings above, wearing this symbolic garment has no meaning to a non-Jew.

Finally, rabbis set limits around ritual actions, and here, too, they shared a rationale. Many of the actions that rabbis limit take place during the Torah service: opening the Ark, carrying the Torah through the congregation in procession, unwrapping and wrapping the Torah before and after the Torah reading, and lifting the Torah after the Torah reading. Most liberal congregations allow non-Jews to open the Ark, and some allow non-Jews to wrap and unwrap the Torah. However, few (if any) allow non-Jews to carry the Torah through the congregation or to lift it following the Torah reading. The rationale appears to be same as in the previous examples: the closer the action puts the actor to the Torah and the more the actor represents the Jewish community, the more likely the action will be reserved for Jews. So long as that rationale is clear—as with the blessing specific to Jews—the boundary is also clear. However, some of these actions are less easily categorized: Does the person holding the Torah while the Haftarah is read represent the Jewish community or not? What about the person opening the Ark? As a result, there is more variation within and between denominations and congregations regarding these actions. (For example, one Conservative congregation allows non-Jews to hold the Torah while the Haftarah is read, while some Reform congregations do not.)

Rabbis across the denominational spectrum apply two principles in making these decisions, although their interpretation of these principles leads to very different conclusions. First, only Jews are allowed to say words, handle objects, or perform actions that are incumbent on Jews but not on non-Jews. Second, only Jews are allowed to act in a leadership capacity. Beyond those two principles, rabbis differed in the boundaries they set around other parts of the service, with some allowing non-Jews to participate in minor roles. However, even these general principles can be bent when the non-Jew is a participating member of the congregation and the parent of a bar or bat mitzvah.

INCLUSION AND PARTICIPATION: THE NON-JEW IN THE CONGREGATION

Whatever Jewish knowledge non-Jewish spouses bring to their marriages—be it formal learning or cultural narratives picked up from the media and Jewish friends—they enter the marriages without being a Jew, effectively lacking a tribal membership card. Like Jews, non-Jewish partners bring personal history and experience of their childhood religions (if any), as well as attitudes toward religion itself. In the Reform and independent congregations I observed, around half of the bar or bat mitzvah services I attended were for children of intermarried families, as was one of the Conservative bat mitzvahs.[11] Eight of the families I interviewed were intermarried, and I was able to interview seven non-Jewish parents (five mothers and two fathers) representing a remarkable diversity of race, nationality, culture, and religion: African American, Japanese Shinto, Iraqi, Catholic, and Protestant. In each case, the families had committed to raising Jewish children but still incorporated some aspects of the non-Jewish parents' background.

For example, Mitsuke and Michael Hershel are members of Conservative B'nai Aaron. Mitsuke is Japanese and was raised with some Shinto training. Like Aziza Orlansky, she saw little meaning in organized religious practice,[12] but she supported Michael in raising their daughter, Emily, as Jewish.[13] Like other non-Jewish parents I interviewed, Mitsuke took the responsibility of raising a Jewish daughter seriously. At the same time, the family incorporates Japanese art and culture into their home life, and Emily attended Japanese school as well as Jewish religious school. The family does not perceive this as a conflict: though Emily embraces her Japanese heritage, she feels fully Jewish as well. As Emily studied for her bat mitzvah, Mitsuke was responsible for managing the children's Jewish education, Emily's preparation for bat mitzvah, and much of the planning for the party. As was the case with a number of non-Jewish parents, her knowledge of Judaism grew as Emily learned.[14]

Before turning to how these parents participate in the service, it is important to understand their role in the congregation. For that context, I return to Reform Sukkat Shalom and the Berkowitz family as exemplars. Deborah's b'nai mitzvah cohort of twenty-four included the children of eleven intermarried families, of whom the Berkowitzes are relatively typical. Jacob is Jewish; Christine is not. When they married, they agreed—at Jacob's request—that their children would be raised as Jews. Throughout their marriage, they have observed major Jewish holidays, and Jacob has passed on to their children his Jewish family history and stories from his youth. Jacob, Christine, and their three children settled in the Bay Area just a few years ago and only then found a congregation that suited Jacob's Jewish sensibilities as well as made Christine comfortable as a non-Jew. In Christine's words, "we really did more research when we moved here and visited more Reform synagogues, and it was just kind of a feel[ing] of welcoming. . . . And from my point of view, being a non-Jewish member, feeling like I was still part of the community and a member."

Christine's path to engagement in congregational life is also typical. At first she lacked confidence: "I didn't really know this terminology, I needed to become more familiar with certain routines and traditions. . . . I felt the need to observe because I wasn't familiar with some of the customs and was cautious about . . . saying something that would make me really stand out . . . but I found people to be very open." Over time, she became more involved, particularly volunteering for holiday celebrations and as a classroom parent. Her older son's bar mitzvah and Deborah's bat mitzvah affected her sense of being a mother raising Jewish children: "It was a very moving, beautiful experience . . . an acknowledgment that they wanted to be part of the Jewish community. . . . There was an obvious, a real spiritual change for them, which was wonderful."

Whatever their denomination, almost all congregations allowed, accepted, or welcomed the participation of non-Jews in social and educational programs. At

Sukkat Shalom, non-Jews took part in services and holiday celebrations, classes, and social action activities. Jacob describes his family's participation this way: "Attending services is one thing that we do and feel very comfortable with. I think the kids feel very comfortable, as does Christine." He noted that in addition to volunteering in religious school, Christine had participated in an Introduction to Hebrew class, which increased her comfort level with services.

As their children prepared for bar or bat mitzvah, these non-Jewish parents understood their role to be one of providing support for their Jewish child—that is, of being a supportive outsider, rather than an entitled insider. Christine said: "I don't read Hebrew, and I don't really understand what the prayers are about. I'm kind of learning as she's learning, so my biggest concern was: 'How can I truly support her and guide her through this process when this is all new to me too?'"

Similarly, the Aldrichs belong to large Reform Beth Jeshurun. John, the non-Jewish father of Rebekah, was concerned that he would not know "what was going to be required of [him] as a parent during the whole process." To educate himself, John attended several bar or bat mitzvah services, which gave him both confidence and perspective: "I saw kids who really knew their stuff and . . . kids who went through the motions . . . and you could see the difference. And Rebekah . . . totally did a great job and knew her stuff, and her having one parent who's not Jewish—I thought [it] was kind of going to rub off on the whole process and it didn't."

Neither John nor Christine felt entitled to participate in services, but both felt obligated to support their Jewish families and took pride in their children's accomplishment. Neither expressed the expectation that they would or should take part in the service itself—although both did. According to rabbis, Jewish parents are more likely to press for the full inclusion of all family members, whether Jewish or not.

Rabbi Josephson, of Conservative B'nai Aaron, explains how he talks to intermarried families in which the Jewish partner requests that the non-Jewish spouse be allowed an *aliyah*, something no congregation allows: "If they [the non-Jewish partners] are going to stand there and say the *aliyah*, they didn't make that choice [to be Jewish], so it doesn't make any ritual sense. That's something almost all non-Jews get, but most of the Jews in the intermarried situation become upset about."

Being part of a community is the single most important reason families gave for remaining members of their congregations. This communal feeling often develops as parents, whether Jewish or not, participate in congregational life, most commonly (as was the case with Christine) through helping in the religious school but also through attending religious and social events. This is true even at Orthodox Adat Yitzhak. Daphne Schechter, the non-Jewish partner in an intermarriage, studies with Rabbi Teitelbaum, volunteers in the gift shop, and takes classes. In addition, she enjoys "the social activities, because they help me to deepen my relationships with people, and that's really important to me." When Daphne, Christine, or John attend services, bake challah, or attend a congregational dinner, they are not overtly singled out as non-Jews.[15] However, the situation changes during religious rituals in general and during the bar or bat mitzvah service in particular. While rabbis establish rules that apply to all services, because bar or bat mitzvah is a life-cycle event that has an explicit role for parents, it presents distinct challenges, and rabbis must find appropriate roles for people who, though non-Jewish, are both parents of a bar or bat mitzvah and community members.

NON-JEWISH FAMILY, FRIENDS, AND PARENTS IN THE BAR OR BAT MITZVAH SERVICE

The rabbi of a large Reform congregation told me:

> Generally we have Jews role model rituals that only Jews are commanded to do. A non-Jewish father might hold the kiddush cup, but the child, both because of Hebrew background and because the child is Jewish, would lead the prayer. A non-Jewish mother would lead the introductory reading, but the daughter or son would light the candle. During a Torah service, Jews would dress and carry the Torah; non-Jews would be able to open and close the Ark. There's an English reading that's clearly an alternative to the Torah blessing for the non-Jewish parent in the new Reform siddur . . . and that is something that might be nice to introduce in the future.

The bar or bat mitzvah service, particularly as enacted in Reform and other liberal congregations, can include moments for family participation. Some are part of the usual service, most notably being called to the Torah, so Shabbat service rules apply. Others are extraliturgical and thus offer relatively neutral ways to include non-Jews. Rabbis effectively divide non-Jewish participants into two categories: the bar or bat mitzvah child's parent and other family members or friends. Incorporating the non-Jewish parent into the service requires the most negotiation, but families may also want to honor non-Jewish relatives or close friends in the service (as they do Jewish relatives and friends). While the places in services to honor Jews are well established, this is not the case for non-Jews, but rabbis may find creative ways to include them. For example, in the vignette from Deborah's bat mitzvah above, Jacob's (Jewish) parents passed the Torah to Jacob and Christine, both of whom had contributed to Deborah's Jewish upbringing. Christine's parents were not part of that chain and did not participate at that moment. Later in the service, Christine's father read an English poem on gratitude, a neutral addition that allowed him to participate.

Conservative B'nai Aaron draws the boundaries more strictly. Here Rabbi Rosen, the senior rabbi, explains how he manages non-Jewish relatives: "Lately we've been getting people with non-Jewish relatives, asking: 'What can they do, Rabbi?' What has satisfied people so far is to let them help out at the door. They can give out the programs, they can greet people. So far everybody has said, 'Oh that's a good solution, Rabbi, thank you.' I really feel that there is an important boundary there." Allowing non-Jews to greet guests and act as ushers provides a role for family members without encroaching on the boundary of the service. Rabbi Rosen sets stricter boundaries than is the case at many Conservative congregations, where rabbis find some roles for non-Jews within the bar or bat mitzvah service itself. In one unusual example, a Conservative rabbi allowed non-Jews to read the set of prayers for country, peace, and Israel. She gave the following example: "We had a congregant who had a friend who was a Bedouin from Israel, so let me tell you, her Hebrew was fluent! I found it amazing—here was someone who had fought in the Israeli Army and . . . wow!" This is interesting, not only because it is a rare example of a non-Jew reading in Hebrew, but also because it points out the place of Hebrew as both a sacred language for Jewish prayer and study and the language of Israel as a nation-state, in which Hebrew is a secular language for all citizens, Jewish or not.

Wherever rabbis set boundaries for non-Jewish guests and extended kin, those participants played relatively minor roles. Setting these boundaries for non-Jewish parents is more difficult. In Reform and Conservative congregations, there are several moments highlighted in most bar or bat mitzvah services: presenting a tallit to the student, giving a speech or blessing, passing the Torah (which is almost universal in Reform congregations but less so in Conservative ones), and being called to Torah for an *aliyah*. Because the first two moments involve primarily parental, rather than Jewish, roles, both Reform and Conservative congregations allow non-Jewish parents to participate in them. The latter two moments link parental roles with Judaism, as both symbolize passing Judaism from one Jewish generation to the next. In deciding how or if non-Jewish parents can participate, rabbis balance the role of the non-Jewish parent who is raising a Jewish child with the Jewish character of the moment.

At Sukkat Shalom, Rabbi Doron is quite clear about why he includes non-Jewish parents in passing the Torah: "Usually when we pass the Torah down the generations, I give the Torah to the mother or father, and I involve the non-Jewish parent. I say that they're as much a part of that chain of generations as the Jewish parent." When Christine held the Torah, her role within this specific Jewish community was made real. This is one solution for Reform and other liberal congregations.

In contrast, one Conservative rabbi simply tries to avoid the issue: "[Passing the Torah is] an option, but it's incredibly awkward if there's a non-Jewish parent. They're not up there [on the bimah] for that. Most of the non-Jewish parents choose not to do it. . . . [There's] awkwardness with the non-Jew—it kind of puts it in their face, so I discourage it." For this rabbi, though the non-Jewish parent may be supportive, Judaism passes through the Jewish parent. Furthermore, as another rabbi pointed out, one parent may be supportive, while another is not. How could he judge who was worthy to hold the Torah? For these rabbis, eliminating the Torah passing resolves the dilemma.

The Torah service raises other concerns. Under the norms followed in most congregations, non-Jews are not present on the bimah when the Torah blessings are chanted. The bar or bat mitzvah service complicates this. Parents often receive the penultimate *aliyah*, with the bar or bat mitzvah child receiving the final one, so they are present as the child recites those blessings upon chanting from Torah. When both parents are Jewish, their parental and Jewish roles coincide. This is not the case in an intermarriage, and so rabbis work to honor the parental role while still respecting the Jewish nature of the moment.

Some Conservative and most (if not all) Reform congregations call multiple people for each *aliyah*, distinguishing Jews from non-Jews by careful wording. This is the case at Sukkat Shalom, where Rabbi Doron called Jacob forward using his Hebrew name and added "accompanied by Christine Berkowitz." This distinction is subtle, but the attentive listener would have noted that Christine has no Hebrew name and did not say the blessing (although she did read the English translation). Such a listener would probably conclude, therefore, that although Christine was included, she is not Jewish. Both actions—finding ways to include the non-Jew but also to signal that the inclusion is partial—matter and are noted by the community in ways that can confuse or clarify relationships.[16]

Other liberal rabbis take similar approaches to participation. For example, one Reform rabbi told me: "We have an English blessing we have [the non-Jewish parents] do. Sometimes they do the *aliyah* anyway. It happens—we explain it and all that, but it just happens." While congregational rules are designed to circumvent non-Jewish participation in this blessing, the rabbi will not embarrass the parent who is caught up in the moment. This is only one response—other rabbis (most often Conservative) allow only the Jewish parent on the bimah.

As rabbis find ways to incorporate non-Jews who have helped raise Jewish children into a quintessentially Jewish service, they—and the families—are breaking new ground. All rabbis in my study attempted to find an acceptable and respectful place for a non-Jew that did not violate their understanding of Jewish boundaries. All rabbis in the Bay Area, regardless of denomination, face the difficulties of resolving the place of the non-Jew in the bar or bat mitzvah. In the Orthodox community, resolving the place of girls in bat mitzvah services presents a similar type of negotiation between participation and protecting ritual boundaries.

A ROLE FOR WOMEN: DEVELOPING THE ORTHODOX BAT MITZVAH

Like including the non-Jew on the bimah, the Orthodox bat mitzvah is a response to the question of who has the right to enact Jewish practice authentically. In the case of the non-Jew on the bimah, membership in the Jewish people conferred the right to act in particular ways, with the non-Jewish parent acting as a supportive outsider. In the case of the Orthodox bat mitzvah, the boundary is not drawn between Jew and non-Jew but between two groups of Jews who have been assigned different roles in enacting Judaism.

Judaism's strict and separate gender roles are hardly unique in religious practice: it is much rarer to find a religion that is completely gender-neutral. However, as with all religions in the late twentieth century, the different branches of Judaism have struggled to assimilate the changes in thinking and practice related to women's roles in society. During the 1970s and 1980s, all Jewish denominations except Orthodox adopted formal policies of egalitarian practice, with Reform Judaism including women in prayer as equals with men and ordaining the first female rabbi in the United States in 1972, while Conservative Judaism included women as equals and ordained its first female rabbi in 1985. Enacting these general policies resulted in challenges at the congregational level about matters as diverse as language, dress, and authority. However, though complicated, these questions rarely result in discussions of rules about bar or bat mitzvah participation.[17]

In these non-Orthodox congregations, men and women sit together, rather than on separate sides of the sanctuary. Both men and women may lead services and read Torah. This formal indifference to gender extends to bar and bat mitzvah students as well. Few rabbis acknowledge differences between boys and girls, except to note that girls tend to be more mature in their approach to learning. A Conservative rabbi made a typical comment to me: "Boys are just as serious about the learning, but in a group setting, they goof off a lot more. So they probably feel the same way about the learning, but the manifestation of their interest is radically different. I don't see any differences when I see them one-on-one."

In these congregations, boys and girls are expected to learn similar amounts of material and to enact the service in similar ways. The differences that exist are not specific to Judaism but rather reflect larger cultural trends and expectations, such as modes of dress. However, rabbis, parents, and students all expect both boys and girls alike to undergo the same preparation and enact the service in the same way.

Not so in Orthodox Judaism. Because Orthodox Judaism places obligation to Jewish law—or God—higher than personal choice, rabbis cannot simply replace gender distinctions with egalitarian practice: these boundaries are central to their view of the religion itself. Yet, particularly in modern Orthodox settings in which congregants live secular lives, egalitarian expectations have found their way into Jewish practice. In particular, reading Torah has come to have particular importance and resonance, and families expect their children, whether male or female, to have some opportunity to perform that act. As with the non-Jew in Shabbat services, rabbis—pushed by parents' desires—make decisions about how and when women can participate in Shabbat services.

When men are present, they are obligated to lead the service, an obligation that applies to prayer and text reading but not necessarily to interpretation. Thus, in many Orthodox congregations, a woman may give a *d'var* Torah or other speech to a mixed group, even though she may not lead services or read Torah in that same mixed group.

Orthodox congregations have developed several solutions that enable women to lead services and read Torah. Some Orthodox congregations develop women's minyans, which are composed entirely of women. In these congregations, a women-only bat mitzvah may take place on Saturday morning, parallel to the men's service. This enables the girl to lead as much or as little of a full morning service as she wishes but also results in two different experiences: one for males and another for females. A different approach is that taken at Adat Yitzhak, in which girls lead an early afternoon service. In this case, services for boys and for girls are quite different. Before turning to a description of the services, I should describe the congregation's Shabbat morning practice.

ADAT YITZHAK: BALANCING WOMEN'S ROLES AND JEWISH LAW

The morning Shabbat service at Adat Yitzhak begins early. Only a few men are present, seated on their side of the *mehitzah*, a chest-high glass divider running the length of the sanctuary. It formally divides men from women, but in fact, each group can easily see and talk to the other. This style of divider is typical of Modern Orthodox congregations in the Bay Area.[18] While only men led the services, both men and women followed along in both siddurim and Hebrew Bibles. And both men and women entered and exited the room and engaged in (usually brief) side conversations. So while women do not lead these services, they are nevertheless engaged in the service content.[19]

Rabbi Teitelbaum strives to maintain a sense of wholeness for the Shabbat service, whether there is a bar mitzvah, a bat mitzvah, or any other life-cycle event taking place. Therefore, little changes during a bar mitzvah service.

According to him, "the way we do our services has a very specific structure and format that goes back a few thousand years, so if [a bar mitzvah family wants] to incorporate a poem or something like that, we can do that easily around the time of the presentation or at kiddush, at lunch, but not during the service itself. . . . The service is what the service is, and we're going to stay with that."

Lay leaders, male relatives and friends, and the boy himself all participate through the end of the service, the only difference from the usual Shabbat service being that many participants have a connection to the family. At the end of the service, the boy typically delivers a speech of some length. This is followed by an extended lunch, after which the congregation gathers for the afternoon service.

The bat mitzvah is quite different, as Sarah Levy's day illustrates. On a Saturday morning in March, twelve-year-old Sarah is ready for her bat mitzvah service, which begins with a traditional Shabbat morning service led by male members of the congregation, including Sarah's father and older brother. As the service concludes, Rabbi Teitelbaum calls Sarah forward to deliver a *shi'ur* (a lesson lasting about thirty minutes on a specific topic of Jewish interest), during which she describes the laws for building a sukkah (a temporary hut built for the holiday of Sukkot). When she finishes, Rabbi Teitelbaum says a few words of praise, and the congregation adjourns for a kiddush lunch, during which Sarah's parents deliver a few words of praise and blessing.

After that, the *minhah* (afternoon) service takes place. It includes a brief Torah reading that previews the following week's Torah portion—in this case, the first thirteen verses of the book of Leviticus. This is a service for women only (with the exception of Sarah's father and grandfather, who stand discreetly in the rear), so the rabbi gathers all the men into a small side chapel to allow women access to the main sanctuary.

Sarah's classmates and other women spread out on both sides of the *mehitzah*, while Sarah takes her place next to Dinah—the rabbi's wife and Sarah's tutor— and begins the service. She leads the prayers with excited competence, omitting those for which a minyan (ten adult men) is required. When it is time to read the thirteen verses of Torah from the upcoming week's portion, she and Dinah simply uncover the Torah, without the usual procession around the room.

The thirteen verses Dinah is chanting are divided into three sections. Dinah calls forward first a friend of Sarah, then Sarah's mother, and then Sarah herself before each of the three readings. Each recites a blessing that does not include any reference to a obligation: Sarah's actions are considered voluntary, not obligatory.

Following the readings, Sarah and Dinah return the Torah to the Ark, and Sarah leads the last few prayers, with loud and enthusiastic participation by her friends. At the conclusion of both services, men and women come together in the sanctuary. After the afternoon service, Sarah's father hugs her, and her accomplishment is described to the rabbi and the other men.

Rabbi Teitelbaum's rationale for this model balances the authority of Jewish law, his concern for the community, and the expectations of families, as he explains: "Because women in our community don't read Torah for men, [a morning bat mitzvah service] would mean splitting our community into a women's service and men's service right at the moment when we are all together. The majority of girls have done a *minhah* service."

While Sarah was delighted with her bat mitzvah service, this model does not satisfy all families with girls, particularly those who are not Orthodox in their own practice. Some of these families want their daughters to read Torah in an egalitarian manner. Rabbi Teitelbaum cannot allow this in the synagogue.

Because of the mixed nature of the congregation, part of Rabbi Teitelbaum's role was to balance the different expectations of the groups in the congregation with his own understanding of God's rules and the needs of each individual. He did so by setting firm boundaries for Jewish practice in the synagogue while accepting with (apparent) equanimity differences in individual family practice. So while he will not allow an egalitarian bat mitzvah in the synagogue, he will prepare girls for the ritual and enable the family to hold the service outside the synagogue.

This is another way to set boundaries, defining them by space, not role. In doing this, the rabbi is able to maintain a place where the authority of Jewish law holds, while still supporting his individual congregants' choices. There is still one drawback: Shabbat morning services are, as Rabbi Teitelbaum pointed out, the time the congregation comes together. An off-site bat mitzvah that draws people from the community results in splitting the congregation for that day. Nevertheless, from both the rabbi's and the family's perspective, an off-site venue enabled the family to meet its members' individual needs without compromising the rabbi's beliefs or the congregation's expectations.

Rabbi Teitelbaum also worked to broaden the definition of bar or bat mitzvah beyond the service itself. This is not uncommon: as discussed above, most rabbis focus on bar and bat mitzvah as representative of more extensive Jewish learning and practice. However, in this case, a more extensive approach also enabled Rabbi Teitelbaum to provide other, more Halakhically acceptable ways for families to think about bat mitzvah, as noted in chapter 2.

The most common model for boys, he notes, is a familiar one: "Boys do some bit of Torah reading, [and] opt to read some Haftarah—[it] depends on the education of the child. Many choose to lead services. Boys are more oriented that way."[20]

Most of the girls follow the *minhah* service described above. In addition, many of the girls and some of the boys take on mitzvah projects, which vary from learning about and practicing blessings before eating or learning about elements of Shabbat practice to visiting the elderly and sick children or collecting money, food, or other requested items for the poor. Again, these projects are a common part of bar or bat mitzvah preparation, but they can take on greater significance for the girls than for the boys. Natalya Ruben's mother, Marcia, explains her goals for her daughter: "I really wanted her to understand the importance of doing *chassidish* [charitable] activities, even though they weren't fun. Different people express different aspects of their Judaism differently, but this is what I wanted, as her mother, to give to her."

Natalya enjoyed spending time with her mother, but she especially enjoyed working with the rabbi's wife to learn prayers and texts: "I liked that I got total option over [*sic*] what I wanted to learn. I could learn the *parsha* [weekly portion], I could learn Mishnah [early commentary]. . . . I wanted to learn something related to my bat mitzvah and my birthday, and we researched Sukkot. . . . I could do anything I wanted, and that seemed really cool. I chose to do a book, and I'm glad I did."

The process meant a lot to her: "I never really had to do a project that really affected me before. Every project I've done was for school, and it's never been something where you get judged on it. It was also on my own time, it wasn't homework. My *drash*—if I didn't do a good job on it, I would be presenting it to my whole community. I wanted to do well on it. I also liked making my book. I was proud of it."

Natalya did not feel her bat mitzvah service had gone particularly well: "I got through it, but I was thinking, 'yeah, this isn't really working.'" However, neither she nor Marcia focused on the day itself. Rather, Marcia was happy that they had spent time working together on community projects, while Natalya was most pleased with research that resulted in her own book. The fact that the service was not at the center of the event gave this family more freedom to explore other aspects of Judaism. In theory, this is also true for boys, but here the difference between being obligated and having a choice matters: the boys expressed more concern over their performance than did the girls.

While the *minhah* service is an option that some girls are happy with, that was not the case with Sasha Kasinsky: "I don't like that I'm not allowed to read from the Torah. I was a girl, so my guy family besides my immediate family like my dad and my brother, they could not hear me. They come from New York and they could not hear me, they could only hear my speech. But I practiced all my other stuff and they could not hear it. I was a girl, and that was why, and I think that's wrong because I'm a feminist."

Sasha and Natalya had a similar preparation and similar services but very different responses. In both families, leading a bat mitzvah service was an assumed part of Jewish life. In Marcia's words: "It was a nonissue. That's what you do. It's a community norm. And she wanted it." In determining the boundaries for women's participation in the service, Rabbi Teitelbaum takes these differences into account with varying degrees of success. In doing so, he is guided first by Jewish law (as interpreted by Orthodoxy) and then by his concern for the congregants. The boundaries he sets are thus both rigid and nonjudgmental: neither his nor his congregants' personal feelings are the point; the rules are determined by God, and his job is to interpret and follow them. As a result, while unwavering in his approach to Judaism, he is unfailingly sympathetic to his congregants and passionate about teaching all students, whatever their personal practice. And by attempting with limited success to shift the meaning of bar or bat mitzvah from the service to the age itself, he minimizes the importance of the service.

Nevertheless, as the cases of Natalya and Sasha show, girls and their families have different responses to rabbis' decisions, with the response depending on each family's approach to Judaism, feminism, and Orthodox practice more generally. Whatever their response, these girls approach the bat mitzvah as an insider, with the right to accept or critique particular Jewish practice.

COMPARISONS AND CONCLUSIONS

The cases of non-Jews and of Orthodox girls on the bimah both require rabbis to balance including a previously excluded group with defining and protecting essential group boundaries. Both cases illustrate how denominational policy is interpreted, modified, and changed at the congregational level as leaders and the laity negotiate their different positions. Like the bar or bat mitzvah itself, these changes begin with the people but require the attention of the leaders. No matter what the denomination, the rabbi interprets what is and is not allowed, as the contrast between Rabbi Teitelbaum's approach and that of his more judgmental colleague demonstrates. This negotiation between laity and leadership results in changes to the bar or bat mitzvah ritual as rabbis work to accommodate the needs of non-Jewish parents or of Orthodox girls. These changes, in turn, affect the congregation's composition as stricter or more open attitudes attract different types of members.[21]

However, the most interesting results from this comparison are the shared elements of symbolic group definition that emerge. In both cases, rabbis follow two key principles: only those obligated (whether that be all adult Jews or all adult Jewish men) may say prayers that include words of Jewish obligation or take the role of leading the Jewish community in prayer or text. Whether rabbis believe (as do Reform Jews) that enacting these commandments is a matter of individual choice or whether they believe (as do Orthodox Jews) that it is incumbent on Jews to follow these God-given commandments, they expressed the belief that these acts are particular to the Jewish people. Similarly, leading services and reading texts are understood to be incumbent on members of the Jewish community—a non-Jewish leader of a Jewish service makes little sense.

The decisions that rabbis make follow from their interpretations of these two principles. In liberal communities, the definition of a Jew includes children of one Jewish parent of either gender; in Conservative and Orthodox Judaism, only children of Jewish mothers or converts are Jews.[22] However, in both cases, the bar or bat mitzvah student is considered a legitimate member of the community and able to lead a service. Similarly, while congregations differ in the roles they assign to non-Jewish parents (and non-Jewish relatives more generally), all rabbis attempt to acknowledge the role of these parents, within the limits of the symbolic boundaries.

In the same way, Orthodox rabbis work to acknowledge women in both Jewish life and in religious services within the limits of their interpretation of Jewish law. This has led to separate services for men and women and different words to state women's voluntary acceptance of a commandment. Here, as with non-Jews, the boundaries are around who is or is not obligated to perform particular commandments and who may or may not lead a Jewish congregation in prayer. But this also points out the differences: these girls are Jews, and some of them, like Sasha, not only understand their place in Judaism to be identical to that of men but also feel that they have the right—by virtue of being Jewish—to insist on that place.

The various ways rabbis determine who participates in the bar or bat mitzvah service exemplify both how the leadership and the laity negotiate changes to the boundaries of Jewish rituals and what boundaries to that participation emerge. First, denominational policy—in concert with broader cultural norms—shapes the institution and institutional practice that are the context in which these decisions are made. Without the increased rate of intermarriage and without the Reform ruling on patrilineal descent, this issue would not exist or would have a very different shape. Shifting gender roles in Judaism were influenced by and developed together with shifting gender roles in the dominant society.

Second, these larger cultural shifts affect people who want to maintain Judaism and also be included in ways that, for traditional Judaism, seem transgressive. These contradictions are mediated in synagogues by leaders who are not only representatives of Jewish tradition (however interpreted) but who also have relationships with their congregants. Thus, as intermarriage becomes normalized in liberal American congregations, new categories are being created that acknowledge the non-Jewish member of the Jewish community. Public worship is the place where inclusion is most difficult, and it is here that limits are most difficult to navigate.

Third, a rough consensus has evolved—at least for the moment—across denominations that draws boundaries between Jew and non-Jew with regard to leading prayers and reading sacred texts in Hebrew and reciting prayers that allude to obligation or chosenness. This consensus speaks to a fundamental center of Jewish identity marked by language and obligation to a people.

7 · WHOSE BIMAH IS IT, ANYWAY?

Public Shabbat Service or Private Bar or Bat Mitzvah Ritual

In his address to the 2007 Union for Congregations Biennial Convention, Rabbi Eric Yoffie, then president of the Union Reform Congregations, called on Reform movement professional and lay leaders to revitalize Shabbat morning services. As part of that charge, he said:

> Bar mitzvah is the occasion, symbolically at least, when a young person joins an adult community of Jews. But you cannot join what does not exist. A regular community of worshippers, who would be best suited to mentor the child, is not even present. At the average bar mitzvah what you almost always get is a one-time assemblage of well-wishers with nothing in common but an invitation.
>
> And worst of all: Absent a knowledgeable congregation, worship of God gives way to worship of the child—and self-serving worship is a contradiction in terms.

Rabbi Yoffie describes one kind of bar or bat mitzvah service—a series of private events that occur weekly in large Reform congregations—from the standpoint of the leadership. In these large congregations with weekly bar or bat mitzvah services, such as Beth Jeshurun, rabbis see a different set of friends and family at each event, with little congregational participation.

For example, at one large Reform congregation, the weekly bar or bat mitzvah service often includes two students, each with 150 to 200 guests, making for an ever-changing population with only the leaders—and occasionally a few congregants—constant from week to week. The sense of a private event came through to visitors as well, as the cantor of that congregation described to me: "My saddest moment was my first year here, when I had this couple whose wedding I was doing and they just wanted to hear me lead services. At the time there was an usher's bench by the door, and they just sat there, watched the service, and left right afterward. I said to them later, 'It was so nice to see you, but I wish you'd come in a little more.' They said, 'Oh, we just felt so bad, because we weren't invited.'"

Though a bar or bat mitzvah service can produce a "one-time assemblage" for rabbis and other attendees, this is not the case for the children's families. To them, the attendees represent an individual family's web of relationships, of which the congregational community is one piece.[1] Yet Rabbi Yoffie's point is valid: when the Jewish community, as represented by the congregation, is not present to acknowledge entry into adult Judaism, does that not diminish the Jewish character of the ritual?

Rabbi Yoffie's remarks assume the contemporary model for Shabbat observance, in which the primary Shabbat service takes place on Friday night, with Saturday morning services lightly attended or nonexistent. The missing Shabbat service results in a space in which the bar or bat mitzvah service becomes, de facto, a private event. To create a "regular community of worshippers" that would welcome the bar or bat mitzvah student, these long-standing patterns of Reform worship would first have to change.[2]

But the regular Shabbat morning service does not need to be reinvented: it already exists in Conservative and Orthodox congregations that follow the traditional model. In these congregations, congregants expect to have consistent Shabbat morning services led by knowledgeable lay leaders or clergy. Bar or bat mitzvah services complicate that expectation: they bring additional people to the congregation, introduce young leaders with unpredictable levels of confidence and skill, and change the usual dynamic of the service. When bar or bat mitzvah services occur infrequently, they provide moments of interest and excitement. When they take place frequently, they can feel like intrusions into community worship. While Reform and similar congregations face the problem of building community, Conservative and Orthodox congregations face the problem of balancing public worship with private ritual.[3]

Bar or bat mitzvah is not the only peak life-cycle event that is marked within a regular service. Aliyot are regularly used to mark important moments including naming babies, weddings, and to anniversaries of loved ones' death.[4] Yet it is the very structure of bar or bat mitzvah, in which the peak life-cycle event is incorporated into much of the regular congregational service, that creates this tension. Equally important, congregational characteristics—denomination, size, and culture—determine the balance between public and private aspects of the service.

Denominational norms largely determine whether a congregation follows a traditional model, as do Conservative and Orthodox congregations, or a contemporary one, as do Reform, independent, and other congregations. In the traditional model, the congregational Shabbat service serves to bring the community together and reinforce Jewish values and community through consistent ritual practice. The bar or bat mitzvah service uses this same service to enact a peak moment in an individual family's life—a moment that, for the family at least, is emphatically not usual. The combination of these two similar services results in tension between the consistent weekly services and individual peak ritual.

In the contemporary model, the bar or bat mitzvah and the congregation's Shabbat service are separate: one takes place on Friday evening, the other on Saturday morning. For many lay participants, there is no conflict—each group in the congregation has its needs met. Leaders see things differently, as Rabbi Yoffie so eloquently expresses. From this standpoint, the community is necessary: how can a child join a Jewish community if that community is absent? The tension here is between leadership and laity, as leaders attempt to educate and regulate congregants.

Whether congregations follow the traditional or the contemporary model, all of them are affected by the size of the bar or bat mitzvah cohort. The effect of a few rituals each year can leave either type of regular service unaffected, while one or more rituals every week will significantly affect the service. While congregations deal with small or large cohorts as a matter of course, few reflect on how cohort size directly affects the service.[5]

These two dimensions—denomination and size—are integral to each congregation, acting like independent variables to structure what is possible, as congregations balance public and private aspects of the service. Within these constraints, congregational culture, along with the relationships among the participants, further determines the balance. Families' expectations for the ritual are shaped both by congregational expectations and by congregants' experiences of bar or bat mitzvah in other places.[6] Other congregants may value the regular service, the minyan service, or various secular activities. Finally, rabbis have the most authority to effect change and not only mediate between the different groups but also choose when or how to enact denominational policy. The balance between public and private aspects of the resulting service is thus determined by institutional characteristics within which participants negotiate their different needs and values.

This chapter focuses on the institutional dimensions of denomination and size, as their effect is largely taken for granted and therefore deserves a careful examination. Because traditional and contemporary patterns for Shabbat observance lead to different expressions of the tension between private ritual and public service, I discuss each separately, before turning to how rabbis act to mediate the difficulties that result from size, congregational culture, and conflict among participants.

INTEGRATING SHABBAT SERVICES AND BAR OR BAT MITZVAH RITUAL: THE TRADITIONAL MODEL

Congregation Shomrei Tzedek, a Conservative congregation with about 700 families, follows the traditional pattern. Though the congregation works hard to increase Friday evening attendance with special music or programs for families with young children, when there are no special programs, Rabbi Brenner said, "We tend to draw a minyan at best."

Attendance on Saturday morning is far higher. Rabbi Brenner told me: "Our typical non-*simcha* [happy event, often a life-cycle ritual] Saturday morning attendance tends to be between 150 and 200 people.... We tend to have a very traditional lay-led participatory service, so there's a lot of singing, we do full Torah reading.... The associate rabbi and I will ... announce pages, and we'll do teaching and explanation throughout the service. With some regularity we have lay people who give *drashot* or talks. We have a rotation of Torah and Haftarah readers, but nine of us do it with greater regularity than anyone else."

Shomrei Tzedek is typical of Bay Area congregations that follow the traditional model.[7] Friday services are brief and conclude in time for attendees to head home for dinner. Some congregations use these evening services to experiment with innovations, provide community Shabbat dinners, or develop special programs for children. However, both of the congregation's rabbis are most invested in Saturday morning services, which is when the congregational community comes together both to worship and to connect with each other. On Saturday mornings, individuals' connection to community and Judaism is reinforced by congregational customs and active lay participation in services, regular attendance by congregants, and eating together following services.

Services at B'nai Aaron and Adat Yitzhak exemplify this pattern. As noted above, the Shabbat morning service is the primary service for both congregations and these services are well-attended, with around 120 people regularly attending at B'nai Aaron and 150 attending Adat Yitzhak. Both had fairly good demographic representation, although B'nai Aaron skewed somewhat older, with fewer men than women attending, while Adat Yitzhak had many more young families, with fewer women attending. Whether formally or informally, congregants at both congregations took or were given the responsibility for welcoming visitors, so that members noted my presence as a visitor at regular Shabbat morning services, and congregants made an effort to help me follow the service. Finally both congregations assumed the presence of children, although in different ways. B'nai Aaron was more intentional in how children were treated, with one corner of the sanctuary was set aside for young children and their parents. On some weeks, teachers supervised an alternate service led by older children; on other weeks they remained in the sanctuary for much of the service, with children of similar ages sitting together. At Adat Yitzhak, children were free to enter and leave the service. Some moved from the men's to the women's side and back; others played outside or in chatted the halls. Women supervised children playing outside, and on some weeks, the rabbinic intern led a very casual prayer practice session.

As at most other congregations that follow the traditional model, congregants at both B'nai Aaron and Adat Yitzhak felt the Shabbat services belonged to them. Each congregation had customs taken for granted by regular attendees: specific melodies that never changed or particular moments when individuals could choose melodies or style, prayers performed in specific ways, and people with specific roles.[8] For example, at Orthodox Adat Yitzhak, one elderly man always led the opening section of the service. Though his distinctive accent was difficult for me to understand, it was clear that the congregation viewed him with respect and honor. Over time, his presence came to reassure me that all was as it should be in the congregation. Other customs also act as barometers for a congregation's and its congregants' well-being.[9]

At both congregations, lay leaders led the service and chanted the Torah and Haftarah portions, with rabbis being part of the regular rotation. When not leading services, they prayed with the congregation or quietly greeted both congregants and visitors. Their primary role on Saturday mornings was to teach the weekly texts. Both Rabbi Joseph at B'nai Aaron and Rabbi Teitelbaum at Adat Yitzhak introduced the Torah and Haftarah readings, noting particular points of interest, and they also delivered the d'var Torah.

One feature of these traditional services is the kiddush luncheon following the service, a meal explicitly open to all attendees. On most Shabbats, these lunches were simple—including, for example, soup, bread, various salads, and cookies served on disposable plates. When a bar or bat mitzvah or other celebratory event (an anniversary, baby naming, pre-wedding blessings, or a Jewish holiday) took place, the lunches featured more elaborate and plentiful dishes served more formally. In either case, congregants gathered, ate, and talked for well over an hour at these meals.

A sense of belonging—both to a congregation and a people—is reinforced for both service leaders and participants through enacting a standard liturgy as interpreted by congregational custom. The rabbi's ability to communicate Jewish history and philosophy deepens this communal sense.[10] Finally, breaking bread together strengthens the sense of community and provides an ending to the morning's ritual. However, each of these communal experiences depends on the presence of a regular community, a community that bar and bat mitzvah services change by altering the composition of the attendees, the nature of the service, and the communal feel of the luncheon.

The addition of a substantial number of guests alters the ability of the congregation to respond as a community. Guests attend because of their connection to the family rather than any connection to the congregation. These guests may be familiar with the service or not; they may know congregational melodies and customs or not. In any case, their presence raises the question of how much explanation of Jewish or congregational practice is necessary. In addition, with many additional guests, paying attention to visitors becomes more difficult, a situation common at other life-cycle events as well.[11]

During a bar or bat mitzvah service, roles previously filled by lay leaders or the rabbi—leading prayers, chanting texts, and/or giving the d'var Torah—are filled to a greater or lesser degree by the bar or bat mitzvah student and family. This changes both the mood of the service, which acquires the sense of risk that accompanies a rite of passage, and the nature of congregants' participation, as even guests knowledgeable about Judaism are unlikely to know congregational customs. The rabbi's d'var Torah, which draws on expert knowledge and experience, may be replaced or supplemented by a bar or bat mitzvah speech that, no matter how carefully prepared and thoughtfully written, still relies on a thirteen-year-old's knowledge and experience. Bar or bat mitzvah students also lead portions of the service that are led by congregants during other weeks, displacing these regular leaders. And bar or bat mitzvah services are likely to include some additions to the service, even if just the rabbi's words of welcome to the guests.

As with other special moments, the kiddush luncheons following a bar or bat mitzvah service are more elaborate than usual and include the family's guests. While all of those I interviewed saw more and better food as an improvement, they also noted that it becomes more difficult to relax with their fellow congregants at a lunch after a bar or bat mitzvah service.

A Shabbat morning service that includes a bar or bat mitzvah thus integrates two events with contradictory goals—one strives to be standard, the other to be special—and rabbis and congregations respond differently to the resulting tension. At one end of the spectrum, the bar or bat mitzvah service and the regular service remain separate, with congregants avoiding services when a bar or bat mitzvah takes place. This is the case at Conservative Am Hayim, with around 600 member families and an annual bar or bat mitzvah cohort that ranges from twenty to fifty. Most weeks, somewhat over 100 people attend services, with congregants leading services and reading from the Torah. So that fewer regular Shabbat services would be affected, Rabbi Weinberg instituted a policy of double b'nai mitzvah, with each service including two students. However, when these b'nai mitzvah services do take place, the effect on the congregation is substantial. Any such service results in additional people attending the service, but at Am Hayim the number of extra guests doubles, further diluting the regular community of worshipers. The result, according to Rabbi Weinberg, is that "there are many congregants who do not come to shul. . . . When there are b'nai mitzvah, it sometimes seems like everyone in the congregation is a guest of the b'nai mitzvah, and there are a small number of congregants who are actually participating in person."

Though the double b'nai mitzvah means that fewer Shabbat mornings are affected, it also means that when a b'nai mitzvah takes place, congregants have fewer opportunities to participate. Because the students split service leading, only one section of the service is open for congregants to lead. In a congregation used to leading, this is not viewed favorably. In fact, the luncheon is the only part of the bar or bat mitzvah service that the congregation views positively, and even here, according to the executive director, the feeling is mixed: "Truly, I think people look forward to a slightly more elaborate kiddush [luncheon], but our regulars are irked by the disruption of regular services."

At Am Hayim, the number of guests simply overwhelmed the number of regular attendees, changing the balance between congregation and guests substantially. With few members attending the bar or bat mitzvah services, it would be difficult to convince a substantial enough number to attend and effect a change in that balance. Instead, though some congregants do attend Shabbat services that include a bar or bat mitzvah service, most of the attendees are guests of the family, so the service has the feel of a private event.

Another Conservative congregation retained a congregational feel most of the time, as the rabbi explained: "The absolute number of congregants does not change, but total number of people does. So there are usually about 200, then there are usually about 100 more there for the bar/bat mitzvah." Maintaining that feeling is a congregational priority, although one that is not always met: "There are moments where it doesn't feel the same. This past Shabbat was one of them, and it was really hard." This quote captures what is lost for the regular attendees when the service begins to feel more like a private event than a community service. Should that experience become a regular occurrence, it would not be surprising for congregational attendance to decline during bar or bat mitzvah services.

Different rabbis and congregations address the change in the composition of attendees in different ways. At one Orthodox congregation, attendance can rise from 150 to 250 people at a bar or bat mitzvah service, and many of the attendees, according to the rabbi, "have not been in a traditional setting before." As a result, while the service itself does not change, the rabbi may assist guests in making their way through the service: "[The congregation] has its melodies, we usually do them. We announce more pages, we do more basic explanation, just one line: 'This is the silent meditation, which is followed by a repetition.'" A number of rabbis mentioned these one-sentence instructions that orient guests but may also disrupt the service movement. To manage this, some congregations print explanatory booklets for visitors and guests. At Conservative B'nai Aaron, one of these booklets includes transliterations of basic prayers, along with brief explanations of choreography and meaning. As a result, Rabbi Josephson spends little time orienting guests to the service.

When guests arrive with different customs from those of a given congregation, rabbis must also negotiate between differing sets of expectations, as another Conservative rabbi explained:

> You got seventy-five people coming from Israel and Monsey,[12] all saying "my service is different . . . we don't do *imahot*." That's a fight, a terrible fight. But I'm trying to accommodate the needs of the family at that moment, along with those of the congregation. We'll leave a pause so that they [the congregation] can say the mothers. . . . On the other hand, I could have an intermarriage, and all of a sudden I've got the Episcopal High Church there. I'm going to try to accommodate the needs of the family. It totally changes the nature of the congregation. And I'm not one of those who says, "We do what we do, and you plug into this."

Though a good illustration of the variation between guests, the rabbi's statement requires some parsing. The congregation's practice is to include the *imahot*, Jewish foremothers, in a prayer that refers to the *avot*, Jewish forefathers. This is a relatively recent addition in liberal American Judaism, part of the move to recognize Jewish women's roles throughout Jewish history. Most Israelis are unfamiliar with the addition; few, if any, Orthodox Jews accept the change. Thus, the rabbi must decide between offending the family and guests or offending the congregation. His solution is to pause briefly, so that individuals can choose to insert the mothers or not. Non-Jewish guests of intermarried families create the opposite problem: their lack of familiarity with Jewish practice may require more explanation than is comfortable for regular attendees. In either case, rabbis face the problem of balancing the congregation's needs with those of the bar or bat mitzvah family.

Changes to the service itself as a result of the bar or bat mitzvah ritual are another area of potential conflict. In chapter 2, I discussed how the bar or bat mitzvah service developed from the regular Shabbat service; in chapter 6, I discussed the specific roles of parents in the service. Those serve as the context for the subject here: how those changes affect others in the congregation. These changes fall into three categories: the quality of teaching represented by the *d'var* Torah, interruptions or changes to the service itself, and the level of congregational service leadership.

Because rabbis or other experts are responsible for teaching text or other lessons during the Shabbat service, when that expertise is replaced by the bar or bat mitzvah speech, the regular attendees lose an important piece of their service. At the same time, the speech is a central part of the bar or bat mitzvah ritual, symbolically demonstrating the student's mastery of a particular type of Jewish learning. Nonetheless, these students are still just thirteen, and their words—no matter how carefully researched and well presented (and some were very, very good indeed)—reflect both their age and experience. Rabbis manage this moment in two different ways: some give the bar or bat mitzvah speech pride of place; others treat the speech as a supplement to their regular *d'var* Torah.

Rabbi Teitelbaum, of Orthodox Adat Yitzhak, favored the first approach. His students may choose to present a *shi'ur*, as discussed in chapter 6. These lessons typically explain an area of Jewish law that particularly appeals to the student (for example, one girl lectured on the laws of Purim because she was born near the holiday) or expand on the Torah portion. In either case, Rabbi Teitelbaum maintains his role as a teacher providing context for the Torah and Haftarah readings, as well as responding with an adult perspective to the student's words.[13]

Rabbi Josephson, at Conservative B'nai Aaron, follows the second approach. Bar and bat mitzvah students are responsible for relatively short speeches that they prepare with mentors drawn from the congregation. Whether or not there is a bar or bat mitzvah, Rabbi Josephson presents a topic raised by the Torah portion. These are structured in an inclusive manner: the rabbi prepares extra material drawn from current and historical Jewish sources for congregants to refer to and conclude with a congregational discussion. Both the consistency of a weekly *d'var* Torah delivered by the rabbi and its inclusive format contribute to keeping the congregational aspect of the service central.[14]

Though it might seem that the first approach focuses more on the bar or bat mitzvah student and the second more on the congregation, in fact, the situation is more complicated. Changes in other aspects of the service matter as well. Thus, congregants at Adat Yitzhak regularly attended bar or bat mitzvah services, most (but not all) congregants at B'nai Aaron attended them, and few regulars at Am Hayim did so. One of those reasons is the difference in how the three congregations treat bar or bat mitzvah additions to the service.

Previous chapters have listed moments that mark bar and bat mitzvah services. Not surprisingly, the number of these special moments, the amount of time spent on each, and their content help define the nature of the service. Traditional model services include fewer of these moments, most often the parents' speeches, rabbi's blessing (which often responds to the bar or bat mitzvah speech), and presentation of gifts. Some Conservative congregations include a tallit presentation; a few include passing the Torah from one generation to the next. In contrast, some Orthodox congregations have no special moments in the service. This was the case at Adat Yitzhak: the service remained unchanged, although the service leaders and Torah readers were (male) friends and family of the bar or bat mitzvah.[15] However, all speeches, including the bar or bat mitzvah speech or *shi'ur*, took place at the conclusion, and parents gave their speech during the kiddush lunch.

Both B'nai Aaron and Am Hayim did include a number of these moments in their bar and bat mitzvah services: a welcome to the family, tallit presentations, parental speeches, rabbi's blessings, and presenting congregational gifts. The amount of time and attention given to these moments helps explain the difference in congregants' attitudes toward the bar or bat mitzvah service. A third factor that contributes to the difference is how prayer leadership changes during these services.

Because two students share the bar or bat mitzvah service at Am Hayim, lay leadership is almost completely eliminated. In contrast, at B'nai Aaron, though much of the service is assigned to the bar or bat mitzvah family, the congregation reserves several sections of the service for lay leaders and congregants.[16] Rabbi Josephson told me: "[At] my first shul we had a real issue with the regulars tending to stay away when there was a bar mitzvah—this does not happen with us. I think that the fact that we prevented the bar mitzvah from just taking over everything definitely helped. . . . We've made a conscious effort to get across that the bar mitzvah is participating in the community, it's not the bar mitzvah for the families." By saving some portions of the service for lay participation, congregants are included, albeit not as fully as when no bar or bat mitzvah ritual takes place.

As rabbis work to balance the needs of the congregation with those of the bar or bat mitzvah families, their options are structured by the traditional model of service, in which the congregation's service is also the bar or bat mitzvah service. As a result, rabbis must integrate and balance two services that take place in same space, with the same liturgy, and with many of the same people, but with very different goals. Within that defining structure, the balance between the two services is determined by the underlying congregational culture along with the choices rabbis make regarding the place of the bar or bat mitzvah speech, the number and length of special bar or bat mitzvah moments, and the integration of lay leadership.

FINDING THE COMMUNITY ON SATURDAY MORNING: THE CONTEMPORARY MODEL

Congregations following the contemporary model face a different problem. As noted above, work patterns in the early twentieth century resulted in Friday evening becoming the primary service for Reform congregations (Sarna 2004, 194), in what I have called the contemporary model. Because the congregational community gathers Friday evening, Saturday morning services are minimally attended, leaving an open space into which the bar and bat mitzvah services fit. While families are, of necessity, focused on their peak event, the long-standing pattern enables the privatization to continue. Though attendance is most often low, Shabbat-related activities do take place in many of these congregations.

Some congregations engage in extended Torah study sessions, in which the weekly Torah portion is discussed. In and of itself, this is not unusual: at congregations across the denominational spectrum, congregants gather to study Torah.[17] However, particularly in the contemporary model, some congregants who attend Torah study make a point of not attending services (that is, their Jewish engagement is with text study, not community worship).

In other, often relatively small, congregations, Shabbat services take place only for a bar or bat mitzvah. The rabbi at one small Reform congregation explained: "We only have Saturday morning services when there is a bar or bat mitzvah. . . . The bar or bat mitzvah is there on the Friday night as well and they help do that service . . . as well." In small congregations, because the congregant pool is limited, attendance even at Friday night services can be challenging: at this congregation only 25–40 people typically attended. However, a bar or bat mitzvah Saturday morning service will draw up to 100 people.

Still other congregations hold minyan services led by rabbis or lay leaders that are replaced by the bar or bat mitzvah service. This is the case at Sukkat Shalom, as Rabbi Doron explains:

> It's much more intimate [than Friday services]. People sit in a couple of semi-circles; sometimes there's more Torah study than a Torah service. We use [the minyan service] as an opportunity to actually teach about the liturgy as we go along. . . . When the cantor leads, it's more liturgy oriented, and when I lead, it's a little more Torah oriented and discussion oriented. . . . The hidden agenda for those morning minyans is that at least a subset of that group will attend the bar and bat mitzvahs after they make Saturday mornings a part of their ritual week. . . . About a half a dozen now attend bar and bat mitzvahs at least occasionally.

These informal services contrast with the roughly twenty-five services a year that are held in the sanctuary, either for bar and bat mitzvah services or services with participation by a religious school class. These have a relatively formal feel due to the frontal nature of pews and bimah, more structured service leading, and the larger attendance—over 100, as compared to 10–30 at the minyan service.

Attendees at minyan services typically develop their own small community with unique customs and regular attendees (usually older adults). This was the case at Sukkat Shalom, where—except for one parent-child pair from the bar and bat mitzvah cohort, attending at Rabbi Doron's behest—attendees were in their fifties or older and attended as individuals, rather than with other family members.

In a third pattern, most often seen in larger congregations, minyan and bar or bat mitzvah services took place concurrently to meet the needs of different constituencies. One typical large Reform congregation held a lay-led service attended by 10–20 people in its small chapel, while the larger bar or bat mitzvah service was held in the large sanctuary. The rabbi led these services, which were attended by 200–400 people, almost all of whom were guests of the family. On the few weeks when no bar or bat mitzvah took place, around 100 people attended the service.[18] As at Sukkat Shalom, these minyan services were attended largely by older adults, usually as individuals, constituting what Rabbi Yoffie called a "regular community of worshippers."

All but Conservative and Orthodox congregations fall into the contemporary model. However, for at least the past decade, Reform leaders at the denominational level have developed initiatives that urge congregations to adopt new patterns of Shabbat worship, with the intent of increasing attendance, knowledge, and participation at both Friday evening and Saturday morning services (Union for Reform Judaism 2015b; Yoffie 1999 and 2007). Rabbi Yoffie called on leaders to develop a culture of Shabbat morning attendance and to create bar and bat mitzvah services that are integrated with that congregational service.

This is easier said than done, as the case of Reform Sha'arei Hesed illustrates. The congregation is large, with a membership of around 700 families and an annual bar and bat mitzvah cohort of around sixty, and it follows the model of concurrent services. Most Saturdays, the congregation holds two services: the bar or bat mitzvah service, which takes place in the primary sanctuary, with one of the two rabbis and the cantor officiating; and a lay-led minyan service, which takes place in the synagogue library, often attended by one of the rabbis.[19]

Over the past several years, Rabbi Segal has introduced changes to the structure of Saturday morning services, meeting with some resistance at each point. Prior to her tenure, the congregation held both Saturday morning and Saturday afternoon bar or bat mitzvah services, thus enabling each student to have an individual ritual. From Rabbi Segal's perspective, the afternoon service lacked certain characteristics required to give it the necessary meaning.[20] When Rabbi Segal eliminated the afternoon service, she had two students share the service.[21]

It was not an easy change: "Introducing doubles was a major trauma, so what the kids do is meant to be as similar as possible: everybody gets to do everything. . . . Now that we've been doing it this way for a number of years, people are more accepting. The kids seem to really like it because they have a buddy. The parents have been more of a problem."

As at Conservative Am Hayim, at Sha'arei Hesed around 200–250 people attend these double bar or bat mitzvah services, with almost all of the attendees being guests. However, because congregants (up to 250) attend on Friday evening, with a small number of regulars (15–30) attending the Saturday minyan service, the conflict between regular attendees and bar or bat mitzvah families does not exist here. Rather, several groups of congregants each meet (or not) separately to fulfill individual goals: the private bar or bat mitzvah ritual, the small minyan service, and the largest group of all—those who do not attend. Though the lack of attendance is affected by the fact of b'nai mitzvah rituals, those rituals are part of a larger problem: although leaders see the Shabbat morning service as central to Jewish practice, most congregants do not. Thus, increasing congregational attendance at Saturday morning services was the first and primary goal of Sha'arei Hesed's lay and rabbinic leadership.

The leaders began by introducing community Shabbat morning services several times during the year, as Rabbi Segal described to me: "We have rescued some Saturday mornings from the bar mitzvah calendar. . . . We're trying to make a big fuss about them in order to make people think they can come to services on Shabbat morning. For example, in July we're going to a park and doing something outside. People . . . don't have the habit [of attending on Saturday] anymore. If we can get people to think of always coming, then maybe we could have a big enough group [for Saturday morning services]." By surrounding the service with music and an informal environment, leaders intended—with some success—to appeal to both families with children and those who had little familiarity or comfort with services.

The needs of those groups are very different from those of the lay-led service attendees. The congregation's website includes this description: "Between Simchat Torah and Shavuot . . . services are held in the chapel as an alternative to the Bar or Bat Mitzah service in the sanctuary. Beginning at 10:30 am . . . services are predominantly lay-led, with congregational volunteers leading the service as well as the Torah and Haftarah readings." Though intended to be welcoming, the description implies that is an established community and there is a high level of participation, both of which can be intimidating. Rabbi Segal said, "Some people are afraid that they don't know enough and if they go, they'll be asked to do something." This knowledgeable community has little obvious overlap with those likely to attend services held in a park.

A related problem would make it difficult to combine the minyan service with the bar or bat mitzvah service. Minyan members value their particular customs, which serve to bind the members together, and these customs do not apply to a bar or bat mitzvah service. Rabbi Segal commented: "Some people want me to cancel the minyan because it's divisive. But I don't think those people would come to the bar/bat mitzvah service every week, and I don't think they should be forced to come. Also, I don't think that even if all thirty sat in the first two rows it would change things. Until you have enough people to change the feeling in the sanctuary—which to me is fifty to seventy-five people, people who are going to come regularly, who are going to sing loud, who are going to know what's going on—then it's only in a mythic sort of way that you can make the bar mitzvah a congregational service. Right now the overwhelming number of guests don't participate that way even if they come from local congregations."

By dissolving the minyan, the small community would, necessarily, be diluted. Furthermore, there would be no point to that dissolution: effecting change in the feel of the bar or bat mitzvah service would require a strong base of regular congregational attendance such as exists in the traditional model. By itself, the minyan could not constitute that base.

If the nature of the bar or bat mitzvah service was the problem, then another approach would be to change that service. Some lay leaders suggested limiting the bar or bat mitzvah student's participation to a single *aliyah*. Rabbi Segal disagreed, pointing out that the ritual did matter to families, including those same lay leaders: "That's what they want now that their kids are grown. When they're asked about their most meaningful Jewish moment, they answer that it was when their kids had b'nai mitzvah and did everything. So I don't think people are clear within themselves: what they want for others isn't what they want for themselves."

The example of Sha'arei Hesed illustrates how an institution and its members affect the ability to change ritual, particularly when those changes are top down. Denominational leaders provided the impetus for making Shabbat morning the primary congregational service, a policy enthusiastically embraced by Sha'arei Hesed's lay and professional leaders. Through the community Shabbat was successful, it did not lead to changes in congregational custom. Suggested changes to the content of and attendance at bar and bat mitzvah services had even less success, as leaders ran into the reality that most of the congregation was perfectly satisfied with the status quo.

Independent Or Hadash took another approach to integrating congregants and guests at bar and bat mitzvah services. With a culture of service participation (once a month, services are entirely lay-led, which encourages regular attendance) and a religious practice that falls somewhere between Conservative and Reform practice,

Or Hadash congregants are somewhat familiar with regular Shabbat morning services. Nevertheless, Saturday morning services are more lightly attended than Friday night services (25–40 people and 40–100 people, respectively), although Saturday morning Torah study, which precedes the service, regularly attracts 20 people, about half of whom attend bar and bat mitzvah services.

Bar and bat mitzvah services are led by the rabbi and the student. However, as in some traditional services, congregants and members of the bar and bat mitzvah cohort participate in the Torah service. By creating a space in the service for congregants, leaders increase the chance that they will attend. In addition, the bar or bat mitzvah speech is structured as a discussion about a question raised and introduced by the student, along with commentary gleaned from family and friends. The speech leads into a discussion with the service attendees. In theory, this structure can engage anyone present. In practice, regular attendees and members of the bar and bat mitzvah cohort modeled the first few responses, with guests participating as the discussion proceeded.[22]

There is no question that the primary congregational Shabbat service at Or Hadash takes place on Friday night. The bulk of the congregation consists of families with school-age children. It is common for families to have competing secular activities on Saturday morning, so regular attendees then tend to be older and drawn from a relatively small pool. Nevertheless, both the culture of high participation, similar to that in congregations following the traditional model of services, and customs that informally require congregant participation result in a model that, while still contemporary, leans toward the traditional in congregant attendance and participation.

Nevertheless, Or Hadash, Sha'arei Hesed, and other congregations following the contemporary model exist with a very different set of norms regarding the public and private balance of the bar or bat mitzvah service than do congregations following the traditional model. Contemporary congregations face tension between groups of participants regarding the meaning of the Shabbat morning service. Bar and bat mitzvah families assume, with some justification, a privatized ritual. Other congregants assume that their individual needs will be met, whether they be at a service or on the soccer field. And leaders see the service and regular attendees as having a central role in the meaning of Shabbat, as well as in the meaning of the bar or bat mitzvah service. The tension is thus in finding a way to bring the separate groups together in the pews. In the traditional model, the community is already sitting in the pews, and the problem is managing the two different goals of the same service. In either case, however, the size of the congregation and of bar and bat mitzvah cohort adds a second dimension.

SIX OR SIXTY: THE EFFECT OF SIZE
ON THE SHABBAT SERVICE

Gan Emek, an independent rural congregation with a membership of around eighty families, holds between two and four bar or bat mitzvah services a year. Rabbi Yardena serves as the part-time rabbi, leading services every other Friday evening and integrating eight to ten Saturday morning learning services into the religious school program (for a total of about a dozen Shabbat morning services each year).[23] Rabbi Yardena teaches each bar or bat mitzvah student individually, the bar or bat mitzvah family participates in planning the service, and the congregation helps organize the event. Rabbi Yardena sums up the congregational approach: "B'nai mitzvah have always been a big deal in this congregation. Everyone is always invited, and a lot of people turn out. So it's a very supportive communal atmosphere."

Numbers matter. Neither congregational nor cohort size can be ignored: congregation size dictates available resources, congregants' needs, and congregational culture; and cohort size dictates how often bar or bat mitzvah services take place and hence their effect on Shabbat services.[24] Yet in most congregations, the effect of cohort size is taken for granted: congregational leaders simply manage the students, rather than considering how numbers structure what is possible. This chapter's opening quote illustrates this: Rabbi Yoffie assumed a large cohort, an assumption that shaped his comments.[25] But that is not Rabbi Yardena's world: at tiny Gan Emek, bar and bat mitzvah rituals are moments when the whole community can join together to make a Jewish time and space for all.

Cohorts can be divided into three categories.[26] Small cohorts can be defined as having fewer than ten students. Seventeen congregations in this study, varying in size from 80 to 200 families, have cohorts of this size. Medium cohorts can be defined as having between ten and thirty students. Sixteen congregations, varying in size from 150 to 625 families, have cohorts of this size. Large cohorts can be defined as having more than thirty students, and nine congregations, ranging in size from 300 to 2,400 families, have cohorts of this size. Congregation and cohort size are only roughly correlated: no small congregation has very large cohorts, nor does any very large congregation have small cohorts, but aside from those extremes, there is substantial variation. Each of these categories of cohort size affects the relationship between congregational and bar or bat mitzvah services differently.[27]

Small congregations, such as Gan Emek, typically offer fewer religious services than larger ones. Some small congregations offer Shabbat services every other week; others hold them weekly, alternating between Friday evening and Saturday morning services. At small congregations, bar and bat mitzvah rituals are rare and usually individualized, which enables them to retain a sense of novelty and excitement. Because the community is small, people form more intimate connections with each other: families know who is likely to attend and who can be relied on to help and in what ways. As a result, bar and bat mitzvah services become events that unite the congregation and affirm not only the family but also the ongoing existence of the congregation and the hope for the Jewish future. As the service leader of another small congregation said: "People really show up. It's radically different than in other congregations I've been part of where it's like: 'Oh, not another one!' Members who know the family well and members who don't know them so well all show up and they get the *oneg* [food and drink following a service] set up. It's a major big deal."

This personal, individualized bar or bat mitzvah stands in contrast to those in large congregations, whether they follow the traditional or contemporary model. In large congregations, bar or bat mitzvah services take place weekly and, by definition, are routine events. The effect of size is amplified in the contemporary model. Because Friday night services remain the congregation's primary service, the differences in perspective between leaders and the bar or bat mitzvah family are intensified: the absence of other congregants both encourages families to see the bar or bat mitzvah service primarily as a peak family event and results in rabbis and cantors seeing a different congregation every week.

Furthermore, in large congregations, it is easy to remain anonymous: there is no expectation that strangers who share a congregation will also share a bar or bat mitzvah. Thus, Conservative Am Hayim, with cohorts of 40–60 students, has congregants who expect to engage in regular Shabbat worship and feel displaced when a bar or bat mitzvah takes place, while Reform Sha'arei Hesed, with a similar-size cohort, has minyan attendees who feel no need to attend bar or bat mitzvah services that have no consistent community; rather, the minyan is their community.

The size of the cohort also affects students' sense of community and dictates how individualized or routinized the preparation and service are. A cohort of three students will act as three separate individuals, as at Gan Emek, where the rabbi tailors the bar or bat mitzvah preparation and service to each student's needs and interests. In contrast, a cohort of eighty may be split into smaller groups, as at Beth Jeshurun. A large cohort necessitates a greater degree of standardization and concomitant bureaucracy, simply to ensure that no student is lost in the crowd. Tracking and managing students affects the nature of preparation, as well as the bar and bat mitzvah services, which become more uniform. This enables staff members not only to track the progress of students and families but also to control the tendency toward comparisons between students, with the resulting competition for the best bar or bat mitzvah.[28]

With both large and small cohorts, the effect of size is clear: small cohorts tend to unify congregations in individual, community-centered rituals; large cohorts tend to lead to more routinized rituals that, at least potentially, act to split congregations into interest groups. What of the case of the medium-size cohort? This category was, in some sense, the most interesting because at this size, the cohort effect was minimized. These cohorts were large enough to create a community of families who—if the congregation developed appropriate programs—could support each other through the event, as well as a cohesive cohort. This size also had implications for the service: so long as bar or bat mitzvah services and regular services were roughly balanced, weekly attendees (whether they chose to attend bar and bat mitzvah services or stay away) were not likely to feel displaced. Because medium cohorts had little impact on the service, it is in these congregations that the effect of the rabbi's role as mediator becomes clear.

MAINTAINING THE STATUS QUO OR
EFFECTING CHANGE: THE RABBI AS MEDIATOR

Chapter 2 briefly discussed the role of the rabbi, particularly with regard to how rabbis affected bar or bat mitzvah preparation and enactment. This chapter places the ritual within the congregational frame and necessitates a broader view of both the rabbi's role and the people who play that role. As with the leaders of other institutions, rabbis act as the public face of the congregation, communicate its vision or mission, enact a range of activities to achieve that vision, and mediate between congregants. As do comparable leaders in other religions, rabbis have an element of the sacred in their work: their role embodies the values and narratives of the religion.[29] The individual who plays the rabbi's role takes on its sacred and secular elements, which gives that individual great responsibility. Though congregants may perform leadership acts—leading services, chanting Torah and Haftarah, and delivering speeches—ultimately it is the rabbi who ensures that the acts are performed correctly with regard to Jewish and denominational rulings, content, and level of preparation. The case is similar with regard to education: though rabbis—except in very small congregations—work with teachers and education directors who deliver content, it is the rabbis who determine the direction of the education. In the Reform movement, for example, rabbis determine whether the congregation will enact the Shabbat initiative described above or the B'nai Mitzvah Revolution discussed in chapter 5. In the Conservative movement, rabbis determine which of two patterns for reading the weekly Torah portions (completing the full reading each year or completing it on a triennial cycle) the congregation will adopt.

Rabbis also determine—as a result of personal preference as well as of rabbinic training and Jewish practice—what aspects of Judaism to emphasize. These aspects interact with congregational culture to determine the degree to which a rabbi can effect change.[30]

Within denominational guidelines, these congregational cultures can be powerful, as congregations develop very different institutional identities. Independent Or Hadash, for example, describes itself as a "participatory" congregation, an adjective that applies to the number of congregants who regularly lead services and to a communal approach to other programs and events. Bar and bat mitzvah services fit into this approach: cohort families help each other with their services, and the congregation participates in the services at a relatively high rate for contemporary model congregations. A large Reform congregation describes itself as "innovative" and regularly experiments with new educational and religious programs. New programs are the norm there, as they are not at another congregation that defines itself as "traditional."

Within this broad understanding, congregational culture determines how congregants view both services and bar or bat mitzvah, so that apparently similar congregations may have very different attitudes toward the ritual. This was the case with two large urban congregations, each with bar and bat mitzvah cohorts of around fifteen. At the first congregation, the rabbi expressed frustration with a culture that was unwilling to change to accommodate the ritual: "Within my congregation there's . . . resistance. But if we don't serve these kids and these families better, there won't be a congregation."

The second congregation had a very different attitude. "I don't have a situation in which the regulars don't come if there is a bar [or] bat mitzvah," explained the rabbi. "In fact, we expect the kids to be here four to six times before their bar or bat mitzvah with their parents. They come to Torah study, Shabbat service, and therefore some of them are adopted by some of the regulars. They [the regulars] are really excited to see little So-and-so, whom they've gotten to know over the last few months. . . . It's the ideal, it doesn't always happen."

Along with general attitudes, congregations develop fixed customs that become difficult to change. The elderly man who regularly opened the service at Orthodox Adat Yitzhak is an example of this: replacing his voice with someone else's would represent a loss to the attendees. Similarly, congregations develop bar or bat mitzvah customs that are difficult to change. For example, according to the cantor at one large Reform congregation, bar and bat mitzvah parents "revolted" when leaders attempted to minimize the private nature of the ritual by eliminating individualized booklets describing the student and service.[31]

Whether part of the regular Shabbat service or the bar or bat mitzvah service, specific customs—such as when the congregation joins in a melody, other patterns of participation, and the language of specific prayers—all contribute to creating a mood of authenticity and authority that can limit a rabbi's ability to effect change. Nevertheless, the rabbi ultimately makes the decisions that mark a service as bar or bat mitzvah or congregational. While these decisions tend to follow denominational norms (for example, Orthodox congregations do not include passing the Torah through the generations) and be affected by size limitations, there is still ample room for variation.

For example, at Orthodox Adat Yitzhak, Rabbi Teitelbaum keeps Shabbat services similar, whether or not there is a bar mitzvah: "I might go out my way to explain more—we're talking sixty seconds more, maybe two minutes over the course of the service, like the mechanics." Yet another Orthodox rabbi institutes a number of changes: welcoming the family, having parental speeches, and including parents and grandparents when the Torah is carried through the congregation. For both rabbis, following Jewish law is of primary concern; however, they interpret how to enact that law differently.

It is one thing to mediate conflicts between congregants and bar or bat mitzvah families; is it another to both mediate and be a party to conflict. Yet this is not uncommon, as rabbis make changes with more or less care. The dual role of leader and participant is, in and of itself, a matter of negotiation, with rabbis determining how much of the power vested in their role they can—or should—cede to the congregation. One approach is that taken by Rabbi Teitelbaum at Adat Yitzhak, where there is no religious practices committee and no negotiation. Rather, he is the sole interpreter of Jewish law within the synagogue walls and to those who choose to follow his rulings outside those walls. Individuals who attend and/or join Adat Yitzhak make personal religious choices (including, for example, going elsewhere for a bat mitzvah), but these choices are not a matter of negotiation with the rabbi, nor do they affect Jewish practice within the synagogue itself.

The situation is different at independent Or Hadash, where Rabbi Melmed actively encourages participation in determining religious practice. With the goal of creating a pluralistic Judaism in one congregation, congregants rely on an active religious practices committee, Rabbi Melmed's religious expertise, and the congregational value of Jewish pluralism to negotiate these different Jewish choices. That participatory model was stretched when the heightened emotions around bar and bat mitzvah came into play in an issue mentioned repeatedly by different interviewees: the question of whether and when photographs could be taken in the synagogue on the day of the bar or bat mitzvah service itself. It is worth noting that this conflict did not arise around either preparation or the service itself: interviewees explicitly or implicitly ceded that responsibility to Rabbi Melmed. Rather, it concerned balancing individual family needs with the Jewish practice of other congregants. The conflict and its resolution illustrate how different needs of congregants, family, and rabbi around the event of bar or bat mitzvah are negotiated.

Few congregations (and none of those whose representatives or members I interviewed) allow photography at Shabbat services: it turns the sacred nature of worship into a secular performance. Furthermore, Jewish practice aside, the use of photography at a congregational service becomes distracting. Yet rites of passage are typically recorded, which results in a contradiction between the two goals of the service. In Conservative and Orthodox congregations, formal photographs take place during the rehearsal. In Reform and similar congregations, while the service may not be photographed, photography may take place before or after the service.

This latter option was what families at Or Hadash requested. However, Rabbi Melmed's personal religious practice does not allow for being photographed on Shabbat. He was also opposed to photography in the synagogue on Shabbat, arguing that those photographs might include others who shared his reservations. Thus, the issue of photographing the rite of passage conflicted with the nature of the Shabbat day itself and with Rabbi Melmed's personal practice. The congregation's Religious Practices and Bar and Bat Mitzvah Committees discussed the issue at some length. Families wanted pictures with the rabbi. The rabbi refused unequivocally: he had no intention of allowing his personal practice (or anyone else's) to be compromised. This stand created a dilemma: if the congregation had decided to allow photography without regard to personal religious practice, it would have been antithetical to the congregational value of religious pluralism—irrespective of the rabbi's role. In the end, the participants reached a compromise: any photographs with the rabbi would take place prior to Shabbat, while photographs taken on the day itself needed the permission of those being photographed. This solution resulted in a pluralistic religious approach that respected individual religious practice, the preferences of the regular attendees, and the needs of the bar and bat mitzvah families.

RITUAL AS A MEANS OF CREATING UNITY OR DIVISION

I began this chapter with Rabbi Yoffie's call for changing the nature of the Reform Shabbat morning service, services that are currently virtually owned by bar and bat mitzvah families. However, his words assume a contemporary service model and a large congregation. The situation in a small, rural congregation is very different from that in a large, urban congregation, and different again in an Orthodox congregation. These institutional characteristics of denomination and size, particularly cohort size, are difficult—if not impossible—to change. Yet, despite the way they structure the tension between private ritual and public service, they are taken for granted.

The issue of who "owns" the service is where much of the obvious conflict around bar or bat mitzvah is centered. This makes sense: the ritual is the public display of all that has come before and represents to family, congregation, and Jewish community the possibility for a Jewish future. Though that existential fear underlies all the tensions, here it speaks to how the ritual affects the community itself. Depending on how the tensions between the public and private aspects of the service are balanced, the ritual can serve to unify or divide the congregation. How that happens is matter of negotiation between participants, mediated by the rabbi.

8 · A VERY NARROW BRIDGE

Bar and Bat Mitzvah and Connecting to the Jewish Future

Bar or bat mitzvah has played an important role in mediating continuity and change in American Judaism, as its central ritual. It has contributed to reshaping the American synagogue, the emphasis of the Jewish life cycle, and the lives of individual American Jewish families. Given its importance, it is not surprising that both the ritual and its influence are of great interest to Jews individually and to the greater Jewish community. However, different people bring their own perspectives to the ritual, its importance, and its meaning, leading to an incomplete understanding. Though a more comprehensive approach, my research has led to a more complete understanding of the relationships and tensions that make up the bar and bat mitzvah system. The first section of this final chapter summarizes these relationships and tensions.

The second section turns to the nagging question at the heart of bar or bat mitzvah: the effect of the ritual on Jewish continuity. For two reasons, my research largely and quite deliberately focused on the ritual in the congregation. First, I found it surprising that, though bar or bat mitzvah has shaped American Jewish life in important ways, social science research had barely touched on the subject. Second, it is impossible to separate the ritual's effect—positive or negative—from other aspects of students' lives after the ritual: there are simply too many confounding factors. Yet the question must be addressed. This section does so, providing a method for approaching the issue and some preliminary results.

Throughout this study, my intention has been to remain dispassionate, reporting rather than prescribing. Yet the people who gave so generously of their time and who allowed me to participate in their lives want to understand practically what they can do to improve bar or bat mitzvah. For them, I offer the last section of the book, in which I make a set of policy recommendations for the future of the ritual.

FROM BAR MITZVAH BARGAIN TO BAR AND BAT MITZVAH SYSTEM: A SUMMARY

This book began by arguing that American bar mitzvah developed from the bottom up, with its strength being largely a result of how it enabled Jewish families to assert Jewish allegiance in an American context. The bar mitzvah bargain resulted from the Jewish elite's placing bar or bat mitzvah within the congregation. In doing so, Jewish leaders approved the ritual, giving it greater weight in the eyes of parents. And by taking on the bar or bat mitzvah as a congregational project, leaders gained the ability to teach children, theoretically achieving the larger goal of giving the next generation the essential tools for leading a Jewish life. The result was two different visions of bar or bat mitzvah: a goal in and of itself and a means to a Jewish end. These two visions—which need not be mutually exclusive—underlie the place of bar or bat mitzvah in the American Jewish psyche. Debating the merits of the two visions has little point; both have meaning to American Jews. It is more productive to understand the interplay of these visions as underlying the relationship among the ritual, congregation, and participants. That relationship is structured by a set of inherent tensions that, with its constituent parts, makes up the bar and bat mitzvah system.

The book first defined the constituent parts (ritual, congregation, and participants) and then defined and developed each of four tensions. Different chapters have focused on understanding these different elements of the whole. I began by describing each constituent, first comparing different contexts provided by congregations, particularly with regard to size and denomination; then developing the relationship between the Shabbat service and the bar or bat mitzvah ritual; and finally describing the roles and responsibilities of each group of participants—students, parents, and teachers. Though the constituent parts can be considered alone (see, for example, Davis 1995; Ellman 2004), they are interrelated, with each shaping and being shaped by the others in an ongoing relationship structured by the four tensions explored later in the book.

As noted above, participants ascribe four different meanings to the ritual: a change of status associated with turning thirteen, an affirmation of Jewish identity, the accomplishment of a difficult Jewish task, and a celebration of the student and his or her new status. Teachers, families, and students negotiate these different meanings throughout the preparation for and performance of the ritual.

Rituals create a reality that exists only when those participating believe in that reality. Enacting a ritual badly breaks that spell. Thus, whatever bar or bat mitzvah means to participants, the ritual requires that the student perform with some degree of competence. Rabbis and teachers—and most families—also expect students to have gained some broader knowledge of Judaism. Teachers and rabbis, of necessity, balance the process of learning and doing Judaism with a ritual performance.

In addition to how the ritual is performed, congregational leaders (largely rabbis) determine who is allowed to perform what parts of the bar or bat mitzvah service. In the wake of the cultural and demographic changes of the past several decades, congregations face the problem of both including previously excluded groups—women in Orthodox Judaism and intermarried families in liberal Judaism—and determining boundaries that protect the Jewish quality of the ritual.

Bar or bat mitzvah is peculiar in the way that it adds a life-cycle ritual to a regular congregational service. Though other life-cycle events are acknowledged in that regular service, bar or bat mitzvah is the only one in which the participant plays such a large role in the service. As a result, congregations negotiate public expectations for the congregational service with those for the private elements of a family life-cycle event. This tension manifests itself very differently in congregations with a contemporary style of worship and those with a traditional style: in the former, there is little congregational participation in Saturday morning services, leaving a time and place for a more privatized ritual; in the latter, a strong congregational presence means that leaders must find a balance between the public and private aspects of a service held in common by the congregation and the family.

Understanding the relationships between the constituents and the tensions that shape these relationships enables both laity and leadership to better understand the limits of change and continuity, and to give each tension its due, I have considered them separately. However, as negotiating one tension changes the nature of the constituents, those changes can have a ripple effect on the entire system. For example, if the quantity of material for which a student is responsible changes, that affects the content of the ritual, which can then implicitly affect its meaning. At the same time, that change is likely to affect the curriculum and nature of tutoring. The power of this system is that it enables participants to consider constituent parts and tensions at many different levels, resulting in a better understanding of the potential consequences of change in any one area. With the overarching system in mind, I now turn to how the system can be used to understand the challenges of Jewish continuity.

FROM A NARROW BRIDGE TO A WEB OF RELATIONSHIPS

On Sunday mornings at Conservative B'nai Aaron, Shelley Weinstein (introduced in chapter 5, where I discussed how she helped Mindy Simon rehearse for her bat mitzvah service) teaches prayers and chanting to the sixth-grade class. Early one Sunday morning in March, I sat in the corner taking notes as sleepy students entered the room. They ignored me as they roused themselves to gossip, pull out notebooks, and settle themselves around long tables. Shelley was an enthusiastic teacher and, despite the early hour, drew the students into the subject matter—learning the melodies for chanting Haftarah. By the end of the hour, despite bouts of rowdiness, most students were paying attention.

After the lesson, as the students left in a burst of noise, Shelley turned to me: "How are we doing?" Despite her evident enthusiasm, despite the fact that early on a Sunday morning she was able to hold squirming preteenagers' attention, she wanted to know that her efforts mattered.

Shelley was not the only teacher who asked that question. In one form or another, her question and the underlying concern was echoed by teachers and rabbis at every congregation I observed. All wanted to confirm that their work mattered: that the ritual is meaningful, the students competent, the community engaged, and the appropriate people included.

At the conclusion of my interviews with parents, many asked a different question: "You have seen a lot of bar and bat mitzvahs," they would say. "Out of all of them, wasn't my child's exceptional?"[1] These parents wanted independent confirmation of their own sense of wonder. They wanted me to confirm that I, too, saw what they saw: an emerging adult, a new and surprising mastery of difficult material, and an expression of Jewish identity.

But underlying both questions is the deeper question of how bar or bat mitzvah matters to Jewish continuity. The leaders wonder: If we use bar or bat mitzvah, not only for itself, but as a means of teaching Judaism to the next generation, can we ensure that the Jewish people and Judaism will endure? The parents ask: If I spend time, money, and effort on this event, will it ensure my child's Jewish identity? In different ways, both leaders and families are really asking about whether bar or bat mitzvah matters and if so, in what ways. The simplest—and most unsatisfying—answer is that the very time, money, and effort expended by all parties demonstrate that it matters, at least in the moment. Yet that answer does not speak to how the ritual will affect Jewish connection, identity, and continuity in the future.

I have argued that bar or bat mitzvah retains its power for Jewish families because it symbolically promises that there will be a Jewish future. However, determining whether and how the ritual will affect students' Jewish identity, practice, and connection in the future is no easy task. Questions about Jewish identity and practice abound and have even been categorized into a question bank that covers subjects from abortion to Zionism (Jewish Survey Question Bank n.d.).[2] Yet even if these questions had been framed with bar or bat mitzvah in mind, it is impossible to untangle the effect of that event from other aspects of the students' lives and make any causal connection. Research on the subject is mixed. A comprehensive research project directed by Jack Wertheimer (2007) includes mixed results from parents, children, and teens, as well as teachers.[3] Barry Kosmin and Ariela Keysar (Keysar and Kosmin 2004; Kosmin and Keysar 2000) have conducted longitudinal studies providing some evidence that students who have taken part in bar or bat mitzvah rituals develop strong Jewish identities.[4] These data give good information about how students change as they mature but cannot show the effect of the bar or bat mitzvah itself apart from other cultural and Jewish influences.

Nevertheless, the question of the Jewish future was simply too important to ignore, so my interviews included several questions addressing that issue. I asked parents and students if they anticipated any changes in family life or student participation in congregational life or Jewish life more generally as a result of the bar or bat mitzvah, and specifically what they thought might change. Since interviews with families took place within a few months of the event, these questions really address how the event left parents and children feeling about Judaism. I asked rabbis and education directors about opportunities in the congregation for post–bar or bat mitzvah programs, whether formal or informal, as well as rates of student participation in such programs. This gave a sense of how congregations and leaders understood the years following the ritual. While the answers help understand how each group sees life after bar or bat mitzvah, those all-important questions remain unanswered: Does bar or bat mitzvah matter? If so, how? And how do we know?

One way to address the questions has to do with the multiple meanings attributed to bar or bat mitzvah: a status change that occurs when a child turns thirteen; public affirmation of Jewish identity; a successful accomplishment of a difficult Jewish task; and a celebration of the child, the accomplishments, or the new status. Of these, the celebration is the only one bound to the ritual moment. The other three meanings point toward future participation in a Jewish community and can be used to understand how to think about the future engagement of bar or bat mitzvah students. First, then, these meanings need to be defined to show how they are—or can be—enacted by students after the ritual. Then, by explicitly framing these questions from the congregation's perspective and tying them to these three meanings, the relationship between what is possible and how that relates to bar or bat mitzvah becomes clear.

Bar or Bat Mitzvah as a Change of Status:
Creating Opportunities for Adult Jewish Practice

Bar or bat mitzvah has been criticized for being a rite of passage with no real change of status. Births, marriages, and deaths all produce changes in responsibilities and relationships. What does bar or bat mitzvah do? How does the change of status change the individual? In chapter 4 I showed students wrestling with this very question. For many, the answer was elusive: they believed the new status led to greater responsibilities, but most of them did not see those responsibilities as particularly Jewish. There were exceptions, including Orthodox boys who expected to participate in daily minyan services several times a week, students who planned to fast on Yom Kippur, and some who had been part of a *shiva* minyan (gathering for mourners). For most students, however, their congregations gave them little chance to demonstrate their new status regularly.

At least in part, the fact of the bar or bat mitzvah ritual implies that being a Jewish adult is enacted primarily in those services. This is, indeed, something that congregations encourage. Or Hadash expects students to chant from the Torah at a friend's bar or bat mitzvah. Beth Jeshurun and other congregations encourage students to chant from the Torah during the High Holy Days—Rosh Hashanah and Yom Kippur. Still others encourage students to read their bar or bat mitzvah portion each year (or every third year) on the proper date. These acts are more symbols of adulthood than real life changes. However, if the change of status was largely enacted through participation in service, then only a few students were likely to feel that change. Instead, most of the students I interviewed took their new status seriously, yet they had no desire to enact Judaism regularly through services.

Bar or Bat Mitzvah as an Affirmation of Jewish Identity:
Individual Expression to Community Connection

While the change of status is largely about Jewish practice (that is, about what a student can do), affirmation of Jewish identity is about who that student is (that is, about his or her informal ties to Jewish culture, history, community, and people). It can be no more than the thin connection of symbolic ethnicity Herbert Gans (1979) describes. The reflections of these parents from Sukkat Shalom exemplify this type of connection:

[The best thing about Judaism is] just being sort of an outsider and not having people like you around in your community. It's definitely the cultural [aspects]. I think that's what I think [is] . . . best.

I love the cultural aspects of it [Judaism] because that was the part I was steeped in more as a child. The gatherings, the food, the celebration—that aspect of it.

However, that identity can be much thicker, informing every part of a person's worldview, as the examples of the Seuss and Orlansky families illustrate. This much variation in meaning results in definitions that can cover the whole of Jewish life or a simple statement of affiliation. This can also been understood to be the most individual of the meanings: "I identify as a Jew." When parents or rabbis talk about their children choosing to be Jewish as adults, they are talking about their children's individual choices, the self-creation that is part of modern identity formation. Because it is largely individual, it is also the meaning that can be best captured in demographic data. Those data are clear: the thicker the web of a family's Jewish practice and engagement, the more likely the children will remain engaged in Judaism after bar or bat mitzvah.

Congregations serve as catalysts for that engagement in Jewish life by creating communal bonds. Identity may be individual, but to be sustained, it must be expressed and reinforced in groups. Congregations offer Jewish spaces, connections, and communities that attempt to engage both post–bar or bat mitzvah youth and their families. In other words, the flip side of individual Jewish identity is community connection and engagement, which congregations are uniquely suited to deliver. Furthermore, although families in my study joined congregations for a variety of reasons that included the rabbi, their children's education, and the denomination, the single most important reason they remained members was for a connection to a Jewish community.

Sometimes that sense of community can be invoked at the bar or bat mitzvah service. At large Reform Beth Jeshurun, students from a grade above and a grade below the bar and bat mitzvah cohort participate in the ritual, welcoming others or being welcomed by others into the bar and bat mitzvah program. And at a very small Renewal congregation with fewer than 100 affiliated families, congregants look forward to the few bar or bat mitzvah services that take place. Following the Torah reading, as a way to include the community and demonstrate support for the student, the cantor "asks everyone to stand up and get close to the bimah, shoulder to shoulder . . . and make a web, so there's a big circle around the bar/bat mitzvah. There's a communal blessing that we sing, and we ask the young person to look around and take in the love that they're seeing and tuck it away for times they'll need that support. . . . That's the moment when people start crying." Both of these exemplify how individual congregations develop distinctive customs, the effect of which depends on previous connections.[5]

One common path to connection brings students' connection to the supplementary school to the next level, with teenage assistants, called *madrichim*, helping in classrooms. Those who fill these spots relearn past material through teaching, and they can also continue to build connections with their peers. Programs specifically for teens are another avenue for connection. These include youth groups and teen education programs. In both cases, the programs combine aspects of community building, education, and practice. Depending on the size and inclination of the congregations involved, they can be sponsored by one congregation or several. Though most congregations offered some combination of these options, participation varied widely. For example, enrollment in post–bar or bat mitzvah educational programs varies from 20 percent to 80 percent of a given congregation's bar and bat mitzvah cohort.

Following the ritual, congregations cannot compel students to participate in programs.[6] Rather, participation becomes a matter of family and individual choice, which leads to the obvious question: Given that post–bar or bat mitzvah participation is de facto a matter of choice, what factors encourage students and families to participate? Responses from students, parents, and rabbis lead me to a preliminary conclusion: It is not the number of programs a congregation creates that matters, but rather how effective congregations are in creating long-lasting connections and communities for the students and their parents. These programs begin prior to the bar or bat mitzvah year and create connections between members of the bar and bat mitzvah cohort and sometimes the students' parents. When these programs do not exist, families make choices guided by individual family circumstances: families that are deeply engaged in Jewish life will continue to be; families less engaged will remain so.

In chapter 5, I touched on some examples of family education. There the focus was on how these programs prepared families for the bar or bat mitzvah, rather than on how they connected families to the congregation and each other. Some of these programs connect the individual student and family to another person or group. In one such program, students meet with, interview, and give a place in the bar or bat mitzvah service to a congregational elder. In another example, students meet with adults who teach them about an area of mutual interest. In both of these cases, the goal of the relationship is to develop a mutual interest or bond between two individuals to create a lasting connection.

A more communal connection can occur with intensive family preparation programs, such as that at Or Hadash. In this program, each family is responsible for a different task, which ensures that they work together. Above, I described the session in which families discuss each other's mottos. The exercise explicitly taught how Jewish knowledge is passed on over time and between people. Implicitly, the structure of the exercise ensured that families would work together and depend on each other. First, each family contributed mottos to the group, meaning that the members of each family must first consider their family culture and how to present it. Then two families worked together to collect and organize the material. Finally, the whole group used the collected mottos not only as a way to experience Jewish learning but also as a way for families to learn about each other. Through these types of activities, as well as through dividing up the tasks necessary to provide the kiddush luncheon, parents and children experience the effect of community, which can lead to longer lasting connections to the congregation. In addition, by structuring the program so that families work together to achieve mutual goals, they also develop a pool of knowledge that enables them to solve problems common to bar or bat mitzvah planning.

This effect is no small thing, as one father told me: "We have this wonderful tradition at our shul of families helping, and it was so nice, you just didn't have to worry about anything. If you want to talk about one of the best things, it is tremendous on so many levels, and you don't even realize it until you're actually having your own and you realize that this is really an amazing gift that these people have given you."

In contrast, Beth Jeshurun, with its large bar and bat mitzvah cohort, structures its equally intensive preparation program so that each family chooses from an array of activities. As a result, there is little opportunity for either parents or students to develop a sense of community around the shared experience, and parents' comments reflected this.

One strong component of Reform Jewish philosophy is universalizing an ethic of caring for community, from the Jewish people to the wider community, whether local or global. Beth Jeshurun expects students to enact this value by choosing from a range of sponsored activities. Another large Reform congregation took a different approach. Each bar and bat mitzvah cohort pooled their gift money. Each student then researched a different cause and presented it to the group. The class used that information to decide to which causes they would donate and how the collected money would be divided. Though the program's explicit purpose is to teach the responsibility of giving, the implicit purpose is to create a situation in which each member of the group is responsible for helping the others to reach a common, collective goal. The education director attributed the fact that 80 percent of the students entered the post–bar or bat mitzvah program in the year following their bar or bat mitzvah to the close bonds formed through this program.[7]

Congregations have long recognized that connecting families to the congregation matters. Thus, it is not surprising that many congregations have created programs intended to build those connections. However, understanding the relationship between individual Jewish identity and community connection is not so easy, particularly since creating that individual identity is an assumed part of the American project of self-creation. As noted above, to be more than symbolic, identity must not only be felt but also enacted as part of a real or imagined community. Sometimes that community consists of family and friends; sometimes it consists of a cultural ethos and activities (such a community is easier to find in New York than it is in the Bay Area). However, congregations create Jewish communities in which members can enact Jewish identity together.

A research agenda for exploring this area would consider how congregations engage post–bar or bat mitzvah students and their families in congregational life.

Bar or Bat Mitzvah as the Accomplishing of a Difficult Jewish Task: Continuing Jewish Learning

The third meaning attributed to bar or bat mitzvah is that of accomplishing a difficult Jewish task, one that implicitly and explicitly includes a strong educational component. It is in enacting this meaning that students learn Hebrew liturgy and texts and develop their speeches. This meaning is about what students know and believe, and for post–bar or bat mitzvah students, it translates into continuing formal education. Like opportunities for a student to demonstrate his or her change of status, the opportunities for continuing education are limited. Most commonly, congregations offer or participate in continuing supplementary school programs, as noted above. These programs serve students in eighth grade through high school, meet for a few hours each week during the school year, and may include weekend retreats with other students. As with educational programs for students in the lower grades, these schools serve the dual function of building community and engaging students in learning—and in the case of schools for young adults, the learning is more advanced. For example, one program introduces itself this way:

> Berkeley Midrasha is the premier Jewish learning and identity building experience for East Bay teens in 8th–12th grade. It offers a broad range of interesting and challenging courses to students with a strong Jewish background and to those with little former training or knowledge—classes ranging from Talmud and Hebrew to Jewish films and drama. The program provides students with the skills and knowledge to become *engaged* and committed *Jewish* adults. Midrasha offers a larger social group of Jewish teenagers than exists at any one synagogue and the opportunity to form lasting friendships. The program provides a warm social environment in the classroom and at weekend retreats. In addition, our faculty provides our students with positive, knowledgeable role models of successful young Jewish adults who are at home in Judaism and the secular world. (Midrasha in Berkeley n.d.)

The program thus offers learning, community, and positive Jewish role models to teenagers across the Jewish spectrum of practice. Both goals and audience are mixed. A student who primarily wants social activities may be uninterested in Talmud or even films, while one who primarily wants learning may find the social activities unappealing. Furthermore, teaching the material to the students with different levels of knowledge offers challenges.

The confirmation year is another way by which congregations engage students. First introduced in Reform congregations to replace bar or bat mitzvah, it now serves as a supplement to the ritual. Tenth-grade students meet with rabbis over the course of a year to develop a deeper understanding of Judaism. Whereas bar or bat mitzvah is an individual service, the confirmation service includes the whole class. It takes place on the holiday of Shavuot, the symbolic moment when the Jewish people accepted the Torah at Mount Sinai. The symbolism of communal acceptance through enacting the service combines elements of identity, community, and knowledge.

Like supplementary school for younger students, these programs require time. Both elementary and high-school students have competing secular activities that can result in missed classes. However, students in elementary school face the requirements of bar or bat mitzvah, which can exert pressure to attend religious school. Students in high school have no such pressure—quite the reverse. As students enter high school, secular priorities become more pressing, particularly as students approach the competitive college application process. Furthemore, post–bar or bat mitzvah students are more likely to be given the choice whether or not to attend post–bar or bat mitzvah programs. Unless the student and family already have prioritized Jewish learning (or have developed the strong community ties discussed above), they are less likely to make the extended commitment that these programs require.

Post–bar or bat mitzvah engagement is a subject ripe for further research. This research could be approached by considering congregations rather than individuals and by using categories derived from the three meanings of bar or bat mitzvah I have been discussing: change of status, interpreted as opportunities for practice inside and outside of the congregation; claiming Jewish identity, interpreted as opportunities for developing community cohesion before, during, and after bar or bat mitzvah; and accomplishing a difficult Jewish task, interpreted as opportunities for ongoing study. Yet academic research has not addressed the ongoing difficulties faced by leaders as they negotiate the tensions of the bar and bat mitzvah system. In the final section of this chapter, I turn to some concrete suggestions for these leaders.

SOME RECOMMENDATIONS FOR THE BAR OR BAT MITZVAH OF THE FUTURE

I have made the case that the relationships among bar or bat mitzvah, congregations, and participants are structured by inherent tensions. Within the congregation, these tensions manifest themselves as problems to be managed, and because each congregation is unique, there cannot be one set of recommendations that applies equally well to large and small congregations and to Orthodox and Reform ones. I can, however, make three general recommendations for leaders: pay attention to context, broaden education's range and methodology, and develop multiple forms of engagement.

First, pay attention to competing perspectives and the possibilities and constraints afforded by a congregation's context. During my preliminary interviews, it became clear that leaders and families had such different orientations toward the bar or bat mitzvah that each group was talking past the other, with families seeing the ritual as a peak event in their families' histories and leaders seeing it as the means to a Jewish end. Each group took its perspective for granted. As a result, there was substantial conflict between parents, who felt unfairly dictated to, and leaders, who felt that parents often attempted to create private events at the expense of the service. For obvious reasons, leaders largely dictate preparation and ritual, and it falls to them to determine how to frame the bar or bat mitzvah ritual. Some leaders attempt to minimize the ritual. Another approach—less common in the Bay Area—is for rabbis to take the families' perspective at the expense of the congregation's. Both these approaches lead to conflict, either between rabbis and families or between rabbis and other congregants. However, congregations where the two perspectives are both acknowledged and integrated, so that the ritual is treated both as a serious Jewish event in and of itself and also as a marker of Jewish accomplishment, had substantially less conflict and resentment than others did.

That sensitivity—or intentionality—also applies to considering the congregational context to understand how it enables or constrains what is possible. Large congregations face different challenges than small congregations do. Similarly, the possibilities and constraints facing Reform congregations are very different from those facing Orthodox congregations. A family that expects egalitarian treatment for their daughter in an Orthodox congregation is sadly misguided. So is a Reform congregation that expects changes to bar or bat mitzvah to lead to changes in Saturday morning attendance.

Second, use a variety of methods to educate the whole family. The short time available for students in religious school makes it difficult to teach Jewish studies, Hebrew, and bar or bat mitzvah preparation material. Some congregations have moved programmatic material online, particularly Hebrew. Students can participate in Wikis and listen to prayers on synagogue websites. Other congregations have students keep journals of home practice of Jewish ritual or of their service experience. All of these are examples of inculcating individual practice and extending the ability to reconcile Jewish learning and bar or bat mitzvah preparation.

Yet learning and teaching are not limited to students. Though the ritual is about the child, it is the parents who drive the process. In every congregation I studied, regardless of denomination, at least one parent I interviewed expressed insecurity and sometimes alienation with regard to his or her own Jewish knowledge. The range of possibilities here is extensive, including family education programs, adult classes held at the same time as the children's classes, and programs focused on the bar or bat mitzvah year. Each type of program has a different purpose, but together they would enable parents to be models of adult Jewish behavior for their children; empower the parents by providing them with new skills and knowledge; and—in the case of bar or bat mitzvah programs—ensure a better understanding of the Jewish nature of the ritual itself.

Third, find multiple ways to integrate both parents and students into congregational life. The place of the bar or bat mitzvah in Jewish life can distort participation. As the examples in the previous section illustrated, some congregations are quite intentional about using the ritual not only to educate parents but also to integrate them into the community. These programs are more common in the Reform movement, and their lack was evident in some of the comments from less-engaged parents in both Conservative and Orthodox congregations. Regardless of denomination, building a web of support before and during the bar or bat mitzvah year strengthened community bonds.

At the same time, preparing for the bar or bat mitzvah can be difficult and time-consuming, and the aforementioned programs would increase the required commitment. Families may feel exhausted following the bar or bat mitzvah. This is a normal response to a major event, be it secular or religious. However, few congregations have developed ways to reengage families following the ritual. Most congregations have post–bar or bat mitzvah programs, as discussed above, but few if any work with students to develop a plan for their individual post–bar or bat mitzvah future. This leaves both parents and students adrift and contributes to the "bar or bat mitzvah and out" mentality that leaders complain about. Thus, applying the same amount of effort to families' experience before and after the ritual is important.

I recognize that all three recommendations ask leaders to navigate between not enough and too much in every area. That is the reality of the bar and bat mitzvah system: as congregants, norms, and congregations' demographics change, the relationship among the participants, ritual, and congregation will inevitably change, too. Still, finding ways to pay attention, to broaden education, and to deepen engagement are overarching goals that congregations can strive to reach.

I conclude with a personal reflection. These days, I attend Saturday morning services as part of my personal practice. Sometimes those services include a bar or bat mitzvah. Of course, it is now impossible for me to attend these services without taking mental notes. I pay attention to how my rabbi welcomes attendees, while also setting rules of etiquette—some of which are ignored. I pay attention to the ratio of congregants to invited guests and watch how each group participates. I listen to the bar or bat mitzvah student and hope that the speech is thoughtful and the Torah chanting is on pitch.

But my attention is often on my two small grandchildren who attend with me. They sit on either side of me, each one braiding and then unbraiding the tzitzit (symbolically knotted strings) on my tallit, just as their mother and aunt did years before. These children, born in the second decade of the twenty-first century, are the second generation to grow up in this congregation. Now they play with their friends in the synagogue courtyard. In a few short years, they will be learning their Torah portions and preparing their own speeches. As the bar or bat mitzvah ritual continues to evolve, I look forward with personal and professional interest to seeing them and their peers become part of the future of American Judaism.

METHODOLOGICAL APPENDIX

The first chapter discussed my rationale and methodology briefly. This appendix uses that material as a starting point to discuss the methodology in more depth. Because it is intended to be read as a stand-alone piece, the introduction repeats some of the material in the acknowledgments and chapter 1.

For an event that consumes so much time, energy, and imagination, surprisingly little is known about bar or bat mitzvah. There is a rough sense of what constitutes the ritual and how students are prepared for it, but this assumed knowledge is at best imprecise and at worst simply wrong. Two examples illustrate the problem. First, reading Torah is an expected part of all bar and bat mitzvah services (except, sometimes, the Orthodox bat mitzvah). However, the amount that a student chants varies from three verses to the entire weekly portion, and no one knows who does how much and why. Second, many people assume that the students are performing a rote act with little real content. While both service content and preparation for the service vary, the reality is more complex, as my research shows. Part of my goal, therefore, was to fill the information gap by simply describing the landscape of bar or bat mitzvah preparation and event. However, the specific elements of that landscape change over time and across places, so my larger goal was provide a way to think about what shapes this landscape by identifying and describing the interactions among the ritual, the congregation as an institution, and the different stakeholders.

Two avenues of investigation enabled me to accomplish both goals. A broad survey of congregational leaders that included rabbis, education directors, and administrators provided information about specific patterns of preparation and enactment, as well as an understanding of how professional leaders understand the place of bar or bat mitzvah in the congregation and the ritual's role in Jewish life. More in-depth interviews and observations at representative congregations enabled me to understand the nature of interactions related to bar or bat mitzvah and how these interactions affected individuals, the congregation, and the ritual. The combination of specific descriptive data and information showing the meaning of and effect on different parties enabled me to understand how the different parties negotiated the resulting tensions.

My work is part of a recent trend in research on lived religions, the study of how leaders and the laity negotiate with religious tradition (Ammerman 2006; Baggett 2009; Benor 2012; Cohen and Eisen 2000; Luhrmann 2012; Thompson 2014) in the twenty-first century. Though my work relies on the general approach toward observing lived religion, Steven Cohen and Arnold Eisen's findings were particularly useful in understanding the development of American Jewish individualism, while Jerome Baggett's study of Catholic parishes provided a particularly good complement to my research. Baggett examines how individuals, doctrine, and leaders mutually shape beliefs and practices in a pluralistic society, providing a model by which to understand how individuals reproduce, renew, and transform religion and, indeed, culture. In a similar way, I used mixed methods to understand relationships among the ritual, participants, and congregation. My research took place in the San Francisco Bay Area, where I conducted extensive interviews, engaged in participant observation, and gathered related contextual material (website data, booklets, and speeches).

Bar and bat mitzvah rituals usually take place in congregations, and congregations usually belong to denominations (nationally, 5 percent are unaffiliated). There are distinct denominational differences in the content and enactment of services, and there are also distinct regional differences in US Jewish communities. Describing both regional and denominational differences would not have been a manageable project. I chose to examine one region—the San Francisco Bay Area—in great detail and across denominations. In the next section, I discuss my rationale for choosing this approach and the Bay Area in particular. In the following two sections, I discuss the two parts of the project: the broad leadership survey and intensive observations at five congregations. I conclude with possibilities for future research.

THE SAN FRANCISCO BAY AREA AS A RESEARCH SITE

As defined by the San Francisco Jewish Federation, the Jewish Bay Area covers a region that extends north of the bay to Ukiah, south to Monterey, and east to Antioch. Like the areas around Washington, D.C.; Philadelphia; and Boston, it has a population of around 215,000 Jews (Kotler-Berkowitz 2013). Since the Bay Area Jewish community's beginnings, dating back to the California Gold Rush, it has had a history of acculturation and diffusion (Kahn and Dollinger 2003) and a distinct lack of the ethnic enclaves that shaped Jewish communities like those in New York, Chicago, and Los Angeles. The rate of intermarriage with gentiles is somewhat higher in the Bay Area (55–60 percent) than it is nationally (48 percent). The rate of synagogue affiliation in the Bay Area (21–22 percent) is notably lower than the national average (40 percent).[1] However, the region supports an active Jewish cultural life that includes many Jewish film festivals, street fairs, Jewish day schools, centers for specific types of Jewish learning (such as meditation), a regionwide adult education program (Lehrhaus Judaica), and synagogues of various sizes and denominations.

High intermarriage rates strongly affect the composition of liberal Bay Area congregations. While the percentages of intermarried families in Conservative and Orthodox families are similar in the Bay Area (5–15 percent in Conservative synagogues and 3–5 percent in Orthodox synagogues) and the United States as a whole (12 percent in Conservative synagogues and 5 percent in Orthodox synagogues), the percentages in Reform and similar congregations in the Bay Area and the United States are very different (40–70 percent and 26 percent, respectively).

The percentages of synagogues identifying with different denominations in the Bay Area also differ from the US averages. Excluding congregations that serve specific populations (for example, the elderly or young single people), those with particular missions (for example, Jewish meditation), and Chabad groups, because these are organized as hierarchical franchises led by individuals or couples, I identified seventy-three congregations, which are categorized in Table 1.[2]

This is substantially different from the US percentages, as shown in Table 2. In the Bay Area only the percentage of Conservative congregations is similar to the national average, while there are far more Reform, independent, Renewal, and Humanist congregations and far fewer Orthodox congregations.

In sum, compared to the United States as a whole, the Bay Area has a smaller percentage of Jews who join synagogues. These synagogues are more liberal, and within those synagogues—particularly for younger families—the intermarriage rate is higher.

TABLE 1.   Numbers and Sizes of Bay Area Congregations, by Denomination

Denomination	Number of congregations	Percent of all congregations	Range in size (family units)	Number of families in congregations	Estimated number of individual members in congregations
Reform	27	37.0	80–2,500	15,000	37,500
Conservative	15	20.5	300 to 700	6,200	15,500
Independent	12	16.4	100–400	1,600	4,000
Orthodox	10	13.7	50–250	1,000	3,000
Renewal	4	5.5	50–400	500	1,000
Reconstructionist	3	4.0	<100	200	400
Humanist	2	2.7	<100	100	200
Total	73	99.8	<100–2,500	24,600	61,600

NOTES: See note 2 for an explanation of how I estimated the number of individual members. Percentages do not sum to 100 because of rounding.

TABLE 2.   Percentages of Bay Area and US
             Congregations, by Denomination

	Percent of all congregations	
Denomination	Bay Area	United States
Reform	37.0	26.0
Conservative	20.5	23.0
Independent	16.4	5.0
Orthodox	13.7	42.0
Reconstructionist	4.0	3.0
Renewal and Humanist	8.2	1.0
Total	99.8	100

NOTES: Percentages for the United States are from Cohen (2006). In the Bay Area, 5.5 percent of congregations are Renewal and 2.7 percent are Humanist. Percentages may not sum to 100 because of rounding.

Jews in the Bay Area are an example of one of the many different types of American Jewish communities. Though New York—which has the largest, densest, and most Orthodox (by percentage) Jewish community—is often imagined as the paradigmatic American Jewish community, it does not represent the variety of practices, beliefs, and identities found in other American communities, such as Chicago, Minnesota, or the Bay Area. By the same token, studies based in small and isolated Jewish communities (for example, Albuquerque) capture the issues facing such communities, but not those of a large ethnic enclave. History, the surrounding culture, size, and density all contribute to Jewish life, and each results in people's different engagement with Judaism.

As a research site, the Bay Area offers much more than simply one choice among many. Its size offers one obvious advantage: there are fewer than a hundred congregations in the region, making it possible to describe completely the Jewish congregational landscape of the area. Understanding bar and bat mitzvah across a complete region provides the opportunity to understand how different variables—notably, size and denomination—shape the ritual in the context of a particular regional culture.

More significantly, both the American religious landscape (see, for example, Hadaway 2011; Putnam 2010) and the American Jewish landscape (Kosmin and Keysar 2013) show increasing levels of individualization and secularization nationally. With its low rate of congregational affiliation and its continuing cultural norms of religious pluralism and individualism, the Bay Area exemplifies these current trends. Examining it provides a window into the American Jewish future. For example, precisely because synagogue affiliation is not the norm, choosing to affiliate requires some self-justification on the part of congregants, with regard to both time and money. Furthermore, both lay and professional leaders of these synagogues are well aware of the difficulties in recruiting new members, which results in substantial efforts in some synagogues to make the case for joining.

High rates of intermarriage introduce another issue that is likely to affect congregations in increasing numbers: how can a congregation remain both distinctively Jewish and include non-Jewish participants in congregational life? Thus, the Bay Area is both a particular space that can be described quite completely and a possible model for Jewish continuity in the increasingly pluralist and secular American religious milieu of the twenty-first century. More generally, the approach of this particular minority group illustrates the tension between distinctiveness and inclusiveness faced by every minority community—religious or ethnic—in a pluralistic society.

Nevertheless, at least some of the patterns of preparation and performance are likely to be specific to the Bay Area. For example, because of the degree of intermarriage in the area's synagogues, non-Jews may be more integrated into congregational life there than in some other regions. However, without data from these other regions, there is no way of comparing these different specific practices, a fact which points to the limitations of the research design.

The alternative to examining one region whose congregations vary in size and denomination would have been to compare practices of one denomination in two or more regions.[3] This design would have captured some regional differences but resulted in a far less complete picture of the ritual. By examining a range of denominations, I have established a set of questions that can be used in other communities and across the denominational spectrum, as well as a set of regional practices that can be used for comparison. The specific patterns change over time, but the tensions that shape those patterns remain. While specific resolutions of these tensions will vary over time and place—as, for example, the rules about what a non-Jew can do on the bimah have changed over the past twenty years—every congregation, whether located in New York, Albuquerque, or the Bay Area, faces the question of who can participate in what way during the service.

FROM CONGREGATIONAL WEBSITES TO INTERVIEWS: THE LEADERSHIP SURVEY

The leadership interviews were intended to gather information on the relationship between bar or bat mitzvah and the congregation from the standpoint of those responsible for developing and administering bar and bat mitzvah programs. I planned to interview individuals playing three key roles (rabbi, education director, and administrator) at each congregation. I first developed and pilot tested the set of interview questions in congregations outside the Bay Area. At the same time, I identified congregations within the Bay Area and gathered basic data about them; then I identified the individuals to be interviewed. I made several attempts to contact each congregation and interviewee, using e-mail, postal mail, and phone. Finally, interviews were conducted over the phone, recorded, and transcribed. In what follows, I discuss each of these steps in some detail.

The initial list of synagogues was taken directly from *Resource: A Guide to Jewish Life in the Bay Area* (Gellman 2008). A publication of the San Francisco Jewish Federation, it collects and organizes denominational lists by subregion, including at least basic contact information. Through a combination of examining websites, then calling to confirm that information, my assistants and I eliminated all congregations that did not fit the profile described in the previous section.[4] In the process, we also gathered website information in three categories: introductory statements, information about services, and descriptions of children's education. This information gives a sense for how the congregation—or at least the person who wrote the text for the congregation—understands the overall congregational goals, the range of its services, and the nature of its education program.

Using the information collected, my assistants and I attempted—with only partial success—to contact each person. We sent letters through the postal service or by e-mail and followed up with several phone calls and an additional e-mail message as necessary. The individual responses are detailed in Table 3 and indicate a response rate from somewhat over half (57 percent) of the congregations, with roughly proportional denominational representation.

The congregations that did not participate in the study are disproportionately small and presumably short on human resources. Most of these congregations (about ten) simply did not respond. The leaders of another subset of these congregations did respond but declined to participate due to time constraints. Finally, a third group expressed a willingness to participate but did not follow through due to scheduling problems.

TABLE 3.   Number of Leadership Respondents, by
             Type of Respondent and Denomination

Denominations (number of congregations)	Rabbi	Educator	Administrator	Total
Conservative (12)	12	11	12	35
Independent (5)	4	4	4	12
Orthodox (5)	5	1	3	9
Reconstructionist (1)	1	0	0	1
Reform (17)	19	17	17	53
Renewal (2)	1	2	2	5
Total (42)	42	35	38	115

Not all of the participating congregations had individuals filling all three roles. Orthodox synagogues, where it is the norm for children to attend full-day religious school rather than supplementary school, rarely have education directors, so this role was missing for all of them.[5] Small congregations often had only one person filling two or more of these roles; in these cases, I asked that person all the relevant questions. Finally, some individuals in participating congregations either did not respond or declined to be interviewed, on the ground of either discomfort (some administrators) or lack of time (some rabbis and educators). The set of interviews that results is not the census I intended to conduct, but rather a survey that is relatively representative with regard to denomination, location (including urban, suburban, and rural areas and with representation from different subregions in the Bay Area), and size.

Each of the three roles contributes a different perspective on bar or bat mitzvah and has a particular set of responsibilities and knowledge. Rabbis are responsible for overall congregational leadership, particularly with regard to religious services and education, including the bar or bat mitzvah event. Education directors are responsible for developing and implementing religious school curricula, which usually include the bar or bat mitzvah program. Even when it does not, religious school programs include teaching material that is a prerequisite for bar or bat mitzvah training. Administrators or executive directors are responsible for basic congregational information, but they also can have a more informal relationship with congregants, and I thought they could reflect the congregants' feelings and views. In what follows, I describe how the interview questionnaires were developed and delivered, first discussing sets of questions common to the different types of interviews and then turning to questions related to specific areas of expertise.[6]

I asked two sets of questions of all interviewees. The first set asked about congregational culture, including questions about demographic characteristics and Jewish practice of congregants, priorities and strengths of the congregation, and decision-making processes and strategies for conflict resolution. While many questions were developed from information gathered from congregational websites, the set of scenarios on congregational decision-making processes was loosely based on Penny Becker's (1999) models of conflict in congregational life.

The second set of questions concerned the place of bar or bat mitzvah in congregational life. The most significant question in this set asked respondents to comment on a list of meanings attributed to bar or bat mitzvah in different sources, including congregational and informational websites; books for bar or bat mitzvah families, Jewish educators, and the general public; and common statements. The respondent was asked which items in the list were heard most commonly in the congregation—that is, the respondents were asked to serve as proxies for the congregants. The answers are, of course, highly subjective.

However, they serve two useful functions: they provide a sense of what the leaders believe the congregation's view of bar or bat mitzvah to be and, more concretely, they can be compared to those given by congregants, lay leaders, and bar or bat mitzvah parents to get a sense of how accurately leaders understand their congregants' perspectives.

I asked rabbis three sets of questions specific to their role. The first set established the normative context for observing Shabbat—that is, these questions concerned when services took place if there was no bar or bat mitzvah. Therefore, I asked questions regarding the content and style of services on both Friday night and Saturday morning, attendance and demographic characteristics of attendees at each, and practices and rules related to participating in the service. The second set repeated these questions for services when a bar or bat mitzvah ritual was included, to help me understand what changed in the service and attendance, and what additional ritual elements were added (for example, passing the Torah through the generations). The third set concerned preparation for and results of the bar or bat mitzvah service. I asked questions about the nature of the preparation for the ritual, rabbis' goals for it, and issues that might come up during the service.

To ensure that the questions in all sets (both common and specific) were both clear and complete, I conducted pilot interviews with three rabbis—one in New Jersey, one in the Detroit area, and one in the Chicago area—each of whom critiqued the questions. In addition, Shawn Landres, then of Synagogue 3000, kindly offered comments and critiques on the questions.

I followed a similar process with the questions for education directors. In addition to the common questions about congregational culture and attitudes toward bar or bat mitzvah, I asked education directors two sets of questions. As responsibility for bar or bat mitzvah often spans the roles of rabbi and education director, one set of questions largely repeated those also asked of rabbis. The second set addressed the content of and attitudes toward the supplementary school program, covering issues of scheduling and curriculum, attendance requirements, and demographic characteristics of the religious school families. To understand attitudes toward the program, I also asked about priorities. For these questions, I asked the educator to speak for him- or herself and then to serve as a proxy for three other groups: parents, children, and congregants not involved in the school.

Depending on their size, congregations employ either administrators or executive directors. In either case, this is the person who is responsible for the administrative work of the congregation and is often the face of the congregation. I expected the individuals filling this role to serve as a proxy for the congregants, as well as providing basic demographic information. In fact, while all were able to do the latter, it was more difficult for them to serve as proxies for the congregation.

In some cases, this was due to personality and perception of role. In other cases, particularly when the congregation employed an executive director, other employees filled that role.

For both education directors and administrators, because many questions had already been vetted in the pilot interviews for the questions directed at rabbis and many others were matters of fact, I conducted only one pilot interview in each case.

Due to the location of many of the congregations, telephone interviews allowed for greatest participation; for consistency, all interviews were conducted by phone. The length of each interview was determined both by the nature of the questions and the constraints on the respondents' time. Typically interviews lasted one hour for rabbis, forty-five minutes for education directors, and half an hour for administrators. Rabbis are responsible for the greatest share of bar or bat mitzvah preparation and enactment, but their time is also the most constrained. Thus, while longer interviews would have allowed me to gather more information, they would also have reduced the number of rabbis willing to participate. Both questions and interviews were designed to balance the information acquired and the rate of participation.

FIVE REPRESENTATIVE CONGREGATIONS: OBSERVATIONS AND INTERVIEWS

The heart of this research depended on observing and interviewing people at five representative congregations. By choosing to observe five congregations, rather than becoming a participant observer in a single congregation, I traded more intimate and complete knowledge of one specific congregation for the ability to compare several congregations that differed in denomination and size. However, since my goal was describe the variety and breadth of practice, this was not a difficult decision to make. In fact, it was more difficult to limit the scope of my observations to only five congregations. Initially, I intended to include large and small congregations of representative denominations, which could have meant studying as many as eight congregations. When it became clear that this was not feasible, I chose four congregations of the most common size (200–500 families) and from largest denominational categories (Reform, Conservative, Orthodox, and independent), which enabled me to compare practices across denominations. In addition, I chose one very large Reform congregation as the effect of size is substantial, both in terms of numbers of students, the routinization of their treatment, and the effect on Shabbat services more generally. I reluctantly decided against observing a Renewal congregation and a small congregation, each of which would have added additional variation.

After eliminating congregations that were atypical due to unusual demographic characteristics (for example, congregations located in Berkeley, with its unusually high educational level) or conflicts, I spent some time attending services around the Bay Area and chose two or three congregations of each type from different locations in the Bay Area. In each case, I first contacted the rabbi to ask permission to observe and interview people. All five of my first choices agreed, although the process for getting permission varied. In three cases, the rabbi simply agreed and allowed me to contact others using his name; in two cases, the question of my participation was taken to congregational boards and approved by them. Approval, in all cases, did not ensure participation; rather, it meant that I could approach teachers, congregants, and bar or bat mitzvah students with approval from the leadership. In what follows, I first discuss my observations, then the distribution of interview participants, and then the interview questions.

At all congregations, I attended Shabbat morning services, some of which included bar or bat mitzvahs and some of which did not. I observed religious school classes and tutoring sessions. I interviewed tutors, teachers, congregants, and families. I collected bar or bat mitzvah handbooks, individual bar or bat mitzvah programs, and parent and student speeches. However, while all rabbis were willing have their congregations participate in the research, my access to observations and ability to find individuals in each category who were willing to be interviewed varied.

Anyone is welcome to attend any Shabbat service, so I could and did attend Shabbat services weekly, rotating through the congregations while taking account of when bar or bat mitzvah services took place. My ability to observe in classrooms depended on the willingness of both education directors and individual teachers.[7] Nevertheless, I was able to observe several times at each congregation (except for the Orthodox congregation, which does not have supplementary school). Both tutoring and d'var Torah meetings required the agreement of both teacher (rabbi, mentor, or tutor) and bar or bat mitzvah family and student. These were difficult to arrange, so there are substantially fewer observations of this type than of services or classrooms.

Despite these limitations, clear patterns emerged in the following areas. First, in all cases, I gained a good sense for the congregation's patterns of Shabbat service enactment with and without bar or bat mitzvah. Similarly, I was able to observe the different organization and culture at each religious school, as well as observing representative classes in the relevant grades (sixth and seventh). At both independent Or Hadash and large Reform Beth Jeshurun, I was able to see how theory and practice came together for both parents and children by observing family education programs. Finally, I observed similarities across denominations in how tutors communicated texts to students—as well as important differences at Beth Jeshurun—and differences in both approach and content regarding rabbis' approaches to the *divrei* Torah. Table 4 summarizes the number of these different observations, while Table 5 summarizes the types of interviewees.

There was a relatively high response rate for the leadership interviews. However, congregant interviews were far more difficult to accomplish, particularly with regard to bar or bat mitzvah families in some congregations. In retrospect, I realize that asking respondents why they chose to participate would have helped explain this, though not completely (people are famously bad at determining their own motives). Despite this lack, I can offer some possible explanations.

First, bar or bat mitzvah rituals are part of professional leaders' responsibilities. Rabbis and education directors, and tutors and some teachers, are invested in preparation for and enactment of the ritual, which would lead to greater interest in reflecting on the process and contributing to my understanding of it. In

TABLE 4.   Observations at Different Congregations, by Type of Observation

Name and denomination	Type of observation					
	Service without bar or bat mitzvah	Service with bar or bat mitzvah	Religious school	Tutoring	Speech	Total
Beth Jeshurun (large Reform)	3	6	6	3	2	20
Sukkat Shalom (Reform)	3	5	4	1	2	15
Or Hadash (Independent)	3	6	6	5	2	22
B'nai Aaron (Conservative)	5	4	4	2	0[a]	15
Adat Yitzhak (Orthodox)	5	4	2[b]	3	2	16
Total	19	25	22	14	8	88

NOTES: Each service, with or without bar or bat mitzvah, took five hours (approximately 9 A.M. to 2 P.M.). Tutoring observations averaged around an hour but varied from twenty minutes to an hour and a half. Religious school sessions lasted around three hours each and included two to three classes of different lengths. *D'var* Torah meetings varied from thirty minutes to more than an hour.

[a]This congregation used mentors from the congregation to develop the students' speeches. I was unable to find a mentor-student pair willing to be observed together.

[b]This congregation had no supplementary school program. However, as part of Shabbat programming, younger students sometimes attended an informal program concurrent with adult services supervised by a rabbinic intern.

TABLE 5. Interviews at Different Congregations, by Subject of Interview

Congregation name and denomination		Interview subjects						Bar or bat mitzvah students	Total
	Rabbis	Education directors	Administrators	Tutors or cantors	Teachers	Lay leaders and congregants	Parents		
Beth Jeshurun (large Reform)	3	3	1	2	2	3	10	5	29
Sukkat Shalom (Reform)	1	1	1	1	2	4	6	3	19
Or Hadash (Independent)	1	1	1	3	2	7	12	7	34
B'nai Aaron (Conservative)	2	1	1	1	1	2	8	5	21
Adat Yitzhak (Orthodox)	1	1[a]	1	1	0	4	12	6	26
Total	8	7	5	8	7	20	48	26	129

[a]This person was the director of a Jewish day school, as noted in the text.

contrast, bar or bat mitzvah affects families for a limited period of time, and they are responsible for only one event per child, rather than for maintaining the system of producing the rituals. This means that they are less invested in understanding the system at the same time that they are trying to navigate a difficult and (for many) new experience. It is not surprising that many chose not to add one more responsibility, particularly one that might have seemed to have little bearing on their lives—or, as one family explained to me, that would actually increase anxiety due to the additional stress of being observed.

There are other possible reasons for differences in participation: regional subcultures, congregational expectations of participation, locations, individual circumstances, or some combination of all of the above likely accounted for some of the differences. In addition, I believe the appeal of a respected leader and in-person appeals accounted for some of the difference. At independent Or Hadash, which had the highest participation rate, the rabbi strongly and actively supported the project. He introduced me and the project to the entire bar and bat mitzvah cohort and encouraged families to participate, as he circulated a sign-up sheet. In contrast, although Rabbi Doron, at Reform Sukkat Shalom, willingly agreed to support the project, he did not actively encourage people to sign up. At Sukkat Shalom, the education director, with substantially less authority than the rabbi, introduced me to the bar and bat mitzvah cohort. In this case, only a few families signed up.[8]

What characterizes those who did volunteer, and how do they differ from those who did not? First of all, in almost every case, the bar or bat mitzvah student was part of making the decision. Some of these students were extremely excited about being interviewed; others did so at their parents' behest. When the student initiated the interview, the reason seemed to be the desire to tell his or her story and reinforce the reality of the event. That is, in some way, the interview itself contributed to the significance of the ritual. This was true not only for students, but also for some parents who were eager to share their unique stories.[9] When parents initiated the interviews, they were more likely to want to make a contribution to the congregation, to the Jewish community, or both. Other parents used the opportunity to talk about difficult issues. In one case, three interviews resulted from one: as I interviewed one family, a friend walked in, became interested in participating, and also referred me to a third person. In other words, participation happened deliberately and by chance, and it occurred among those deeply engaged in Jewish life and those who were engaged for the moment. In all cases, I believe that the event had touched families enough that they wanted to continue thinking and talking about it. That is, this population is likely skewed to reflect the views of those who care about and were touched by the bar or bat mitzvah ritual and who were comfortable in an interview situation.[10]

Lay leader and congregant participation varied substantially from congregation to congregation. The two congregations with the strongest community participation and strongest rabbinic presence had a greater number of lay leaders and congregants participate than did the other congregations. In some congregations, lay leaders work with professional leaders to develop educational programs. Thus, I believed that interviewing these lay leaders would show how bar or bat mitzvah affected congregational life more generally. Congregants who attend services but have no children in bar or bat mitzvah programs provided still another view of the effect of bar or bat mitzvah services on the congregational service. In addition, each congregation's culture led to greater or lesser participation in the life of the congregation. For example, lay leaders do not participate in either religious school or service decisions at large Reform Beth Jeshurun; these are handled by the large professional staff. However, a monthly lay-led minyan takes place alongside the weekly bar or bat mitzvah services, and several minyan attendees agreed to be interviewed. This added to an understanding of their attitudes toward the congregation but shed little light on their views of bar or bat mitzvah. In contrast, at independent Or Hadash, with its culture of high lay participation and engagement, both lay leaders and congregants were willing to participate in my study and quite forthcoming. In fact, this congregation stands out for its unusually high level of participation.

Initially, I intended to interview both teachers and tutors: the former to understand the interaction between classroom and bar or bat mitzvah preparation; the latter to observe the tutoring process. However, my school observations made clear that, while the school does prepare students to begin bar or bat mitzvah training, teachers largely implement programs decided by the education directors, rabbis, and sometimes lay leaders. The few teacher interviews I conducted confirmed this: teachers are largely concerned with the details of teaching, irrespective of the subject matter. In contrast, bar or bat mitzvah training, both speech development and tutoring, is central to the ritual and the goals of the professional leadership. Thus, I made sure that I interviewed tutors (several, if possible) from each congregation to understand their goals, their methods, and the content of each lesson.

The interview questionnaires for the participants fell into three groups. Tutors, cantors, and teachers were grouped with other professional leaders and asked questions related to their roles as well as questions about bar or bat mitzvah and the congregational context. As with the education directors, they were asked to act as proxies for parents and students with regard to the content. These questions were developed to be similar to those asked of the education director, but they focused on each particular role.

Lay leaders, congregants, and parents were grouped together as nonprofessionals. These people share a voluntary approach to congregational life: each person can participate in the congregation to whatever degree they choose.[11] Congregants were asked about their current engagement with the congregation as well as questions about bar or bat mitzvah and the congregational context. Lay leaders answered the same questions, in addition to a brief set of questions regarding their specific role in the congregation. Parents answered the basic questions as well, with the addition of an extensive set of questions about their experience of their child's bar or bat mitzvah. This last set of questions regarding their training, preparation in the week before the event, and response to the day itself. For all these respondents, I posited a relationship between childhood experience of Judaism and bar or bat mitzvah and current Jewish practice and attitudes toward bar or bat mitzvah, so I also asked a set of questions regarding their childhood. While the answers were extremely interesting and worth exploring in their own right, the relationship between childhood and adult experience of Judaism and bar or bat mitzvah more specifically is, at best, indirect and complex. While I generated many of the questions asked of the professional leadership, I consulted previous studies of Jewish practice (Cohen and Eisen 2000; Berman Jewish DataBank n.d.) to ensure that I was asking the standard questions used in the Jewish community. I modified these questions to be general subject prompts (for example, I asked "What Jewish holidays do you observe?" rather than listing the holidays), so that the initial response would be from the respondents. Following that initial response, I asked about specific practices to confirm the answer.

The final category was, of course, the bar or bat mitzvah students themselves. The questions I asked them differed from those I asked other people, since I assumed that the students were engaged with the school and preparation and not with the larger congregational context. As was the case with their parents, I asked about their home and congregational Jewish engagement, including home practice, religious school experience, and other engagement in congregational and Jewish life. I continued with questions regarding bar or bat mitzvah preparation and their experience of the day itself, concluding with their expectations for future Jewish engagement. Much more than the adults, students varied in their ability and willingness to answer. Some were fully as articulate as any adult; others gave brief answers and had difficulty expanding on them. This is not surprising; while adults are familiar with interviews, few children are. In fact, I was more surprised at the number of students who answered the questions comfortably and completely.[12]

In addition to observations and interviews, congregations gave me their guide booklets for the bar or bat mitzvah process (as available), teachers provided worksheets from lessons that I observed, I collected bar or bat mitzvah service programs, and families provided me with copies of parent and student speeches. Of this content, both sets of speeches provided the most interesting and relevant data. Parent speeches provided a sense of how parents viewed the day and their role with regard to both Judaism and their child; student speeches showed the different ways rabbis viewed the speech and its relationship to Judaism.

FUTURE RESEARCH: INVESTIGATING THE MISSING PIECES

While the research generated a substantial quantity of data, that does not mean that all areas are covered equally, as I have alluded to above. Limitations fall into three categories.

First, simply due to finite time and resources, I set parameters that excluded areas that would have provided more information. These include what aspects of bar or bat mitzvah I studied and the region. Above, I explained the reasons I chose to study one region and this particular region. However, a comparison of different regions would provide a better understanding of specific practices and the ways the tensions discussed in this book manifest themselves differently in different regions. Anecdotal evidence suggests that there are regional differences in these practices (particularly with regard to parties, but also to students' levels of competence). Throughout the book, I have argued that the tensions are a constant, while the specific practices that result from negotiating them vary. This is the case even within the Bay Area; understanding the limits of that variation would contribute to understanding the range of Jewish practice and pluralism.

I also chose to limit my observations within each congregation to preparation for bar and bat mitzvah and to the Shabbat service (with and without bar or bat mitzvah ritual). This eliminated looking at the parties, which was no small benefit from my perspective. However, as my interviews with families made clear, parties are an integral part of the families' experience. Since I argue that part of the meaning for the family comes from the fact that it is a peak event, observing firsthand how the ritual and the celebration interact in the life of the family would have provided a more complete understanding of the whole ritual from the family's perspective.[13]

It was not until the research was almost complete that I realized the ubiquity of the mitzvah project, so I did not adequately observe this. I do not believe this omission changed the overall results, but the project adds a dimension to both the preparation for and the meaning of bar or bat mitzvah. These projects—in which the student does some kind of charity work—are both universal and without any consistency: some congregations structure the project, some do not; some consider them central to the student's preparation, some do not. Like the celebrations, they are not central to the ritual itself, but they are another way that participants—whether leaders or families—make meaning out of the ritual. More data on these programs would have helped show if and how they bridge the gap between the universal goal of "doing good" and the specific "Jewish commandment."

A final area excluded from the research concerned observing what happens in the years following the ritual. While I asked my interviewees about Jewish connections and practice following bar or bat mitzvah, this was not the focus of the research. As discussed in the last chapter of the book, congregations invest much time, resources, and energy in the bar or bat mitzvah, but comparatively little in the following period. While there is some research on students' engagement in Judaism in the years following bar or bat mitzvah (Kosmin and Keysar 2000; Keysar and Kosmin 2004), the role of the congregation in continuing to engage these students is not well understood.

Second, my initial proposal and eventual results diverged. Originally, I intended to examine how bar or bat mitzvah acted to unite or divide congregations—that is, to understand connection and community. Thus, my interview questions targeted these areas. This was one resulting tension, but it was overshadowed by the four discussed in the book. As a result, my questions on the tensions that did emerge were less thorough than I would have liked. Thus, there are areas—for example, the range of practice in the Orthodox bat mitzvah—that are less complete than ideal. Again, I do not believe this affects the overall conclusion with regard to tensions and the bar and bat mitzvah system, but the patterns discussed may not represent all forms of negotiation.

Third, the nature of the participation was not random. In particular, the Orthodox community in the Bay Area is very small, and many of the congregations rely on non-Orthodox Jews to survive. In regions with larger Orthodox communities that can be less pluralistic in approach, patterns of practice are likely to be different, and I can imagine the tensions themselves being less conspicuous (for example, the public-private tension may manifest itself quite differently).

As noted above, different groups were more or less motivated to respond. The families who were willing to be interviewed were those who were willing to commit an evening to talking about Jewish topics. While families varied in how engaged they were in Jewish life, all had some interest in and commitment to Judaism. I was not able to observe the truly disengaged: those families of legend who are unengaged in any form of Jewish life and who, following the bar or bat mitzvah, never again darken the synagogue doors. Understanding this group is important—programs like the Reform movement's B'nai Mitzvah Revolution, which set out to fix the bar or bat mitzvah, are largely designed to target these families—so the lack of data on it is significant and likely skews an understanding of the meaning of the ritual toward the perspective of leaders. To capture the disengaged group would require a different kind of research design: longitudinal observations one congregation over a period of several years. In this way, even those families who attended infrequently could be observed.

NOTES

CHAPTER 1 IT'S NOT DUDDY KRAVITZ'S BAR MITZVAH ANYMORE

1. A relatively recent example is the popular *Bar Mitzvah Disco* (Bennett, Shell, and Kroll 2005).

2. A poignant exploration of this is *Thirteen and a Day* (Oppenheimer 2005).

3. For example, McGinity (2014, 167–68) cites several Jewish men who found that their mid-twentieth-century bar mitzvah experiences made them feel more distant from Judaism and the Jewish community.

4. This section relies on Marcus (2005, 82–123) and Hilton (2014). In his first two chapters, Hilton traces history and myth, arguing (as does Marcus) that at each historical point, the ritual was connected to the past, giving it a legitimacy that it would otherwise lack.

5. This is a sweeping claim that ignores the differing contexts that affected Jewish leadership over time and across places. Nevertheless, the larger point regarding the tension between the laity and the leadership stands.

6. There is an extensive literature on both of these topics, some of which appears in the bibliography. A fuller discussion of both topics appears in chapter 6.

7. McGinity (2009) questions the accuracy of that perception, but whatever the reality, the perception existed and, to a large degree, continues to exist.

8. Hilton (2014, 267) points this out as well. The effect of bar or bat mitzvah on intermarried families in Reform congregations deserves more study: the 2013 Pew study on American Jews, *A Portrait of Jewish Americans* (Lugo et al.), shows that the percentage of children of Jewish-gentile marriages who identify as Jews increased following the Reform resolution, with consequences (including possible effects on bar and bat mitzvah) that have yet to be fully understood.

9. These changes also enable the congregation to host other events. However, bar and bat mitzvah celebrations are the most common.

10. Early afternoon (or *minhah*) services are less common, but—as discussed in chapter 6—they are one option for the Orthodox bat mitzvah. Another option that does not occur in bar or bat mitzvah rituals held in Bay Area congregations is the Havdalah bar or bat mitzvah. These services include an afternoon or evening service, then transition to Havdalah (the ceremony marking the end of Shabbat), after which the celebration begins. These are not uncommon in other regions of the United States or in independent bar or bat mitzvah preparation in the Bay Area. However, Bay Area congregational rabbis rejected this option, as discussed in chapter 2.

11. The bar or bat mitzvah speech usually follows the pattern for an adult *d'var* Torah, or commentary on the Torah portion. The relationship is discussed in chapter 2.

12. Some non-Orthodox rabbis noted that they would also add the *sheptarani* to the service if the family so requested. In a few interesting cases, rabbis reinterpreted the difficult language of the original blessing as a way for parents and children to understand the new roles as children become more self-sufficient teens.

13. There are, of course, other reasons for this blessing to be missing; however, most rabbis confirm that it simply has no meaning for families and eliminate it.

14. See the appendix for some discussion of this decision. The appendix contains a complete discussion of methodology, while details about the interviews themselves can be found online at: pmunro.net/main/coming-of-age.

15. As defined by the San Francisco Jewish Federation, which compiles information on Bay Area institutions, the Jewish Bay Area covers an area that extends north of San Francisco to Ukiah, south to Monterey, and east to Antioch. Though other boundaries could be chosen, this one has the advantage of common usage.

16. With around 1.5 million Jews, the New York City region has by far the largest Jewish population in the United States, followed by Los Angeles (519,000); Chicago (292,000); and Broward County, Florida (241,000).

17. In addition, I gathered instructional material, speeches, and website data.

18. The immediate question that follows is: what about very small congregations? Here, too, size offers possibilities and constraints. I was able to talk with several rabbis of very small congregations, and these interviews provided information on how small size affects the bar or bat mitzvah preparation and enactment. I determined that the benefits of adding an additional congregation to observe were outweighed by the disadvantages.

19. For recent examples, see Ammerman (2006), Baggett (2009), and Luhrmann (2012).

CHAPTER 2   DESCRIBING THE CONTEXT

1. This section relies on recent research on congregations, in particular that of Ammerman (2005) and Chaves (2005), but also that of Baggett (2009) and Cohen (2006).

2. For example, a community Shabbat dinner, which includes Shabbat blessings, teaches home worship skills while building communal religious practice.

3. There is an extensive literature on the development of the American synagogue throughout the twentieth century. In particular, this summary relies on Raphael (2011), Sarna (1986 and 2004), and Wertheimer (1987). Additional literature discusses each Jewish denomination's history. See, for example, Gurock (2009), Meyer (1988), and Wertheimer (2000). In addition, each denomination hosts a website that provides Jewish material from a denominational perspective. These primary sources include ALEPH: Alliance for Jewish Renewal (n.d.), Orthodox Union (n.d.), Union for Reform Judaism (2015a), and United Synagogue of Conservative Judaism (n.d.).

4. This is based on comparisons between synagogue and church websites (Munro and Nervik 2013). However, that work is based on comparisons with Protestant churches, most of whose members are nonimmigrant and white. Immigrant churches and black churches are more similar to synagogues in providing places of refuge (see, for example, Mora 2013; Pattillo-McCoy 1998).

5. A case can be made that the key elements of bar or bat mitzvah mirror those of the synagogue, replicating in time what synagogues do in space. The elements that define the space—identification with the Jewish people, linking present with past and future, and encouraging individual interpretation of central Jewish beliefs and practices—also define the ritual, as students learn Hebrew, make statements of connection to the past and future, and are encouraged to give voice to their individual interpretations of Jewish texts and values.

6. How Jewishness is determined is a matter of debate between and within denominations. I summarize the issues in chapter 6, but more complete analyses can be found in Fishman (2004), McGinity (2009), and Thompson (2014). Whatever the degree of inclusiveness, almost all synagogues expect that Jewish heritage, whether by birth or conversion, will constitute some part of membership.

7. While Reform, Conservative, and Modern Orthodox Judaism fit the normative definition of "denomination," Jews use the terms "denomination," "movement," and "branch" interchangeably, with the latter two most common. I use all three terms in this book.

8. To preserve confidentiality, I have changed the names of both congregations and individuals, as well as altering details that do not change the substance of the findings.

9. Alban's model of congregational size, modified to reflect the behavior I observed, was useful here. In this model, the effect of size creates four categories, with the members of each category behaving differently: the small congregation, in which lay leaders provide the parental stability for the family; the pastoral congregation, in which the religious leader focuses the efforts of the congregation; the program congregation, in which lay and professional leaders have and execute a common vision; and the corporate congregation, in which expert professional leaders make the decisions (Alban 2007). Four of the congregations in my study have aspects of the pastoral and program congregation; Beth Jeshurun is clearly a corporate congregation.

10. Larger congregations are likely to have larger bar or bat mitzvah cohorts, but this is not always the case: where demographic characteristics are changing, a congregation might be large but lack families with school-age children.

11. While the rise of postdenominational Judaism is a matter of ongoing research and debate, even nonaffiliated congregations define themselves in terms of denominations (Sales 2011).

12. The history, theology, and philosophy of both Modern Judaism and American Judaism are fields of study in themselves. However, Eisen (1998) provides an excellent summary of the underlying theological and philosophical issues that shaped the development of American Judaism.

13. The Bay Area includes congregations affiliated with the following three smaller denominations. First, Jewish Renewal, as its name implies, attempts to renew and universalize Jewish practice through nontraditional approaches, particularly mystical and meditative practices taken from Eastern religions. There are eight of these congregations in the Bay Area, several of which are fairly large (with around 400 members). Had time allowed, I would have included this type of congregation in the study. Second, Reconstructionist Judaism, based on the philosophy developed by Mordecai Kaplan, rejects the concept of being chosen, seeing Judaism primarily as a culture or civilization (Kaplan [1934] 1994). There are four of these congregations in the Bay Area, each of which has fewer than 150 members. Third, Humanist Judaism sees Judaism as a people, not a religion, and explicitly rejects the concept of a deity. There are three of these congregations in the Bay Area, each of which has fewer than 100 members.

14. Developing new volunteers is often difficult for congregations, and Sukkat Shalom is no exception. Longtime leaders worried that the younger generation was not stepping up to volunteer.

15. For a further discussion of when and why primary service times differ and the consequences that result, see chapter 7.

16. Congregations combine to offer weekly programs for students in eighth to twelfth grades. These programs draw students from many congregations and are housed in one of the participating congregations, but they are not administered through the congregations and were not part of my research.

17. While most congregations expect students to chant from the Torah, Rabbi Doron feels that the chanting inhibits an understanding of what the text means, so his students read, rather than chant, from the Torah.

18. The shares of Jews by denomination are as follows: Orthodox, 13 percent; Conservative, 26 percent; Reform, 34 percent; Reconstructionist, 2 percent; "just Jewish," 25 percent. The

rate of synagogue membership by denomination is as follows: Orthodox, 86 percent; Conservative, 61 percent; Reform, 47 percent; "just Jewish," 15 percent (Ament and Cohen 2010).

19. This excludes Chabad institutions, which do not fall within the parameters of this work because they are not structured as congregations, but as missionary organizations.

20. Men are bound by virtually all Jewish ritual commandments (mitzvahs), while there are only three that are specific to women. The reasoning for men's participation is as follows: because men are required to fulfill these commandments, while women are (arguably) allowed but not required to fulfill them, if a man is present when a woman fulfils a commandment that is not required of her, that action implies that the man is not able to do so. The effect is that women are not allowed to fulfill these commandments when men are present.

21. The relationship between Jewish day schools and congregations is interesting in and of itself. Day school students know about Judaism and have a better grasp of Judaism in some areas (less so in others) and are often less engaged with their age cohort, compared to supplementary school students. Thus, integrating these students into bar and bat mitzvah programs presents a challenge to congregations with some of each type of student.

22. This congregation was the only one where men were in the majority. The fact that men are obligated to perform religious observance while women are not presumably accounts for the difference.

23. In other words, while the congregational membership skews old, those who attend services are more balanced demographically.

24. This goal has not been borne out in practice. The type of relationship—close or distant—when the mentoring began typically remained the case when it was completed.

25. This quote summarizes language I found on the websites of several different independent Jewish congregations, all of which have similar philosophies.

26. Some of these rituals are incorporated into a service. For example, ceremonies welcoming new babies, such as circumcision (bris) for boys or baby naming for girls, often take place at home, but can also be added to the service. Marriage and death are acknowledged within a prayer service, but wedding ceremonies and funeral services are never part of such a service.

27. For example, every service includes a prayer about creation, but in the morning, this prayer praises the creation of light, while in the evening, it praises the nature of the universe that brings on the evening.

28. These sections are: morning blessings and poems of praise; prayers highlighting the Shema, Judaism's central prayer; prayers highlighting different aspects of individual and group relationships with God; reading the Torah and Haftarah portions; and concluding prayers (sometimes including the Musaf section).

29. This section relies on the siddurim of the different denominations and—in the case of Or Hadash—the original siddur developed by the congregation, under Rabbi Melmed's guidance. The prayer books include Frishman (2010), Hammer (2003), Harlow (1985), Leiber (2001), Sacks (2011), and Scherman and Zlotowitz (2003). In addition, works on the history and interpretation of the liturgy include Elbogen (1993), Hammer (1994), Idelsohn (1932), and Reif (1995).

30. In "Setting Boundaries, Building Bridges" (Munro 2012) I explored this topic, examining the different ways that Modern Orthodox and Reform prayer books interpret complex material to engage attendees and bridge the gap between American and Jewish values.

31. These different models are not unique to Judaism. Jerome Baggett (2009, 89–124) notes these different modes of engagement in Catholicism.

32. In 2007, the Union for Reform Judaism, representing the leadership of the Reform movement, put forward the Shabbat initiative, an attempt to move the primary Shabbat service to

Saturday morning. During my research, only a few Reform congregations were attempting to make the switch; most were continuing as before.

33. The Torah is also read on Mondays, Thursdays, Jewish holidays, and at the beginning of each month.

34. In a variation on this model, some congregations read the Torah in a triennial cycle, so that the first third of each portion is read in first year, and so on.

35. In the past few years, I have had reports of some congregations omitting the Haftarah as an expectation. This change speaks to the moving target nature of bar and bat mitzvah. While the ritual remains central, its content reflects responses to the larger tensions listed in chapter 1.

36. I have not found a good explanation for this increase, although one reasonable explanation is increased anxiety from both the laity and the leadership regarding diminishing Jewish practice and identity.

37. For example, most congregations expect students to recite the Shema.

38. These are social action or charity projects undertaken by students to broaden the scope of what it means to become an adult. All congregations in my study encouraged students to engage in some activity; however, in only a few cases were these projects discussed as part of the speech.

39. How rabbis connected with students—or even if they felt it was important to do so—varied. For example, while Rabbi Doron does not expect a lengthy speech, he puts most of his effort into ensuring that students are able to translate the text, as I discuss in chapter 5.

40. In two exceptional cases, birthdays fell near winter holidays, and the rituals were held on Thursdays, which enabled out-of-town guests to attend more easily.

CHAPTER 3 STUDENTS AND PARENTS, RABBIS AND TEACHERS

1. Lay leaders and other congregants also have a limited role, largely with regard to the tension between public service and private event, which is discussed in chapter 7.

2. See Crapanzano (1992, 219–82) for a discussion of circumcision in Morocco, in which the boys undergoing circumcision and their parents show very different reactions to the ritual, due to their different understandings of it. However, the lack of understanding on the part of the one who is changing roles or status is the norm: both marriage and coping with the death of a loved one are experiences that only begin with ritual.

3. Vern Bengston's work is particularly useful here in discussing changes over generations and proposing a model for transmission of religion across those generations (2013, 184–206, especially 193).

4. Some students resist learning the material, and some fight with parents and/or teachers throughout the preparation. However, only very rarely do students not attempt to rise to the occasion on the day itself.

5. For different discussions of the relationship between community and the initiated, see Crapanzano (1992), Gennep (1960), and Turner (1967).

6. Parents' role in their children's Jewish education is discussed at length in the chapters in Wertheimer 2007. In particular, Jeffrey Kress (2007) analyzes the different attitudes parents bring to their children's supplementary school education and the effect these attitudes have on their children.

7. Although both mainline churches and synagogues expect similar levels of financial support from their members, the method of collection is quite different: for synagogues, the financial commitment is a prerequisite of membership, which becomes a sore spot for many Jews.

8. The bar mitzvah bargain assumes that parents join congregations only when they must and leave immediately following their last child's bar or bat mitzvah. There is no doubt that some families leave immediately after their last child's bar or bat mitzvah, but as discussed in chapter 8, the causes are likely more complicated and less causal than commonly assumed.

9. Jewish day schools introduce another set of complications. Most Orthodox, some Conservative, and a few Reform families send children to these day schools. However, these schools also have a substantial proportion of unaffiliated families (many of whom are Israeli and may be secular Jews). The relationship between these families, whose primary affiliation is to the school, and the congregation creates problems of connection for the community, a subject well worth further study.

10. This is less the case for students who attend Jewish day schools.

11. This issue continues to grow in importance in the Jewish community. In particular, the Ruderman Family Foundation, established in 2008, is a nondenominational, international foundation that works to "advance the full inclusion of people with disabilities into society" (Ruderman Family Foundation 2014).

12. For example, it can result in a disrupted classroom and/or an ostracized student. It can also result in the rest of the class working with the student cooperatively. In either case, it requires negotiation by adults to manage the issues.

13. While this is less the case for the Orthodox congregations, as noted in the previous chapter, these congregations are small, so that even in neighborhoods within walking distance of Orthodox synagogues, most residents are non-Jews.

14. This is a reference to Feinstein (2003).

15. This issue is discussed in greater depth in chapter 5.

16. This problem is, of course, mitigated by Jewish day school; however, most of the children in my study were not enrolled in these schools.

17. There is a wealth of online material that supports the fact that this is a common cultural trope. The four benefits listed in the text are taken from "The Benefits of Playing Sports Aren't Just Physical!" (2012), a blog from the American Orthopaedic Society for Sports Medicine.

18. This is the case for the American Jewish community as a whole, as shown by General Social Survey data (GSS: General Social Survey n.d.), the Pew study on American Jews (Lugo et al. 2013), and the congregational work of both Nancy Ammerman (2005) and Mark Chaves (2005).

19. Ironically, these activities also affect the ritual, as examples related to sports, school, and friends make their way into the students' bar or bat mitzvah speeches.

20. Sylvia Fishman (2001) discusses this pattern, in which the primary parent, usually the woman, sets the standard for family religious practice.

21. No parent admitted to joining for the sake of the bar or bat mitzvah ritual.

22. My findings contradicted this attitude, at least in part. As this book describes, the teachers and rabbis at the congregations I observed had developed thoughtful and intentional programs (and those observations were supported by my interviews with the larger sample of participants). Parents, too, commented on the knowledge their children had gained beyond rote skills.

23. The two quotes describing the B'nai Mitzvah Revolution were taken from the mission statement on the organization's website (http://www.bnaimitzvahrevolution.org/) on November 27, 2013. That section has been replaced with a mission statement that reads: "The B'nai Mitzvah Revolution is a network of congregational professionals, lay leaders and educational thought leaders seeking to bring renewed depth and meaning to Jewish learning."

24. My interview questions addressed congregational context. The role of the rabbi in mediating conflict and establishing Jewish priorities was made clear throughout. This finding is supported by Becker (1999) and Swidler (2010).

25. Eliminating Saturday afternoon bar or bat mitzvah rituals, discussed in the previous chapter, is a good example of the kind of decisions rabbis can enact, albeit not without some effort.

26. Following seventh grade, students are expected, albeit with wide variation in follow-through, to continue with community or congregational Jewish high-school programs. When supplementary schools end following seventh grade, it reinforces the idea that bar or bat mitzvah is a graduation. As a result, a few congregations extend religious school through eighth grade in an attempt to decouple the bar or bat mitzvah ritual from religious school.

27. Confirmation still exists as an additional moment in Jewish education.

CHAPTER 4 VARIATIONS ON A THEME

1. This example is a composite, drawn from several rabbis' interviews and presented this way to protect both rabbis and students.

2. For the sake of readability, I refer to the ritual as taking place at age thirteen. However, bat mitzvah at age thirteen is a relatively recent change, resulting from the egalitarian Judaism that developed in the late twentieth century. The earlier custom, which is still observed in Orthodox practice and in some Conservative congregations, designates twelve as the age that girls become bat mitzvah.

3. These commandments include universal strictures (using fair weights and measures, for example) as well as particularistic ones (refraining from consuming leavened products on Passover, for example).

4. Orthodox and some Conservative synagogues conduct daily community services for which a minyan—ten Jewish adult men (and women, in Conservative practice)—are needed. When boys (and girls, in Conservative practice) become bar mitzvah, they can help make up a minyan. This is the most obvious communal change. Adult Jews are expected to fast on Yom Kippur; only some of the students indicated that they would do so.

5. While the cliché "today I am a man," with its implication that bar or bat mitzvah confers full adulthood, is still heard in bad jokes, neither the students nor their parents understood it that way. Rather, they understood it as symbolically marking the beginning of growing up or as taking on Jewish adult responsibilities. This is not coincidental: rabbis of all denominations almost reflexively made this point during interviews with me, while the number of students who, like Shoshana, echoed their words shows the effort leaders have made to change this stereotype.

6. I have no doubt that this sample is skewed toward a somewhat higher degree of Jewish identity than a random sample would obtain (should such a sample be possible). Though a number of families declined to participate due to privacy concerns or time constraints, others simply did not respond. It is not unreasonable to assume that lack of response is roughly correlated to lack of interest.

7. The strict gender roles in Orthodox Judaism result in distinct differences in how these congregations negotiate egalitarian norms with Jewish gender roles, including differences between bar and bat mitzvah. This subject is discussed in detail in chapter 6.

8. The differences between boys and girls in behavior are the focus of extensive research in the sociology of gender and education, including gender as a constructed category, differences in the way teachers treat girls and boys in classrooms, and language. Bar and bat mitzvah

students and their teachers, like all Americans, swim in that particular cultural sea. In both my observations and interviews, gender's role was similar—or even identical—to its role in American culture more generally.

9. A few rabbis did note differences, but these seemed to be idiosyncratic, as with the Orthodox rabbi who declared with certainty that boys were better scholars. His comment was not echoed by any other rabbis.

10. These moments are much more common in contemporary-style congregations; the traditional-style service has fewer options for additions, and its perspective assumes Jewish identity.

11. This preparation also results in bar and bat mitzvah more closely matching Arnold van Gennep's description of a rite of passage (1960).

12. Marc Chaves separately (1994) and with Philip Gorski (2001) addresses the changes in the way Americans think about ultimate authority of God and religious authority. The difference in the way liberal and Orthodox rabbis refer to God and God's authority exemplify these changes.

13. The fact that synagogues are financed through congregants' paying a yearly pledge (or dues) that can run into several thousand dollars leads to the common perception that synagogues are unwilling to challenge families for fear of losing their monetary contributions. While this deserves a more detailed exploration, preliminary information indicates that families with school-age children in religious schools are often subsidized by older members.

14. The exceptions were a very few Orthodox congregations. However, the stringency of the requirement varied, as did the type of project and level of work required by the student or family.

15. Both Isaac Levitats (1949, 153) and Stuart Schoenfeld (1993, 70) give twentieth-century examples, while Michael Hilton (2014) discusses historical background and regulation.

16. See the appendix for details about the interview questions. These results were based on two questions parents answered. The first asked them to state how strongly they agreed that bar or bat mitzvah had a series of meanings. The second asked them to state what the ritual meant to them.

17. Rabbis may contribute to this during the service by welcoming guests to a bar or bat mitzvah, as opposed to a service, or elevating the student's contribution to the service. The tension between public service and private event is significant enough to warrant its own chapter, and a full discussion of the issue can be found in chapter 7.

18. Thirty-five respondents (parents and congregants) felt strongly that bar or bat mitzvah was "a time to celebrate the child and build his or her self-esteem," compared to twenty-three who felt that it was "a chance to have a big and exciting party." (Respondents could rank each possibility separately, so the sum is greater than the number of respondents.)

19. The word translated here as "responsibility" literally means "punishment." In the Bay Area, this blessing was regularly recited in Orthodox congregations. However, Hilton (2014, xii), writing from a liberal British perspective, also found it regularly recited.

20. Historically, this blessing was recited by fathers for sons. In the twenty-first century, it is most commonly recited in Orthodox congregations, where gender distinctions still largely apply. However, in those cases where it is being reinterpreted as discussed above, it can be recited in a more egalitarian manner.

21. I am not implying a direct connection between the blessing and the speeches: liberal Judaism in general has rejected this blessing as uncomfortably harsh (although, as with other traditional practices, it is being reinterpreted and reclaimed in a few congregations). I simply note that both blessing and speech publicly mark the change in family relationships that is taking place.

22. Most Orthodox congregations allow few, if any, interruptions to the regular service, and parental speeches can be considered an interruption.

23. This is comparable to Arnold Eisen's discussion of how Passover's theme of freedom from slavery has been linked to the American value of freedom (1998).

CHAPTER 5   WHAT IF I DROP THE TORAH?

1. This is a phrase that has made its way into Jewish life in the past few years.

2. How individuals—whether children or adults—acquire the cultural tools to become member of a group underlies much of sociology. For this chapter, however, the work of Peter Berger and Thomas Luckmann (1966) provides a general frame for different modes of interacting with social reality, while both Sarah Benor (2012) and Tanya Lurhmann (2012) show the process of acquiring culture (whether language and dress or learning to pray).

3. Some unaffiliated families work with independent tutors from beginning to end, choosing not to affiliate with a congregation. I interviewed one of these tutors to better understand this situation, but these cases do not fall within the parameters of this project.

4. Here, "reading Hebrew" means having the ability to sound out letters to make words—that is, to decode the language—and, ideally, know enough grammar and vocabulary to recognize a few words and roots.

5. Many synagogues develop checklists or other means for testing students' abilities. Though this was the case at Or Hadash, the information often came late—or parents understood its import only when bar or bat mitzvah tutoring was imminent.

6. When I asked education directors to state their overall goals for their schools, their answers fell into these three categories. The question came up indirectly in my interviews of families but had similar results. Riv-Ellen Prell (2007) found similar results in interviewing parents in Philadelphia.

7. While most families in Orthodox congregations, many in Conservative congregations, and a few in Reform congregations send their children to Jewish day schools, these schools serve regions, rather than individual congregations, and so are not part of this study. However, they affect congregations and congregants in two ways. First, because of the high day-school attendance, few Orthodox congregations offer supplementary Jewish education. This places the few students who do not attend day school at a distinct disadvantage. Second, some congregations (especially Conservative ones) have a large percentage of students who attend day school. Integrating these students and their families into congregational culture becomes a serious problem for these congregations. A few students whose families belong to congregations may be taught individually from beginning to end. This model occurs in congregations with few bar or bat mitzvah students, which therefore cannot support a school. In these cases, the rabbi worked individually with each student for around two years, with no clear transition from basic Jewish education to bar or bat mitzvah preparation.

8. Religious school is commonly called Hebrew school, indicating the place of the language in Judaism, as well as the difficulty in learning it.

9. Day schools have the same subject matter, although they teach it in greater depth. For example, the website for Oakland Hebrew Day School (n.d.) lists the subject areas for each grade as Hebrew, Jewish life (holidays and home practice), text study, prayer, Middot (ethics), and Am Yisrael (Israel as a people and place).

10. The *Journal of Jewish Education* is dedicated to the topic. Also see Flexner et al. (2008), Goodman, Flexner, and Bloomberg (2008), Kelman (1992), and Wertheimer (2007).

11. For example, see Weber (1996).

12. Though Vatican II's embrace of the vernacular made Catholicism more accessible, it also decreased—for some—the sacred (meaning extraordinary) sense of worship that Latin enabled, as Jerome Baggett discusses (2009).

13. The ratio of liturgy- to conversation-based programs speaks to congregational priorities.

14. I am emphasizing the structure here because of the emphasis on acquiring these skills. However, classrooms and hallways often have Hebrew posters, which can include liturgical vocabulary, values, or modern Hebrew vocabulary. These experiential elements confirm that the synagogue is a Jewish space, but they do not necessarily contribute to the knowledge of Hebrew.

15. This individualization is discussed further in chapter 7.

16. An experiment at Or Hadash, in which students learned together, was not even the norm there; it was simply an option.

17. About 80 percent of the time, rabbis worked with students. In the other 20 percent of the time students worked with mentors from the congregation or parents or in group classes. Here, I focus only on the normative pattern of rabbis working with students.

18. The structure of the adult *d'var* Torah and how that is modified for a bar or bat mitzvah speech is discussed in chapter 2.

19. The place of Cohanim within Judaism varies by denomination, with Orthodox Judaism both acknowledging and observing the distinction.

20. See chapter 2 for a fuller discussion of the differences in approach between Orthodox and liberal Judaism.

21. The First Temple, destroyed in 586 B.C.E.

22. Unlike many congregations (including both Adat Yitzhak and Or Hadash), Beth Jeshurun has no additional fees for tutoring, which is integrated into the bar and bat mitzvah program. The education director explained with some pride: "The majority of our students never get an outside tutor . . . and we don't charge an extra b'nai mitzvah fee. So obviously there is a philosophical statement there."

23. In this case, in fact, Judith had the capability to learn far more than was expected of her, but the short lesson did not give her enough time to use those skills.

24. The family's guests, whether they have roles on the bimah or are simply attendees, can also interrupt the service through lack of knowledge—that is, through failures of etiquette. This subject is discussed in chapter 7.

25. This implies that the leaders themselves are competent. A rabbi who is not can do great damage to the ritual and the students. Due to my research design, that problem only entered this project peripherally: two parents described unpleasant incidents with rabbis at their own bar mitzvah services. Nevertheless, I would be remiss if I let the assumption of rabbinic competence stand.

26. When Torah is read, it is customary for someone to stand by to assist or correct as needed, as explained below. Correcting Adam's mistakes could be considered simply a usual part of reading from the Torah.

27. Leaders often make the point that the service leader is not performing but leading a congregation (hence, clapping is inappropriate). Yet there is a performance aspect to leading: the same leaders comment on enjoying services where they can simply be congregants, rather than leaders. In fact, the use of "performance" to mean "rote recitation" seems to result from the history of the ritual as described in chapter 1. Since the beginning of the twentieth century, leaders have worked to infuse preparation for and the ritual itself with meaning, so that—as this book describes—the ritual performance often reflects deep preparation. Yet the word "performance" remains tainted.

28. For example, one rabbi described waiting on tenterhooks until a seriously ill student's fever subsided just a day before the event.

29. This was the only student I interviewed who used her own case as an example of an unsuccessful ritual.

30. In some other congregations, corrections to the Torah reading were unremarkable, a usual part of the Torah reading, and students would expect some level of correction.

31. In some congregations, others read from the Torah as well (this was particularly the case in Conservative and Orthodox congregations). That subject is discussed in chapter 7.

CHAPTER 6   WHAT ARE *THEY* DOING ON THE BIMAH?

1. In all denominations, individuals can convert to Judaism, although which conversions are valid is also a matter of debate.

2. This fundamental issue underlies much of sociological theory: Georg Simmel (1996) and Max Weber (1996) address the general topic, and more recently Fredrick Barth (1996) and David Schneider (1996) have added to this understanding. Within the sociology of religion, Rodney Stark and Roger Finke (2000) examine how American congregations address this issue.

3. The literature on gender in Judaism is extensive. It includes seminal works that define issues in Judaism such as B. Greenberg (1981), Plaskow (1991), and Adler (1998), as well as works on historical contrasts and the situating of Jewish gender roles such as Boyarin (1993 and 1997). The roles of women in Judaism fit into a more general consideration of gender in the religious context as discussed in, for example, Davidman (1991), Gallagher (2003) and Mahmood (2005), which show how complicated a role gender plays in Jewish, Christian, and Muslim religious contexts.

4. One common approach argues for an essentialist view of Jewish men and women, each with separate but equal spheres of influence and power; for example, see Aiken (1992). A more complete view of different approaches to women in the synagogue can be found in Grossman and Haut (1992).

5. Both G. Tobin (1990) and G. Tobin and Simon (1999) discuss rabbis' approaches to intermarriage. This subject is very much a moving target, with attitudes shifting toward inclusivity.

6. See, for example, Cohen 1994; Cohen and Eisen 2000; Goldscheider 1986; Mayer 1982 and 1985; Phillips 1998.

7. See, for example, Fishman 2004; Fishman and Parmer 2008; McGinity 2009 and 2014; Phillips 2010; Thompson 2014.

8. This seems to be the case nationally as well (see Kotler-Berkowitz 2013).

9. See the Methodological Appendix for comparative details.

10. This boundary was marked only in the public venue of the synagogue. In families' home observance, it was routinely ignored, with non-Jewish mothers often taking the role of the Jewish mother, which included performing Jewish rituals as needed.

11. The Orthodox congregation made no special arrangements for intermarriage because the issue comes up so rarely there.

12. Unlike Aziza, she was not angry about her childhood experiences, but simply uninterested in religion.

13. In the Conservative and Orthodox movements, children like Emily are most often formally converted at birth.

14. Though Mitsuke's growing interest was typical of the families I interviewed, other anecdotal evidence indicates that this is not always the case: non-Jewish mothers, in particular, can feel put upon and resentful of the added responsibilities. Unfortunately, the nature of my research design meant that these families were unlikely to participate; however, it is an area well worth studying.

15. In fact, many Bay Area congregations do not ask directly when families join if any members are not Jewish. As a result, when I asked administrators what percent of their congregation was intermarried, some could not answer with any precision. Both rabbis and education directors need—and get—this information, but it is often not formally public knowledge.

16. For example, in one case, a non-Jewish father had not understood that the tallit was reserved for Jews. Since he donned one at his son's bar mitzvah, several congregants later asked when he had converted.

17. Barbara Vinick and Shulamit Reinharz (2012) provide anecdotal accounts of bar mitzvahs in different times and places that add depth to an understanding of the ritual.

18. Other forms of Orthodoxy can have higher dividers that prevent communication or place women in the rear or in balconies. The intent here is as much symbolic as actual.

19. I do not want to leave the impression that people of either gender accepted these distinctions uncritically. Many of the Orthodox women I spoke with, both informally at lunches and more formally in interviews, worked in the secular world, where they expected egalitarian treatment. Some had become more observant under the influence of both the congregation and the rabbi and were conflicted about the role of women; others had chosen to give up a more active practice of Jewish prayer to participate more fully in the cultural life of the congregation. In either case, these women worked hard to reconcile the egalitarian and the gendered parts of their lives.

20. This orientation speaks to the gendered expectations in the Orthodox community.

21. This is in line with the findings in Stark and Finke (2000).

22. In the latter case, rabbis work hard to ensure that children of Jewish fathers are formally converted at an early age to avoid questions near bar or bat mitzvah age.

CHAPTER 7   WHOSE BIMAH IS IT, ANYWAY?

1. Without exception, families described their guests to me as "friends and relatives." They generally used a patient, but slightly incredulous tone, as if to say: "Who else would we invite?"

2. Yoffie's sermon implies that the missing community results from the private bar or bat mitzvah service. Friday night became the primary service in the United States because of work patterns of Jews in the early to mid-1900s; both leaders and the laity mentioned competing activities to me as a reason for maintaining this pattern.

3. Conservative and Orthodox congregations share the problem of balancing the two different goals of a single service, but their approaches are somewhat different. Conservative congregations are more likely to have large bar or bat mitzvah cohorts, which result in many Shabbat mornings being affected by the ritual. Orthodox congregations have smaller cohorts but are more constrained by rabbis' interpretations of Jewish law. The resulting tension is similar, however, and so I discuss the two denominations together.

4. There are a number of blessings that can be recited during the Torah service to mark many different life-cycle events. I was interested in how rabbis thought about them in comparison to bar or bat mitzvah—was that ritual viewed as more important (or more private) than other life-cycle events? Most rabbis would include another life-cycle moment in the bar or bat mitzvah service. A few would not, giving priority to the bar or bat mitzvah. A few said they would want to give each event its due and would try to separate them for that reason.

5. For example, Sukkat Shalom was preparing for a cohort of forty students. Though both rabbi and education director discussed the pressure on staff that would result from needing to prepare twice as many students as usual, neither discussed the effect that twice as many bar or bat mitzvah rituals would have on the small group of regular weekly attendees.

6. Families in my study regularly compared their experiences to those they had observed at other congregations both in the Bay Area and elsewhere.

7. My discussion here draws on interviews with rabbis at all participating congregations, as well as observations and interviews at Conservative B'nai Aaron and Orthodox Adat Yitzhak.

8. Jerome Baggett (2009) makes a similar point in his analysis of the different modes of worship in Catholic parishes.

9. On this point, see also Tavory (2013).

10. A rabbi who cannot communicate well, for whatever reason, can have the opposite effect. The role of the rabbi as a leader is one that deserves substantially more study.

11. The only time I was not greeted at Adat Yitzhak was at a service during which an *aufruf* (a brief pre-wedding blessing of the couple) took place. Many attendees were clearly wedding guests, and it seemed that the regulars thought I was, too. This incident points out the difference between a service with guests of an individual family and one with no particular reason for guests, meaning that a visitor is likely there simply to worship. In the former case, guests are treated as the family's responsibility; in the latter case, they become the congregation's collective responsibility.

12. Monsey is an ultra-Orthodox enclave in New York State.

13. Adat Yitzhak is one of several congregations across the denominational spectrum that expects substantial work on the speeches. At Conservative Am Hayim, the rabbi's *d'var* Torah is replaced by a much shorter speech. According to Rabbi Weinberg, students "usually sum up the Torah portion in a paragraph, and then they raise a question or make a point—they make it personal."

14. However, despite this attempt to preserve the service, two of the congregants I interviewed said they avoided the bar and bat mitzvah services.

15. Nevertheless, there was a certain freedom: at one bar mitzvah, a group of musical friends called the boy to the Torah using the traditional melody, but in barbershop quartet style.

16. These include Shacharit (the section of prayer beginning the formal service), at least two *aliyot*, and some of the Torah chanting.

17. This is another topic worth studying: the variation in topic, leadership, approach to the material, attendees, and their attitudes toward Judaism all would shed light on how and by whom these sacred texts are interpreted, as well as the meaning they have for those attending.

18. This is an unusually high attendance for this pattern, but it fits with the individual culture of this congregation. More commonly there are 10–50 attendees.

19. In addition, once a month there is a so-called tot Shabbat service for families with small children, so that on some Saturday mornings, three different services—each with a different constituency—may take place at the same time.

20. Although Rabbi Segal was most concerned with the fact that students who learn the afternoon service will not use it (it is not commonly held in Reform congregations), other rabbis were concerned that these services led directly into the celebration, resulting in the service and celebration being conflated.

21. This is one of two common patterns. The other, enacted at Beth Jeshurun, is to have two concurrent bar or bat mitzvah services.

22. In addition, this is an interesting way for the students to display competence. They manage the discussions, first repeating the question, then responding to it. Rabbi Melmed stands by ready to intervene if necessary—sometimes to correct a misstatement or add to student's response, but (most commonly) to reassure or assist a student who needs support.

23. At the time this research was conducted, the few independent minyans (small groups largely coalescing around services) had no children's education programs or bar or bat mitzvah services and hence fell outside the parameters of the study.

24. See chapter 2 for a discussion of how size affects congregational dynamics.

25. To be fair, while most congregations are small, it is true that most people belong to large congregations (Chaves 2005): the number of bar and bat mitzvah services at Beth Jeshurun is close to the combined total at the other four observed congregations.

26. I developed these definitions based on observations of the effect of numbers of events on the Shabbat morning service and degree of service individualization. However, the categories could be divided further when considering cohort cohesion: three students do not make a community, but ten do. From the other direction, a cohort of thirty-five can remain a single group, while it is likely that a cohort of eighty will be split into more than one group.

27. The size of the bar and bat mitzvah cohort in each congregation also varied from year to year. Thus, a small congregation might have three students one year and twelve the next. However, unless the typical number increases, the feel of the training is likely to remain individualized. That is, the approach to the cohort lags a few years behind the change in numbers.

28. This topic was discussed briefly in chapter 5.

29. This is similar to the role that African chiefs play in constituting the tribe, as Ann Swidler (2010) discusses.

30. At the same time, though rabbis are congregational leaders, congregations also hire and fire rabbis. Thus, rabbis whose views diverge too much from the congregational practice or culture can create irresolvable conflict. At two congregations in my sample, interviewees described high levels of conflict between congregants and rabbi and, while there is no direct causal evidence, those rabbis are no longer at their respective congregations.

31. As it happened, eliminating the booklets did not affect the service at all, as both large cohort size and a culture of Friday night attendance were more important factors in determining who attended the bar and bat mitzvah services: primarily students' families and their guests.

CHAPTER 8   A VERY NARROW BRIDGE

1. And yes, there is only one answer to that question.

2. Despite the incredible variety of questions, bar and bat mitzvah are missing from the list of topics—a remarkable lack.

3. The overall project was to examine the process of Jewish learning. Bar or bat mitzvah entered the book implicitly, but was only referred to directly a few times in the different chapters. In one quote (Kress 2007, 149), a parent spoke of the value of bar and bat mitzvah; in another (ibid., 152), a father assumes a negative experience like his own. The book provides useful context and complementary material with regard to education, but cannot answer the question directly.

4. Kosmin and Keysar's longitudinal study of Conservative-affiliated students who became bar or bat mitzvah in 1994 provides data on changes in students' attitudes and observance patterns following bar or bat mitzvah through high school and college. However, the work is limited, since the authors looked only at Conservative students who have had bar or bat mitzvah services. Further, the authors can establish only correlation between many of the practices, stating that it is not possible to determine causality from their data.

5. Thus, it is more likely that the circle at the small Renewal congregation represents ongoing relationships, while the one at Beth Jeshurun represents one of the symbolic meanings of the ritual.

6. While some congregations ask students to sign contracts promising to continue in one program or another following bar or bat mitzvah, in fact they have no means by which to enforce attendance.

7. While a causal relationship would be difficult to demonstrate, the logic of realistic conflict theory underlies both this program and the one at Or Hadash (Sherif et al. [1961] 1988) and makes that argument plausible.

METHODOLOGICAL APPENDIX

1. My calculations show a higher affiliation rate of 29 percent in the Bay Area, but see below for caveats.

2. My method is as follows. I used Gellman 2008 to generate a list of congregations and information listed about them in the guide, minimally including denomination, address, phone, e-mail address, and (usually) website. I determined the number of families and individuals in each congregation by asking administrators of responding congregations. Overall, this resulted in family sizes of about 2.5 individuals (higher for Orthodox; lower for some other denominations). This is lower than the number in Ament and Cohen (2010). However, it still results in a higher percentage of affiliated families than in Kotler-Berkowitz (2013). While there are several possible reasons for these discrepancies (including optimistic reporting from administrators), for my purposes, the rough numbers suffice.

3. Comparing two or more regions across denominations is simply too large a project and was never considered.

4. The University of California, Berkeley, encourages undergraduates to participate in ongoing research through the Undergraduate Research Apprentice Program. Under the guidance of Claude S. Fischer, I supervised David Reder, Alina Goldenberg, and Kate Morar in gathering website data and assisting in developing interview questionnaires. In 2011–2012, Berman Foundation Dissertation Fellowships in Support of Research in the Social Scientific Study of the Contemporary American Jewish Community provided funding for three research assistants, Kendra Nervik, Cora Tobin, and Crissy Chung, who transcribed the resulting interviews and assisted in coding.

5. One is listed in table 3. In that case, I interviewed the principal of the religious day school to get an Orthodox educator's perspective on bar or bat mitzvah.

6. Interview schedules appear on my website (pmunro.net/main/coming-of-age).

7. For example, on one occasion, I faced an angry teacher who had not been notified by her education director that I would be observing her.

8. During my interviews with lay leaders at Sukkat Shalom, it became clear that there was some conflict between parents and the education director with regard to preparation for the ritual. In the year following my observation, her contract was not renewed. Thus, the fact that she was the person who introduced me might have reduced participation.

9. The variety was truly remarkable.

10. I don't mean to say that bar or bat mitzvah mattered less to those who did not participate— I have no evidence for that—only that in some way, it mattered to those who participated.

11. This sense of choosing when and how to volunteer could also apply to tutors and teachers, most of whom worked only a few hours each week. However, teachers and tutors are paid, which likely creates a different type of relationship with the congregation and the work itself.

12. While I did not formally request demographic information regarding age and economic status, in almost every case, occupation and education emerged during the interviews. That information, along with observation of location of homes, places most of these families in high income brackets, where the "concerted cultivation" approach to child rearing (Lareau 2003, 1–2) would result in this type of interaction.

13. I will note that in my roles as congregant, family member, and bar or bat mitzvah tutor, I have attended more of these events than I can count, so I believe I have a general understanding of these celebrations. Nevertheless, that does not substitute for observations at the five representative congregations.

REFERENCES

Adler, Rachel. 1998. *Engendering Judaism: An Inclusive Theology and Ethics.* Philadelphia: Jewish Publication Society.

Aiken, Lisa. 1992. *To Be a Jewish Woman.* Northvale, NJ: J. Aronson.

Alban. 2007. "Searching for the Key: Developing a Theory of Synagogue Size." January 24. Accessed August 12, 2015. https://alban.org/archive/searching-for-the-key-developing-a-theory-of-synagogue-size/.

ALEPH: Alliance for Jewish Renewal. n.d. Home page. Accessed October 1, 2015. https://www.aleph.org/.

Ament, Johnathon, and Steven M. Cohen. 2010. "2010 U.S. Religion Census: Religious Congregations & Membership Study: Appendix H: Jewish Groups." Accessed October 4, 2015. http://www.rcms2010.org/images/2010_US_Religion_Census_Appendix_H.pdf.

Ammerman, Nancy Tatom. 2005. *Pillars of Faith: American Congregations and Their Partners.* Berkeley: University of California Press.

———. 2006. *Everyday Religion: Observing Modern Religious Lives.* New York: Oxford University Press.

Aron, Isa. 2010. "Supplementary Schooling and the Law of Unanticipated Consequences: A Review Essay of Stuart Schoenfeld's 'Folk Judaism, Elite Judaism and the Role of Bar Mitzvah in the Development of the Synagogue and Jewish School in America.'" *Journal of Jewish Education* 76 (4): 315–33.

Association of Statisticians of American Religious Bodies. 2012. "U.S. Religion Census 1952 to 2010." Accessed October 1, 2015. http://www.rcms2010.org/.

Baggett, Jerome. 2009. *Sense of the Faithful: How American Catholics Live Their Faith.* New York: Oxford University Press.

Barth, Fredrick. 1996. "Ethnic Groups and Boundaries" (1969). In *Theories of Ethnicity: A Classical Reader,* edited by Werner Sollors, 294–324. New York: New York University Press.

Bayme, Steven, Dru Greenwood, and Joel A. Block. 1998. "Intermarriage: Three Views." In *A Portrait of the American Jewish Community,* edited by Norman Linzer, David J. Schnall, and Jerome A. Chanes, 139–64. Westport, CT: Praeger.

Becker, Penny Edgell. 1999. *Congregations in Conflict: Cultural Models of Local Religious Life.* Cambridge: Cambridge University Press.

Behrman House. n.d. *2015–16 Catalog.* Accessed August 15, 2015. http://www.behrmanhouse.com/magazine.html.

Bell, Catherine. 1992. *Ritual Theory, Ritual Practice.* New York: Oxford University Press.

———. 2009. *Ritual: Perspectives and Dimensions.* Rev. ed. New York: Oxford University Press.

Bellah, Robert, Richard Madsen, William M. Sullivan, Ann Swidler, and Steven M. Tipton. 1996. *Habits of the Heart: Individualism and Commitment in American Life.* Updated paperback edition with new introduction. Berkeley: University of California Press.

Bengston, Vern. 2013. *Families and Faith: How Religion Is Passed Down across Generations.* New York: Oxford University Press.

Bennett, Roger, Jules Shell, and Nick Kroll. 2005. *Bar Mitzvah Disco: The Music May Have Stopped, but the Party's Never Over.* New York: Crown.

Benor, Sarah Bunin. 2012. *Becoming Frum: How Newcomers Learn the Language and Culture of Orthodox Judaism.* New Brunswick, NJ: Rutgers University Press.

Berger, Peter L. 1967. *The Sacred Canopy: Elements of a Sociological Theory of Religion.* Garden City, NY: Doubleday.

———and Thomas Luckmann. 1966. *The Social Construction of Reality: A Treatise in the Sociology of Knowledge.* London: Penguin.

Berkeley Midrasha. n.d. Home page. Accessed May 8, 2015. http://www.midrasha.org/.

Berman Jewish DataBank. n.d. Home page. Accessed October 10, 2015. http://jewishdatabank .org.

Blank, Deborah. 1996. "Jewish Rites of Adolescence." In *Lifecycles in Jewish and Christian Worship,* edited by Paul Bradshaw and Lawrence Hoffman, 81–110. South Bend, IN: University of Notre Dame Press.

B'nai Mitzvah Revolution. n.d. "About Us." Accessed October 1, 2015. http://www .bnaimitzvahrevolution.org/about-us.

Boyarin, Daniel. 1993. *Carnal Israel: Reading Sex in Talmudic Culture.* Berkeley: University of California Press.

———. 1997. *Unheroic Conduct: The Rise of Heterosexuality and the Invention of the Jewish Man.* Berkeley: University of California Press.

Canby, Vincent. 1974. "Screen: Dreams Rampant in 'Apprenticeship of Duddy Kravitz.'" *New York Times,* July 15. Accessed February 2, 2015. http://www.nytimes.com/books/97/12/ 21/home/richler-screen.html.

Casanova, Jose. 1994. *Public Religions in the Modern World.* Chicago: University of Chicago Press.

Central Conference of American Rabbis. 1983. "Resolution Addopted by the CCAR: The Status of Children of Mixed Marriages." March 15. Accessed October 1, 2015. http://ccarnet .org/rabbis-speak/resolutions/1983/status-of-children-of-mixed-marriages-1983/.

———. 2004. "A Statement of Principles for Reform Judaism." October 27. Accessed August 12, 2015. https://ccarnet.org/rabbis-speak/platforms/statement-principles-reform-judaism/.

Chaves, Marc. 1994. "Secularization as Declining Religious Authority." *Social Forces* 73 (2): 749–74.

———. 2005. *Congregations in America.* Cambridge, MA: Harvard University Press.

———and Philip Gorski. 2001. "Religious Pluralism and Religious Participation." *Annual Review of Sociology* 27:261–81.

Chertok, Fern, Benjamin Phillips, and Leonard Saxe. 2008. *It's Not Just Who Stands under the Chuppah: Intermarriage and Engagement.* Waltham, MA: Steinhardt Social Research Institute, Brandeis University.

Cohen, Steven M. 1992. "The Marginally Affiliated." In *What We Know about Jewish Education: a Handbook of Today's Research for Tomorrow's Jewish Education,* edited by Stuart Kelman, 115–27. Los Angeles, CA: Torah Aura Productions.

———. 1994. "Why Intermarriage May Not Threaten Jewish Continuity." *Moment,* December, 54–57, 89, 95.

———. 2006. "S3K Report: Members and Motives: Who Joins American Jewish Congregations and Why." *Synagogue Studies Institute.* Accessed October 1, 2015. http:// synagoguestudies.org/s3k-report-members-and-motives.

———and Arnold M. Eisen. 2000. *The Jew Within: Self, Family, and Community in America.* Bloomington: Indiana University Press.

Congregation Sherith Israel. n.d. "Religious School Pre-K–6." Accessed August 15, 2015. https://www.sherithisrael.org/education/youth/religious-school-pre-k-6.

Congregation Sinai—San Jose. n.d. "Standards for Shlichei Tzibbur, Torah & Haftarah Chanters, and Gabbaim." May 1. Accessed May 1, 2015. https://sinai-sj.org/be-a-service-leader-reader/service-leader-standards.

Crapanzano, Vincente. 1992. *Hermes' Dilemma and Hamlet's Desire: On the Epistemology of Interpretation.* Cambridge, MA: Harvard University Press.

Davidman, Lynn. 1991. *Tradition in a Rootless World: Women Turn to Orthodox Judaism.* Berkeley: University of California Press.

Davis, Judith. 1995. "The Bar Mitzvah 'Balabusta': Mother's Role in the Family's Rite of Passage." In *Active Voices: Women in Jewish Culture,* edited by Maurie Sacks, 125–41. Urbana: University of Illinois Press.

Durkheim, Emile. [1912] 1995. *The Elementary Forms of Religious Life.* New York: Free Press.

Eisen, Arnold. 1983. *The Chosen People in America: A Study in Jewish Religious Ideology.* Bloomington: Indiana University Press.

———. 1998. *Rethinking Modern Judaism: Ritual, Commandment, and Community.* Chicago: University of Chicago Press.

Elbogen, Ismar. 1993. *Jewish Liturgy: A Comprehensive History.* Philadelphia: Jewish Publication Society.

Ellman, Bart. 2004. "Defining Community: Bar/Bat Mitzvah Ritual in American Reform and Conservative Synagogues as an Expression of Community Identity Values." *Conservative Judaism* 56 (2): 32–46.

Feinstein, Edward. 2003. *Tough Questions Jews Ask: A Young Person's Guide to Building a Jewish Life.* Woodstock, VT: Jewish Lights.

Fischer, Claude S. 2010. *Made in America: A Social History of American Culture and Character.* Chicago: University of Chicago Press.

Fishbane, Simcha. 1995a. "Contemporary Bar Mitzvah Rituals in Modern Orthodoxy." In *Ritual and Ethnic Identity: A Comparative Study of the Social Meaning of Liturgical Ritual in Synagogues,* edited by Jack Lightstone and Frederick Bird, 155–68. Waterloo, ON: Wilfrid Laurier University Press.

———. 1995b. "A Female Rite of Passage in a Montreal Modern Orthodox Synagogue: The Bat Mitzvah Ceremony." In *Renewing Our Days: Montreal Jews in the Twentieth Century,* edited by Ira Robinson and Mervin Butosvsky. Montreal: Vehicule.

Fishman, Sylvia Barack. 2000. *Jewish Life and American Culture.* Albany: State University of New York Press.

———. 2001. "Women's Transformations of Public Judaism: Religiosity, Egalitarianism, and the Symbolic Power of Changing Gender Roles." In *Who Owns Judaism? Public Religion and Private Faith in America and Israel,* edited by Eli Lederhendler, 131–55. New York: Oxford University Press.

———. 2004. *Double or Nothing? Jewish Families and Mixed Marriage.* Waltham, MA: Brandeis University Press.

———and Daniel Parmer. 2008. *Martrilineal Ascent/Patrilineal Descent: The Gender Imbalance in American Jewish Life.* Waltham, MA: Brandeis Unversity Press.

Frishman, Elyse. 2010. *Mishkan T'filah: A Reform Siddur.* New York: Central Conference of American Rabbis.

Gallagher, Sally K. 2003. *Evangelical Identity and Gendered Family Life.* New Brunswick, NJ: Rutgers University Press.

Gans, Herbert J. 1979. "Symbolic Ethnicity: The Future of Ethnic Groups and Cultures in America." *Ethnic and Racial Studies* 2 (1): 1–20.

Geertz, Clifford. 1973. *The Interpretation of Culture.* New York: Basic.

Gellman, Steve. 2008. *Resource: A Guide to Jewish Life in the Bay Area.* San Francisco: San Francisco Jewish Community Publications.

Giddens, Anthony. 1991. *Modernity and Self-Identity: Self and Society in the Late Modern Age.* Stanford, CA: Stanford University Press.

Goffman, Erving. 1978. *Presentation of Self in Everyday Life.* New York: Woodstock/Overlook Press.

———. 1982. *Interaction Rituals.* New York: Pantheon.

Goldscheider, Calvin. 1986. *The American Jewish Community: Social Science Research and Policy Implications.* Atlanta, GA: Scholars.

Goodman, Roberta Louis, Paul A. Flexner, and Linda Dale Bloomberg. 2008. *What We Now Know about Jewish Education: Perspectives on Research for Practice.* Los Angeles: Torah Aura Productions.

Goodstein, Laurie. 2013. "Bar Mitzvahs Get New Look to Build Faith." *New York Times,* September 3. Accessed August 14, 2015. http://www.nytimes.com/2013/09/04/us/bar-mitzvahs-get-new-look-to-build-faith.html?adxnnl=1&pagewanted=all&adxnnlx=1378742425-wGD3mpRj6mzUXg47HraUjQ.

Graff, Gil. 2008. *"And You Shall Teach Them Diligently": A Concise History of Jewish Education in the United States 1776–2000.* New York: Jewish Theological Seminary of America.

Greenberg, Blu. 1981. *On Women & Judaism: A View from Tradition.* Philadelphia: Jewish Publication Society.

Greenberg, Steve. 2001. "Between Intermarriage and Conversion: Finding a Middle Way." *Spirit and Story.* Accessed June 13, 2013. http://www.clal.org/ss43.html.

Grossman, Susan, and Rivka Haut. 1992. *Daughters of the King: Women and the Synagogue.* Philadephia: Jewish Publication Society.

GSS: General Social Survey. n.d. Home page. NORC at the University of Chicago. Accessed October 1, 2015. http://www3.norc.org/GSS+Website/.

Gurock, Jeffrey S. 2009. *Orthodox Jews in America.* Bloomington: Indiana University Press.

Hadaway, C. Kirk. 2011. *Facts on Growth: 2010.* Hartford, CT: Hartford Institute for Religion Research. Accessed October 1, 2015. http://faithcommunitiestoday.org/sites/faithcommunitiestoday.org/files/FACTs%20on%20Growth%202010.pdf.

Hammer, Reuven. 1994. *Entering Jewish Prayer: A Guide to Personal Devotion and the Worship Service.* New York: Schocken.

———. 2003. *Or Hadash: A Commentary on Siddur Sim Shalom.* New York: Rabbinical Assembly, United Synagogue of Conservative Judaism.

Harlow, Jules, ed. and trans. 1985. *Siddur Sim Shalom: A Prayerbook for Shabbat, Festivals, and Weekdays.* New York: Rabbinical Assembly, United Synagogue of America.

Hilton, Michael. 2014. *Bar Mitzvah: A History.* Philadelphia: Jewish Publication Society.

Hyman, Paula E. 1995. *Gender and Assimiliation in Modern Jewish History: The Roles and Representation of Women.* Seattle: University of Washington Press.

———. 2002. "Gender and the Shaping of Modern Jewish Identities." *Jewish Social Studies* 8 (2–3): 153–61.

Idelsohn, Abraham Zebi. 1932. *Jewish Liturgy and Its Development.* New York: H. Holt.

Israel, Richard J. 1993. *The Kosher Pig: And Other Curiosities of Modern Jewish Life.* Los Angeles: Alef Design Group.

Jewish Reconstructionist Communities in Association with the Reconstructionist Rabbinical College. n.d. Home page. Accessed October 1, 2015. http://www.jewishrecon.org/.

Jewish Resource Guide. 2015. *Resource: A Guide to Jewish Life in the San Francisco Bay Area.* Accessed August 17, 2015. www.jewishresourceguide.com.

Jewish Survey Question Bank. n.d. Home page. Accessed October 5, 2015. http://jewishquestions.bjpa.org/Questions/topic.cfm.

Joseph, Norma Baumel. 2002. "Ritual, Law, and Praxis: An American Response/a to Bat Mitsva Celebrations." *Modern Judaism* 22 (3): 234–60.

Kahn, Ava F., and Marc Dollinger, eds. 2003. *California Jews*. Waltham, MA: Brandeis University Press.

Kahn, Rabbi Stephen. 2002. "For Officiating at Intermarriages: The Voice of Zipporah." September 16. Accessed October 14, 2013. http://www.interfaithfamily.com/news_and_opinion/synagogues_and_the_jewish_community/For_Officiating_at_Intermarriages_The_Voice_of_Zipporah.shtml.

Kaplan, Mordecai. [1934] 1994. *Judaism as a Civilization*. Philadelphia: Jewish Publication Society.

Karp, Abraham J. 1998. *Jewish Continuity in America: Creative Survival in a Free Society*. Tuscaloosa: University of Alabama Press.

Kaufman, Debra R. 1991. *Rachel's Daughters: Newly Orthodox Jewish Women*. New Brunswick, NJ: Rutgers University Press.

Kelman, Stuart, ed. 1992. *What We Know about Jewish Education: A Handbook of Today's Research for Tomorrow's Educators*. Los Angeles: Torah Aura Productions.

Keysar, Ariela, and Barry A. Kosmin. 2004. *"Eight Up" The College Years: The Jewish Engagement of Young Adults Raised in Conservative Synagogues 1995–2003*. New York: Jewish Theological Seminary.

Kosmin, Barry A. 1999. "Coming of Age in the Conservative Synagogue: The Bar Mitzvah Class of 5755." In *Jews in the Center: Conservative Synagogues and Their Members*, edited by Jack Wertheimer, 232–68. New Brunswick, NJ: Rutgers University Press.

———and Ariela Keysar. 2000. *"Four Up": The High School Years, 1995–1999: The Jewish Identity Development of the B'nai Mitzvah class of 5755*. New York: Jewish Theological Seminary.

———. 2013. *Religious, Spiritual, and Secular: The Emergence of Three Distinct Worldviews among American College Students*. Hartford, CT: Trinity College.

Kotler-Berkowitz, Laurence. 2013. *Comparisons of Jewish Communities: A Compendium of Tables and Bar Charts*. Storrs, CT: Berman Institute.

Kress, Jeffrey S. 2007. "Expectations, Perceptions, and Preconceptions: How Jewish Parents Talk about 'Supplementary' Religious Education." In *Family Matters: Jewish Education in an Age of Choice*, edited by Jack Wertheimer, 143–80. Waltham, MA: Brandeis University Press.

Lareau, Annette. 2003. *Unequal Childhoods: Class, Race, and Family Life*. Berkeley: University of California Press.

Leiber, David, ed. 2001. *Etz Hayim: Torah and Commentary*. Translated by the Jewish Publication Society. New York: Rabbinical Assembly, United Synagogue of Conservative Judaism.

Lev, Tsafi. 2011. "Delaying Bar Mitzvah Till Age 25." MyJewishLearning. November 8. Accessed August 14, 2015. http://www.myjewishlearning.com/blog/rabbis-without-borders/2011/11/08/delaying-bar-mitzvah-till-age-25/.

Levitats, Isaac. 1949. "Communal Regulation of Bar Mitzvah." *Jewish Social Studies* 11 (2): 153–62.

Levitt, Laura, and Miriam Peskowitz. 1996. *Judaism since Gender*. New York: Routledge.

Lewit, Jane, and Ellen Epstein. 1991. *The B'nai Mitzvah Planbook*. Chelsea, MI: Scarborough House.

Liebman, Charles S. 1973. *The Ambivalent American Jew: Politics, Religion, and Family in American Jewish life*. Philadelphia: Jewish Publication Society of America.

Lugo, Luis, et al. 2013. *A Portrait of Jewish Americans: Findings from a Pew Research Center Survey of U.S. Jews.* Washington: Pew Research Center. October 1. Accessed December 15, 2013. http://www.pewforum.org/files/2013/10/jewish-american-full-report-for-web .pdf.

Luhrmann, Tanya Marie. 2012. *When God Talks Back: Understanding the American Evangelical Relationship with God.* New York: Alfred A. Knopf.

Mahmood, Saba. 2005. *Politics of Piety: Islamic Revival and the Feminist Subject.* Princeton, NJ: Princeton University Press.

Marcus, Ivan G. 1996. *Rituals of Childhood: Jewish Acculturation in Medieval Europe.* New Haven, CT: Yale University Press.

———. 2005. *The Jewish Life Cycle: Rites of Passage from Biblical to Modern Times.* Seattle: University of Washington Press.

Mayer, Egon. 1982. *Children of Intermarriage: A Study in Patterns of Identification and Family Life.* New York: American Jewish Committee, Institute of Human Relations.

———. 1985. *Love and Tradition: Marriage between Jews and Christians.* New York: Schocken.

McClain, Ellen Jaffe. 1995. *Embracing the Stranger: Intermarriage and the Future of the American Jewish Community.* New York: Basic.

McGinity, Keren R. 2009. *Still Jewish: A History of Women and Intermarriage in America.* New York: New York University Press.

———. 2014. *Marrying Out: Jewish Men, Intermarriage, and Fatherhood.* Bloomington: Indiana University Press.

Medding, Peter Y., Gary A. Tobin, Sylvia Barack Fishman, and Mordecai Rimor. 1992. "Jewish Identity in Conversionary and Mixed Marriages." In *American Jewish Yearbook 1992*, edited by David Singer, 3–76. Philadephia: Jewish Publication Society.

Meyer, Michael A. 1988. *Response to Modernity: A History of the Reform Movement in Judaism.* New York: Oxford University Press.

Mora, Christina. 2013. "Religion and the Organizational Context of Immigrant Civic Engagement: Mexican Catholicism in the USA." *Ethnic and Racial Studies* 36 (11): 1647–65.

Munro, Patricia. 2012. "Setting Boundaries, Building Bridges: Liturgy as Interpretation." Paper presented at the annual meeting of the American Society for the Study of Religion, Phoenix, AZ, November 10.

———, and Kendra Nervik. 2013. "Places of Refuge; Places of Renewal: Meaning and Content in Jewish and Protestant Congregational Websites." Roundtable discussion at the annual meeting of the American Sociological Association, New York, August 11.

Oakland Hebrew Day School. n.d. "Grades 1–5." Accessed October 1, 2015. http://www .ohds.org/our-school/grades-1-5/.

Oppenheimer, Mark. 2005. *Thirteen and a Day: The Bar and Bat Mitzvah across America.* New York: Farrar, Strauss and Giroux.

Orthodox Union. 2015. Home page. Accessed October 1, 2015. https://www.ou.org/.

Pattillo-McCoy, Mary. 1998. "Black Church Culture as a Community Strategy of Action." *American Sociological Review* 63 (6): 767–84.

Philips, Benjamin T., and Sylvia Barack Fishman. 2006. "Ethnic Capital and Intermarriage: A Case Study of American Jews." *Sociology of Religion* 67 (4): 487–505.

Phillips, Bruce A. 1998. "Children of Intermarriage: How 'Jewish'?" In *Coping with Life and Death: Jewish Families in the Twentieth Century*, edited by Peter Y. Medding, 81–127. New York: Oxford University Press.

———. 2010. "Splitting the Difference and Moving Forward with the Research." *Contemporary Jewry* 30 (2–3): 257–61.

———. 2011. "A Demographer Considers the Twenty-First Century." *CCAR Journal, spring.* Accessed August 15, 2015. http://www.ccarnet.org/media/filer_public/2011/11/08/demographerconsiders.pdf.

Plaskow, Judith. 1991. *Standing Again at Sinai: Judaism from a Feminist Perspective.* New York: HarperOne.

Prell, Riv-Ellen. 1989. *Prayer and Community: The Havurah in American Judaism.* Detroit, MI: Wayne State University Press.

———. 2007. "Family Formation, Educational Choice, and American Jewish Identity." In *Family Matters: Jewish Education in an Age of Choice*, edited by Jack Wertheimer, 3–33. Waltham, MA: Brandeis University Press.

Putnam, Robert. 2010. *American Grace: How Religion Divides and Unites Us.* New York: Simon and Schuster.

Raphael, Marc Lee. 2011. *The Synagogue in America: A Short History.* New York: New York University Press.

Reif, Stefan C. 1995. *Judaism and Hebrew Prayer: New Perspectives on Jewish Liturgical History.* Cambridge: Cambridge University Press.

Reimer, Joseph. 2007. "Beyond More Jews Doing Jewish: Clarifying the Goals of Informal Jewish Education." *Journal of Jewish Education* 73 (1): 5–23.

Roof, Wade Clark. 1993. *A Generation of Seekers: The Spiritual Journeys of the Baby Boom Generation.* San Francisco: HarperSanFrancisco.

———. 1999. *Spiritual Marketplace: Baby Boomers and the Remaking of American Religion.* Princeton, NJ: Princeton University Press.

Ross, Tamar. 2004. *Expanding the Palace of Torah: Orthodoxy and Feminism.* Waltham, MA: Brandeis University Press.

Ruderman Family Foundation. 2014. Home page. Accessed July 8, 2015. http://www.rudermanfoundation.org/.

Sacks, Jonathan, trans. 2011. *The Koren Siddur.* Jerusalem, IL: Koren.

Sales, Amy L. 2007. *Lessons from Mapping Jewish Education.* Waltham, MA: Fisher-Bernstein Institute for Jewish Philanthropy and Leadership, Brandeis University.

———. 2009. "Future of the Synagogue." *CCAR Journal* 56 (4): 116–24.

———, Nicole Samuel, Annette Koren, and Michelle Shain. 2010. "Deep Change in Congregational Education." *Journal of Jewish Education* 76 (4): 358–78.

———. 2011. "Future of the Denominations: Analysis and Possibilities." *Reform Jewish Quarterly* 88 (2): 36–48.

———. 2012. "Reinventing Jewish Education for the 21st Century." *Journal of Jewish Education* 78 (3): 182–226.

———, Nicole Samuel, and Alexander Zablotsky. 2011. *Engaging Jewish Teens: A Study of New York Teens, Parents, and Practitioners.* Waltham MA: Maurice and Marilyn Cohen Center for Modern Jewish Studies, Brandeis University.

Salkin, Jeffrey K. 1996. *Putting God on the Guest List: How to Reclaim the Spiritual Meaning of Your Child's Bar or Bat Mitzvah.* Woodstock, VT: Jewish Lights.

Sarna, Jonathan, ed. 1986. *American Jewish Experience.* Teaneck, NJ: Holmes and Meier.

———. 1998. "American Jewish Education in Historical Perspective." *Journal of Jewish Education* 64 (1–2): 8–21.

———. 2004. *American Judaism: A History.* New Haven, CT: Yale University Press.

Saxe, Leonard, Elizabeth Tighe, Benjamin Phillips, and Charles Kadushin. 2007. "Reconsidering the Size and Characteristics of the American Jewish Population: New Estimates of a Larger and More Diverse Community." Waltham, MA: Steinhardt Social Research Institute, Brandeis University.

Schachter, Lifsa. 2010. "Why Bonnie and Ronnie Can't 'Read' (the Siddur)." *Journal of Jewish Education* 76 (1): 74–91.

Schein, Jeffrey, and Susan Wyner. 1996. "Mediating the Tensions of 'Bar/Bat Mitzvah': The Cleveland Experience." *Journal of Jewish Communal Service* 72 (2): 163–70.

Scherman, Nosson, and Meir Zlotowitz, editors. 2003. *The Complete ArtScroll Siddur: Weekday/Sabbath/Festival: A New Translation and Anthologized Commentary*. Brooklyn, NY: Mesorah.

Schneider, David M. 1996. "Kinship, Nationality, and Religion in American Culture: Toward a Definition of Kinship." In *Theories of Ethnicity: A Classical Reader*, edited by Werner Sollors, 282–93. New York: New York University Press.

Schoem, David. 1992. "The Supplementary School." In *What We Know about Jewish Education*, edited by Stuart Kelman, 163–68. Los Angeles: Torah Aura Productions.

Schoenfeld, Stuart. 1986. "Theoretical Approaches to the Study of Bar and Bat Mitzvah." In *Proceedings of the Ninth World Congress of Jewish Studies*, 119–26. Jerusalem: World Union of Jewish Studies.

———. 1987. "Folk Judaism, Elite Judaism, and the Role of Bar Mitzvah in the Development of the Synagogue and Jewish School in America." *Contemporary Jewry* 9 (1): 67–85.

———. 1990. "Some Aspects of the Social Significance of Bar-Bat Mitzvah Celebrations." In *Essays in the Social Scientific Study of Judaism and Jewish Society*, edited by Simcha Fishbane, Jack N. Lightstone, and Victor Levin, 277–304. Montreal: Department of Religion, Concordia University.

———. 2010. "Too Much Bar and Not Enough Mitzvah? A Proposed Research Agenda on Bar/Bat Mitzvah." *Journal of Jewish Education* 76 (4):301–14.

Sherif, Muzafer, O. J. Harvey, B. Jack White, William R. White, and Carolyn W. Sherif. [1961] 1988. *The Robbers Cave Experiment: Intergroup Conflict and Cooperation*. Middletown, CT: Wesleyan University Press.

Simmel, Georg. 1996. "The Web of Group Affiliations" (1908). In *Theories of Ethnicity: A Classical Reader*, edited by Werner Sollors, 37–51. New York: New York University Press.

Sklare, Marshall. 1964. "Intermarriage and the Jewish Future." *Commentary* 37 (4): 46–51.

———. 1993. *Observing America's Jews*. Edited and with a foreword by Jonathan D. Sarna. Afterword by Charles S. Liebman. Hanover, NH: University Press of New England.

Smith, Christian. 2003a. "Theorizing Religious Effects among American Adolescents." *Journal for the Scientific Study of Religion* 42 (1): 17–30.

———. 2003b. "Religious Participation and Network Closure among American Adolescents." *Journal for the Scientific Study of Religion* 42 (2): 259–67.

Spickard, Paul A. 1992. "The Changing Status of Children of Jewish Intermarriage in the United States." In *Jewish Assimilation, Acculturation, and Accommodation: Past Traditions, Current Issues, and Future Prospects*, edited by Menachem Mor, 191–203. Lanham, MD: University Press of America.

Stark, Rodney, and Roger Finke. 2000. *Acts of Faith: Explaining the Human Side of Religion*. Berkeley: University of California Press.

Stern, Rachel. 2013. "Bully on the Bimah: Bar Mitzvah, No Matter What?" MyJewishLearning. November 6. Accessed August 14, 2015. http://www.myjewishlearning.com/blog/southern-and-jewish/2013/11/06/bully-on-the-bimah-bar-mitzvah-no-matter-what/.

Swidler, Ann. 1986. "Culture in Action: Symbols and Strategies." *American Sociological Review* 51 (2): 273–86.

———. 2010. "The Return of the Sacred: What African Chiefs Teach Us about Secularization." *Sociology of Religion* 71 (2): 157–71.

Tavory, Iddo. 2013. "The Private Life of Public Ritual: Interaction, Sociality, and Codification in a Jewish Orthodox Congregation." *Qualitative Sociology* 36 (2): 125–39.

Thompson, Jennifer A. 2014. *Jewish on Their Own Terms: How Intermarried Couples are Changing American Judaism.* New Brunswick, NJ: Rutgers University Press.

Tobin, Gary A. 1990. "Structural Change, Jewish Identity, and Interfaith Marriages of American Jews." *Conservative Judaism* 43 (1): 3–11.

———, and Katherine G. Simon. 1999. *Rabbis Talk about Intermarriage.* San Francisco: Institute for Jewish and Community Research.

Tobin, Joseph J., David Y. H. Wu, and Dana H. Davidson. 1989. *Preschool in Three Cultures: Japan, China, and the United States.* New Haven, CT: Yale University Press.

Trager, Karen. 1996. *Hebrew through Prayer 1.* West Orange, NJ: Behrman House.

Turetsky, Yehuda, and Chaim I. Waxman. 2011. "Sliding to the Left? Contemporary American Modern Orthodoxy." *Modern Judaism* 31 (2): 119–41.

Turner, Victor. 1967. *The Forest of Symbols: Aspects of Ndembu Ritual.* Ithaca, NY: Cornell University Press.

Union for Reform Judaism. 2015a. Home page. Accessed October 1, 2015. http://urj.org/.

———. 2015b. "The Shabbat Initiative." Accessed August 16, 2015. http://urj.org/cong/holidays/shabbat/.

United Synagogue of Conservative Judaism. 2015. Home page. Accessed October 1, 2015. http://www.uscj.org/.

Van Gennep, Arnold. 1960. *The Rites of Passage.* Translated by Monika B. Vizedom and Gabrielle L. Caffee. Introduction by Solon T. Kimball. Chicago: University of Chicago Press.

Vinick, Barbara, and Shulamit Reinharz. 2012. *Today I Am a Woman: Stories of Bat Mitzvah around the World.* Indianapolis: Indiana University Press.

Wasserman, Michael. 2012. "The New Middle Ground: A Challenge to Conservative Judaism." *Conservative Judaism* 63 (3): 3–13.

Waters, Mary. 1990. *Ethnic Options: Choosing Identities in America.* Berkeley: University of California Press.

Waxman, Chaim I. 1994. "Religious and Ethnic Patterns of American Jewish Baby Boomers." *Journal for the Scientific Study of Religion* 33 (1): 74–80.

———. 2010. "Beyond Distancing: Jewish Identity, Identification, and America's Young Jews." *Contemporary Jewry* (30):227–32.

Weber, Max. 1996. "Ethnic Groups" (1922). In *Theories of Ethnicity: A Classical Reader,* edited by Werner Sollors, 52–66. New York: New York University Press.

Weiner, Julie. 2014. "After Lull, Intermarriage Debate Reignites." Jewish Telegraphic Agency, January 28. Accessed January 29, 2014. http://www.jta.org/2014/01/28/news-opinion/united-states/after-lull-intermarriage-debate-reignites.

Wertheimer, Jack, ed. 1987. *The American Synagogue: A Sanctuary Transformed.* New York: Cambridge University Press.

———. 2000. *Jews in the Center: Conservative Synagogues and Their Members.* New Brunswick, NJ: Rutgers University Press.

———. 2007. *Family Matters: Jewish Education in an Age of Choice.* Waltham, MA: Brandeis University Press.

Wuthnow, Robert. 1988. *The Restructuring of American Religion: Society and Faith since World War II*. Princeton, NJ: Princeton University Press.

———. 2005. *America and the Challenges of Religious Diversity*. Princeton, NJ: Princeton University Press.

———. 2007. *After the Baby Boomers: How Twenty- and Thirty-Somethings Are Shaping the Future of American Religion*. Princeton, NJ: Princeton University Press.

Yoffie, Eric. 1999. "Realizing God's Promise: Reform Judaism in the 21st Century." Sermon delivered at the 65th Union of American Hebrew Congregations Biennial Convention, Orlando, FL, December 15. Accessed August 11, 2015. http://urj.org/about/union/leadership/yoffie/archive/ysermon/.

———. 2007. "Sermon by Rabbi Eric H. Yoffie at the San Diego Biennial, December 15, 2007." Union for Reform Judaism. December 15. Accessed August 15, 2015. http://urj.org//about/union/leadership/yoffie//?syspage=article&item_id=6079.

INDEX

Abrams, David (Or Hadash), 73–74

Adat Yitzhak (Orthodox), 22–23; bar or bat mitzvah, 23, 34–35, 60–61, 68, 70–72, 85–87, 91–92, 95, 132–133, 191n13; beliefs and practices, 22–23, 63, 191n11; education programs, 23, 54; gender roles, 117–121; intermarriage, 107, 112–113; lay leadership, 23; membership, 22–23; participation in study, 171–172, 191n7; services, 23, 127–128, 142–143; staff, 23. *See also* Modern Orthodox Judaism; Orthodox Judaism; Teitelbaum, Rabbi

affiliation: congregational, 7–9, 22, 43, 107, 152, 162, 164, 187n3, 192n4, 193nn1–2; denominational, 9, 18–19, 25, 162, 181n11, 181n13; personal, 5, 152; requirement for bar or bat mitzvah, 4, 6; school, 4, 184n9; voluntary, 3, 17–18, 74. *See also* independent congregations; synagogue membership

age at bar or bat mitzvah, xiii, 1, 59–60, 185n2

Aldrich, John, and daughter Rebekah (Beth Jeshurun), 112–113

aliyah, 7, 30, 102, 108–109, 112, 114–115, 125, 137

American religious life, 8, 10–11, 14, 17, 164–165

American values, 3, 17, 46–47, 60, 63, 74, 187n23

Am Hayim (Conservative), 129–130, 132–133, 136, 140, 191n13. *See also* Conservative Movement; Weinberg, Rabbi

Applebaum, Rosie, and daughter Ellen (B'nai Aaron), 41–43

Apprenticeship of Duddy Kravitz, The (film), 1

Ark, the, 17, 67, 109–110, 113, 118

Aronson, Tina (Beth Jeshurun), 50

assimilation, 3, 106

authenticity: of bar or bat mitzvah ritual, 59, 142–143; of Jewish practice, 3–4, 62, 116

bar mitzvah bargain, 2, 4–5, 86, 147–148, 184n8

bar or bat mitzvah: definition, xiii; educators' roles, 53–55; history of, 2–5, 14; in congregational context, 16–36, 124–145; meanings of, 58–77; parents' roles, 6, 41–51; preparation, 78–101; requirements, 4, 6; rabbis' roles, 51–53, 141–144; ritual, 1, 6–7, 31–35; role in American Jewish culture, 1–7, 144–159; stereotypes, 1, 58, 81, 185n5; students' roles, 39–40; as system, 7–15, 37–38, 55–57, 146–148, 156–158, 173, 177

Bay Area Jewish community: common practices, 6, 35, 91,117, 186n19, 191n6; cultural life, 8, 46–47; demographics, 7–9, 27, 162–165, 180n15; denominational affiliation, 19–27, 163–164, 181n13; diffusion, 46, 100, 162; history, 7, 162; intermarriage, 7–9, 107, 111, 190n15; research site, 8–9, 162–170; synagogue affiliation, 7–9, 43, 163–164, 193nn1–2

Ben-Ami, Rabbi (Beth Jeshurun), 53, 69

Bengston, Vern, 49, 183n3

Berel, Rabbi (Beth Jeshurun), 93

Berkeley Midrasha, 155

Berkowitz, Jacob, Christine, and daughter Deborah (Sukkat Shalom), 102–103, 111–115

Beth Jeshurun (Reform), 26–27; administrative management, 26–27, 53, 87, 140, 174; bar or bat mitzvah, 26–27, 34, 69–70, 76, 85–87, 95–96, 151–152, 188n22; demographics, 26–27; effect of large size, 9, 18, 26–27, 54, 124, 154, 170–172, 181n9, 192n25; family program, 27, 50, 86–87; intermarriage, 50; participation in study, 170–172, 174; services, 27, 53, 174, 191n21. *See also* Ben-Ami, Rabbi; Berel, Rabbi; Lerner, Rabbi; Reform Movement

ABOUT THE AUTHOR

PATRICIA KEER MUNRO is a visiting scholar at the Berkeley Institute for Jewish Law and Israel Studies at University of California, Berkeley, and teaches sociology of religion at Sonoma State University. Her work focuses on contemporary American religion and examines congregational dynamics, intermarriage, pluralist Jewish practice in the United States and Israel, and comparative Jewish-Christian practice and content. Her article on negotiating problems of non-Jewish participation in synagogue life appeared in the January 2015 issue of *Journal of Jewish Identities*. She has presented her work at meetings of the American Sociological Association, the Association for the Sociology of Religion, the World Congress of Jewish Studies, and the Association for Jewish Studies.

Several papers under development further analyze the data collected in this project. An analysis of synagogue website statements shows how Jewish leaders imagine the synagogue's role in Jewish life. A comparison of synagogue and Protestant church website statements explores how different religious content shapes apparently similar institutions in different ways. A third paper analyzes the effect of the diffuse Jewish culture of the San Francisco Bay Area on inculcating Jewish knowledge. Other papers show the effect of Jewish pluralism on attitudes toward Jewish practice and culture and the development of a ritual system generalized from the bar and bat mitzvah system.